China's
Major Mysteries

China's Major Mysteries

Paranormal Phenomena and the Unexplained in the People's Republic

Paul Dong

China Books and Periodicals, Inc.

San Francisco

Published in the United States of America by China Books and Periodicals, Inc.
San Francisco, CA 94110, www.chinabooks.com

A portion of this book was originally published by Prentice-Hall, Inc., as *The Four Major Mysteries of Mainland China* by Paul Dong, 1984.

Library of Congress Cataloging-in-Publication Data

Dong, Paul,
   [The four major mysteries of mainland China]
   China's major mysteries: paranormal phenomena and the unexplained in the People's Republic of China / Paul Dong.
     p.cm
   Originally published: Englewood Cliffs, N.J.: Prentice-Hall, c1984
   Includes bibliographical references and index.
   ISBN 0-8351-2676-5 (pbk: alk. paper)
   1. Parapsychology—China. 2. Unidentified flying objects—Sightings and Encounters- -China. 3. Sasquatch- -China. I. Title.

BF1031.D657 2000
001.94'0951- -dc21   00-029447

Cover design: Linda Revel
Cover illustration by Brian Karvelis

Printed in the United States of America

10 9 8 7 6 5 4 3 2 1

ISBN: 0-8351-2676-5

Figures 10.1, 13.1, 13.2, 13.3, 16.2 and 16.3 courtesy of *The Unsolved Mysteries* by Zhen Wen Bin and Zhou Guoxing, Henan Publishing House, People's Republic of China, 1980.

Contents

Preface

If you were to visit the People's Republic of China today, say, Peking, Shanghai, or Canton, you would probably see quite a different picture of Chinese life than what is ordinarily reported on the news in the West. In China, the "meeting of East and West" is proceeding at a rapid pace. The Chinese people are now intensely interested in subjects that were forbidden to them because of long-standing political attempts to impose an ideology and a uniform mental outlook. The structure of the government and the Communist Party is still there, but China is indeed engaging in vigorous intellectual debate and creative expression that only a quarter-century ago were almost completely suppressed.

The paranormal and the unexplained are the subject of this book. They are now among the subjects that rage in intellectual and popular discussion in China today. Especially prominent are the following four mysteries: UFOs; Exceptional Human Function (EHF)—a newly coined term for unusual psychic abilities; Qi gong, an ancient Chinese breathing technique which can allow one to develop extraordinary abilities; and the Wildman, China's Bigfoot. With the exception of qi gong, these other phenomena have been widely covered in the West, but are only just gaining popular attention in China, the land of my birth.

Because of the influence of Mao Tse-tung, China closed its doors to the West for thirty years. Following Mao's death in 1976, Mao's wife and three others ruled the new Socialist state that had been laid on the foundations of a vast and ancient country with a glorious history. This group later became known as the Gang of Four, and started a policy of non-Westernization. During their strict rule, life for the Chinese people was dull and monotonous, and their knowledge of the world outside was highly censored.

A political struggle deposed the Gang of Four in 1976. China thereupon began to slowly open its doors to the West, and the Chinese people have ever since been greatly attracted to all kinds of unfamiliar things denied to them for decades. They are especially eager to learn about new areas in science and have enthusiastically undertaken research in many traditional and nontraditional areas.

By the late 1970s, among the many new things making their appearance in China were American magazines such as *Life, Scientific American, Omni, Sky and Telescope,* as well as some magazines devoted to UFOs. In the meantime, Coca-Cola and McDonalds also made their way in. Likewise, Hong Kong's best-selling books and magazines, especially the famous *World of Science* and several UFO books, also made their way to the mainland.

Publishing events such as these kindled the interest of the Chinese, who had been kept in ignorance about such developments in the rest of the world, and the inquiring spirit of their ancestors was reawakened. China has a long tradition of scientific and technological inquiry and innovation. A deep interest in pioneering science began to be seen as fundamental research was pursued in areas long deemed forbidden.

One such field was ufology, the scientific investigation of UFO phenomenon. The UFO literature reaching China opened the eyes of people to their ignorance of phenomena that had long been occurring around them—indeed, *to* them. The Chinese began to realize that those strange objects appearing frequently in the sky were called UFOs by the rest of the world. The once censored news broadcasts of the U.S. moon landing in 1969 were acknowledged publicly, along with stories about UFOs. This greatly stimulated public interest and broadened the perspective of the average Chinese citizen.

In 1979, Cha Leping, a physics student in Wuhan University, Hubei Province, wrote to the Readers' Section of the journal *Aerospace Knowledge* to promote the idea of ufology. As a result, the unofficial student-based China UFO Research Organization (CURO) was immediately established with eleven chapters. By the middle of the 1980s, CURO had twenty-eight chapters throughout China.

CURO learned from *World of Science* that I was at the time one of the very few Chinese outside the mainland researching UFOs. At the same time, Peking's second largest newspaper, *Guang Ming Daily,* published an article of mine that translates somewhat awkwardly into English as "Gossip on UFOs." It is not an elegant title in English, but the article certainly drew great interest among my Chinese countrymen, including some members of CURO who wanted to get in touch with me—and soon did.

In 1980 several of my articles on UFOs appeared in the major

Chinese newspaper, *The People's Daily,* which regularly sells 8 million copies every day. My articles were also carried in Tientsin's *Science and Life* (with 1.5 million copies sold per issue), and the third most famous publication in China, Shanghai's *Nature Magazine.* Shortly thereafter, I became an advisor to CURO. I also became the editor-in-chief of *The Journal of UFO Research,* the first publication of its kind in a Socialist country. Upon its publication, the *Journal* immediately sold 300,000 copies.

Thus, I came into a unique position of having access to a vast body of data on UFOs in China, and—as I will show in this book—on three other major mysteries in the land of my ancestors. From 1978 to 1981, Chinese UFO researchers and witnesses provided me with several hundred UFO cases, including nearly two dozen that I personally collected when I visited China for six weeks in 1981, when ufology was just beginning. I consider these cases to be authentic, and follow-up investigations by my colleagues in China have shown them to be more real than ever. They are chronicled in this book.

During the first three years of UFO fever in China (1977-1980), research also began on what Chinese scientists refer to as EHF, or Exceptional Human Function. This began when a fourteen-year-old child, Tong Yu, was found to "see" words with his ears. When news of this was made public, China had within a year discovered more than twenty children with significant EHF ability. These ranged in age from eight to sixteen; only one was older—a twenty-five-year-old woman. An eleven-year-old boy, Sheng Kegong, of Shanxi, could perform mental calculations of twenty-six-digits in twenty seconds, faster than most calculators. Another EHF case was Zhu Mei, a nine-year-old girl who used psychic power to open a lock inside a closed box.

All these incredible displays of exceptional power led people to think about the unpredictable appearances of UFOs and their associated mysteries. UFO researchers in China began to think that there were probably links between these two mysteries—UFOs and psychic phenomena. The public's interest was heightened when Qian Xue Sen, China's "Father of the Missile," published an article on his research into EHF in *Nature Magazine.* When such an eminent man of science spoke with approval of the subject, the entire nation was immediately interested, and the field of study became a legitimate scientific pursuit.

As interest in UFOs and EHF built dramatically, I visited Peking, Shanghai, Canton, and other major cities in China. Everywhere I went I was deluged with questions, requests for lectures, and, best of all, excellent and very precious research materials and photographs. This book is the first full-length account published in the West of China's research into its major mysteries.

Just as UFOs were being linked with psychic phenomena by Chinese theorists of the paranormal, EHF was being linked with another major mystery: qi gong (pronounced "chi gung." Qi gong is an ancient system of breathing exercises that is said to produce profound health benefits as well as phenomenal physiological and physical abilities. Qi (or chi, as in tai chi chuan) is the Chinese word for life force or aether, the vital, invisible energy that gives structure and substance to the entire material universe.

Common knowledge or folk wisdom in China states that qi gong is able to bring about strange powers. This led researchers in EHF to examine experts in the ancient art. The researchers were delighted to find that these qi gong practitioners did indeed have certain remarkable capacities similar to those of the EHF prodigies. The researchers also have begun to correlate specific breathing patterns with particular exceptional functions. They have also found that certain acupuncture treatments also appear to increase EHF in certain ways. Based on my experience, I can personally attest to the power of qi gong to affect health and awaken psychic ability.

During my 1981 trip to China, I lectured on UFOs to an audience of 700 people in Peking, under the auspices of the Astronomical Association. After the lecture, one of the many audience members who questioned me turned out to be a researcher on the Wildman, the Chinese equivalent of Bigfoot, the huge, ape-like creature reported throughout North America, especially in the Pacific Northwest region of the United States. The name of the researcher was Zhou Guoxing, an officer of the Institute of Natural History in Peking, who had been studying Wildman reports in China for over twenty years. Zhou was also the chairman of China's Wildlife Research Association.

Although our conversation began enthusiastically on the subject of UFOs, it soon turned toward Zhou's main interest, and he soon provided me with many reports and photographs on the mystery of the Wildman. I have drawn heavily upon them for this book.

UFOs, Exceptional Human Function, qi gong, and Wildman: these are China's major mysteries. There remains tremendous interest in these topics both in China and the West

I would like to acknowledge with deepest gratitude the cooperation I received from many people and organizations as I collected information and material for this book. I could not have completed it without their kind assistance. I want to give special thanks to the following:

The editor and staff of *The Journal of UFO Research,* Gansu
    Province
The China UFO Research Organization
Peking Evening News science editor Huang Tian Xiang
Astronomy Amateur editor Hung Yun Fong, Peking
Guang Ming Daily science editor Gin Tao, Peking
Mysteries of Nature editor Yeh Gong Seng, Peking
Nature Magazine editorial department, Shanghai
Xin Hua News Agency editor Chang Guong Huen, Peking
Peking Natural History Museum researcher and China
    Wildman Research Association chairman Zhuo Guo Xing
Members of China's Qi Gong and Exceptional Human
    Function Research Association

Paul Dong
Oakland, California
December, 1999

The First Mystery: UFOs

1
The Rise of
UFO Research
in China

Thanks to more than three decades of ufological research, we know that flying saucers are an ancient phenomenon. However, this topic came into public prominence only at the end of World War II—the time when I was a sixteen-year-old country lad in China. In those years I recall hearing people talking about "flying discs in the sky." Some were described as "flying wheels." At that time the term "flying saucer" did not exist in China. People just named the strange aerial objects by their shape, and although the people in my province, Canton, and others spread the news of the unusual phenomenon by word of mouth, very little was recorded on paper.

Nevertheless, from records I have examined, it appears that China noted its first UFO in modern times in 1947. On July 19 of that year, the antiaircraft command base of the Nationalist Government Air Force reported sighting a UFO over Lanzhou City in Gansu Province. It was fifteen meters long, with what looked like a rudder and two jet pipes at the back. It flew somewhat like a modern jet liner. On the same day the Tianjin *Yi Shi Daily* of Hebei Province reported the event. About 8 P.M. people in Gansu saw an unidentified red object, with a diameter of several meters, crossing the sky for about two seconds. This was the first UFO case reported by newspapers before the Liberation. Of course, far more stories were spread by word of mouth.

After the fall of the Gang of Four in 1976, all kinds of publica-

3

tions began to report UFO news from abroad because people were so interested in it. From 1976 to 1978 China experienced numerous UFO witness cases. Especially sensational was a 1977 case in which an army of several hundred men surrounded a UFO. The incident was widely known and talked about within China, but the authorities refused to let any information out to the rest of the world. Here is the way I heard it.

Fujian faces Taiwan Strait. One night a UFO the size of a full moon and gleaming brightly flew across the strait from the direction of Taiwan and landed silently on a hilltop in Tai Yu County in Fujian Province. Two farmers working late at night saw it and ran madly to report it to the army. Three hundred troopers immediately surrounded the hill, and the captain in charge announced, "Don't fire unless I order it!"

A lieutenant behind him asked, "Are we going to capture it?" "Yes, it may be some kind of secret weapon that the U.S. is providing Taiwan and we can capture it as an offering to our country," the captain said confidently.

"Do you think it's damaged?" the lieutenant asked.

"I don't know," the captain said. "We have to be very careful."

The army closed all ground escape routes and sent a vanguard to the hilltop to investigate. As they approached, the UFO became brighter than ever. One of the men could not open his eyes because of the dazzlingly bright light. Many felt dizzy.

"Captain, should we order fire?" the lieutenant asked. "We can't get close to it."

The captain thought quickly and said, "Yes, but order our men to retreat first."

Just at that moment, an indescribable sound came from the UFO—a sound that resembled the howling of the wind and the rattling of running engines. The light brightened as well. The captain then ordered open firing at the target. For a short while, sounds of gunshots reverberated throughout the mountains, but the UFO on the mountaintop remained intact. Meanwhile, it slowly climbed into the air, lighting up the whole vicinity. Twenty seconds later it could no longer be seen. Some people said the light was so bright that the army couldn't look at it directly, so no one could tell whether it rapidly got away or simply vanished in the air.

The story of the Tai Yu County UFO captured public attention and spurred the growth of UFO research groups. Prior to that these groups were always mistrusted by the government and therefore were forbidden. The first UFO research organization was established in 1976 at Wuhan City in Hupei Province. But its leader, Cha Le Ping, was soon too busy with his schoolwork, so the organization was moved first to Peking and then to Fujian Province, where it was supported by the local militia. The military leader, then a captain, has now been promoted to deputy commander, and Fujian Province has become a leading center of UFO research efforts. On one occasion, Mr. Weng Shida, the Peking Observatory researcher on the history of astronomy, a critic of UFO research, gave a speech in Fujian on UFOs. He was very coldly received after the speech and had to slip away quietly. Pro-UFO sentiment was obviously very strong there.

Figure 1.1 Group leaders from all chapters of China UFO Research Organization.

In May 1980 a nationwide China UFO Research Organization (CURO) was established. It soon won official support. The Chinese news agency in Washington, D.C., reported, "Our government in Peking has set up a special commission to investigate this phenomenon." Soon afterward, Gansu People's Publication, a publishing company, established what was described by Western Chinawatchers as "the first UFO magazine in a Socialist country." The first issue of *The Journal of UFO Research*, a bimonthly, immediately sold 300,000 copies when it came out on March 20, 1981. During the buying rush, a UFO fan in Peking who bought three copies commented, "Now we can put away our handwritten magazine, *UFO Exploration.*"

The reason the Gansu UFO magazine sold so well was because of numerous UFO incidents occurring in the skies of China, with Gansu apparently becoming the favorite visitation spot. For example, on October 23, 1978, at 10:40 P.M., several hundred pilots were watching a movie in a large open square at an Air Force base there. Just after the film started, the whole audience looked at the sky in sudden amazement. They saw a huge peculiar object moving from east to west, with two searchlightlike white lights directed forward and one in back. It also seemed to have some kind of nondescript attachment at its center. According to an eyewitness, Zhou Qing Tong, the object could not have been a falling star, locusts or birds, a balloon or an airplane. The eyewitnesses could not be mistaken since they were all Air Force fighter pilots and, as they asserted, "We saw it very clearly." This event shocked the entire nation. Furthermore, according to confidential sources, when the UFO entered the air space above Gansu, two fighter planes were sent to intercept it, but to no avail.

Another incident, equally interesting, was reported by an astronomer, Zhao Shu Xing, who worked in the Yunnan Observatory Solar Research section. On December 25, 1979, at 12:30 A.M., he was observing the sky. The astronomer's fourteen-year-old son, Zhao Xue Ling, and his friend, Lin Yang, were also present, looking at the sky. Out of the west there suddenly emerged a crimson semicircular fireball. "Look, why has the moon become red?" Lin Yang asked. Then he said, "That's not the moon—that's the sun." They began to look for the moon, but couldn't find it. Nor could they find any star—only thick clouds gleaming with color. The man and boys remained there to observe the changing fiery ball. The semicircular object, spinning in a counterclockwise direction, moved at an incredibly high speed toward them, as if it were going to crash into them. As it got closer and closer, the spinning ball constantly changed its color and shape. Finally it became a ringed circle, deep blue on top and crimson red on the underside. This strange object, sometimes spiraling clockwise and sometimes counterclockwise, fluttered on a wavery orbit. At last it disappeared in the direction from which it came. The whole amazing process lasted about five minutes.

This soon came to the attention of Zhao's friend, Gin Tao, who was the editor of the *Guang Ming Daily* science section. He immediately sought verification from others, who confirmed the event.

The Peking Observatory and Purple Mountain Observatory in

Figure 1.2 Zhao Shu Ling and his friend Lin Yang saw a crimson semicircular fireball on December 25, 1979, at 12:30 A.M. in Yunnan Province. The UFO changed its color and shape and became a ringed circle, deep blue on top and crimson red on the underside.

Nanking are world famous. However, the government has invested a huge sum in the most advanced equipment for Yunnan Observatory to do applied astronomical research. This is the reason that a highly trained astronomer's sighting of a UFO was taken quite seriously by the government and the scientific community. The observer, Zhou Zhang Sheng, was a CURO member. He saw a strange object appear frequently in the sky on December 27, 29, and 30, 1979. The December 30 sighting took place in the morning and was especially spectacular. Other astronomers attending a nationwide conference on stellar studies in Kunming (Yunnan's capital) also saw it. The object was round and sent off three trails of bright red-yellow flames. The sun had not yet risen above the horizon. The colorful gleaming fireball looked splendid against the blue sky. All these reports from astronomers, military, pilots, and ordinary citizens caught the attention of the government, since two UFO incidents had taken place over the seat of government, Peking. One happened on a summer night in 1965, when two sparkling objects were seen chasing one another, constantly changing directions. The Air Force and civil aviation authorities were sure they were not airplanes, but could not explain to higher authorities what they actually were.

In autumn 1967, one day shortly after sunset, people in Peking Tung County saw a round flying object giving off a fiery light. It moved at high speed against the wind and then suddenly stationed

Figure 1.3 The author and Mr. Gin Tao, left, science editor of Peking Guang Ming Daily.

itself motionless, high in the sky. It was just like a sunset scene with a burning crimson ball hung in the sky, and it puzzled the authorities.

These events and others led the eleven UFO research groups to advocate the establishment of a China UFO Research Organization. Teachers, scientists, local officials, university students, engineers, and some of the Liberation Army leaders also lent their support to the idea. But leading scientists and officials in the higher levels of the government opposed being officially involved in UFO research. Their reasons were twofold. First, the U.S. government had sponsored UFO research—in the form of Project Blue Book, otherwise know as the Condon Report—without obtaining concrete results. Nor had the French government been successful in its efforts. Second, UFO research was felt to be closely related to matters of national interest and was therefore confidential information. It could not be allowed to leak out. Government leadership in UFO research was therefore decided to be inappropriate.

Thus UFO research was left to unofficial bodies which nevertheless were attached to government unofficially, thereby allowing the government and the military to pursue their classified work covertly.

From November 30 to December 7, 1980, the China Future Research Organization held a meeting at Hefei in Anhui Province. Three UFO research representatives from unofficial bodies were invited. One was China UFO Research Organization consultant Xun Shi Li, who worked in the Latin American Research Institute and had once been the late Chairman Mao's Spanish-Chinese translator. The second representative, Jin Wei, was the head of the Shanghai UFO Research Group; he was also a professor in the foreign language department in Shanghai Jiao Tung University. The third, Zhao Xing Yuan, was the head of the Peking UFO Research Group. The China Future Research Organization, which had six hundred members, was attached to the Chinese Science and Technology Association.

At the meeting, a resolution was passed to accept CURO as one of the subsidiaries of the China Future Research Association. Thus CURO was given a lowly but nevertheless official status. CURO members were quite pleased because they knew well that private organizations had never really existed in China. All kinds of organizations were under government control, including their finances. Now CURO's handwritten magazine, *UFO Exploration*, could obtain $1,000 from the government for each issue. Its name was changed to *Flying Saucer and Its Future*. But soon after the name change, the

Figure 1.4 A conference held by members of Shanghai branch on the subject of UFOs.

magazine's situation took a new turn. The government announced in 1981 that it had a deficit of $500 million and needed to cut the national budget. *Flying Saucer and Its Future* fell prey to the cost cutting. Despite this loss, UFO fans did not give up hope because local governments, such as provincial authorities, could make it up. *The Journal of UFO Research*, published by Gansu Province, satisfied the needs of UFO enthusiasts. It became their main source of intellectual nourishment. In the past, more than half the sighting reports submitted by UFO research groups were rejected by newspapers and magazines. Now a legitimate forum existed.

Figure 1.5
UFO enthusiasts stood in a long line waiting to enroll for membership in the Shanghai Branch.

The entire nation responded to the acceptance of CURO into the China Future Research Association. The number of chapters expanded from eleven to twenty-eight, with an average of about one-hundred or more members each. Hundreds more are still applying. Members include students, aeronautical engineers, astronomers, writers, teachers, and scientists, as well as journalists and magazine editors who could help propagate the work.

Although some high officials opposed UFO research, they could not totally disregard the "silent majority" who actually favored UFO research. CURO began due to the efforts of a member of that majority, Cha Lo Ping, a second-year physics student of Hubei Wuhan University. In September 1979 he and six other students wrote to Peking's *Aerospace Knowledge* monthly magazine to plead for government support of UFO research. One of the editors was sympathetic. He published their letter, thus bringing it greater attention, and wrote in his editorial comment: "We carry this in our magazine to introduce the subject to our readers. Perhaps people of the same interest will knock at your door!" He added, "The world is full of mysteries of every sort. At the present stage it is difficult to deny the existence of UFO phenomena. So many eyewitnesses have reported their encounters that we simply cannot dismiss them as fabricated stories."

As soon as Cha's letter appeared, hundreds of readers wrote to him applauding his suggestions and pleading for the establishment of an academic research organization to explore problems and to undertake research connected with UFOs. After six months of preparation, the first semi-official body for ordinary citizens—the China UFO Research Organization—was set up. Cha was made the president.

The year 1979 was full of controversy about UFOs. Most pro-UFO people were ambiguous on the issue. Shen Yuen Yan, the editor of Social Science Research Institute, wrote an article, "UFOs—An Unsolved Mystery," which was published in the *People's Daily* in November 1978 as a report, without any comment or opinion. *Aerospace Knowledge* published an article on this touchy subject. It was an honest article; printing it was a courageous act on the part of the editor, Xie Chu, who had much material on UFOs. The magazine, which has high status, as it is the official organ of the Aeronautic Institute, Aeronautic Association, and the Third Engineering Department, sold 280,000 copies of that issue. Since the *People's Daily* published an article on UFOs, *Aerospace Knowledge* did as well in promoting interest in this area. Less than a year later, on September 21, 1979, the number two Peking newspaper, *Guang Ming Daily,* whose readers are mainly intellectuals and educators, also published "Do Flying Saucers Exist?" (The author, Zhou Xin Yan, was the editor of the people's broadcasting station technology department). This was the second time a major newspaper expressed an opinion on the subject of UFOs. The article suggested the existence of UFOs and emphasized, "If we don't know about it, then we have to find out." The editor reported that Yuen Chen Zin, a member of the Chinese Academy of Sciences ancient studies department, told him of two UFO cases. In the autumn of 1977, Zin and a colleague from the Academy of Science were in Hupei Shennongjia to investigate

Wildman. One evening about seven o'clock, as he attended a meeting, a high school student rushed in excitedly to report a "monster" flying over the mountain. Many eyewitnesses were talking about it. The sky was not very dark yet and it was clear, without clouds. The people of the countryside all affirmed that the object which just passed them was round and of "washing pot size." It spiraled slowly forward, sending off yellow-white light and giving off fire from its sides. It made no sound. The scene lasted about one minute. Liberation Army officers who were on duty in Hepei, Tang County workmen in a coal-processing factory of Shansi, and teachers in Inner Mongolia also saw the UFO. The soldiers had even pursued it on motorcycles. What they saw was similar to what people in other countries have reported many times. The soldiers said that the flying object was a moonlike ball giving off "foggy gas." After it had remained stationary in the air for a few seconds, it gave off some strong, dark smoke. Then it ascended again, still giving off smoke, and went away.

After this incident became known, a wave of public interest in UFOs swept across the nation.

2
Breaking Through the Barriers to UFO Research

A columnist for the Hong Kong *Ming Pao Daily* who is well known in China, Mr. Zhang Jing Yun, wrote an essay in 1980 entitled "Breaking Through the Barriers to UFO Research." He stated:

> In recent years, mainland China has broken down long-standing barriers to research in many fields. Nevertheless, many barriers remain unbroken, and others once thought demolished have again been demarcated. Let us not be deterred by these obstacles. Scientific research of phenomena such as "reading through the ears" and extraordinary or exceptional human functions will one day carry through to become a legitimate field of inquiry; results will be obtained.

> It sounds as if the door has been opened. For the last three decades, Europe, North America and Asia have talked and written extensively and heatedly about UFOs. Only China has never reported the subject. The reason was that all communication media were strictly controlled. Belief in UFOs was considered mere superstition. Even if one had been found, it would not have been reported. In recent years, when the barriers are being broken, many UFO reports have been released and allowed, showing that the UFO phenomenon is real indeed and that official censorship cannot suppress completely the people's awareness of strange things happening in nature.

> My friend Paul Dong lives far away in the U.S.A. and he is the only overseas Chinese UFO researcher. He brought with him abundant knowledge of such "mysterious" things and stepped through mainland China's broken barrier to UFO research. He first responded to the invitation of *Guang Ming Daily's* "Science Column" and wrote a 5,000-

word article, "Gossips on UFOs," which was published on May 12, 1980, in that newspaper. His article aroused mainland China's keen interest in the wonders of UFOs.

I also cooperated with Paul and wrote a book, *UFO—The Outer Space Visitors*, which was published by World of Science Publishers in Hong Kong.

I was delighted to see Yun's essay in print because it indicated that knowledge of the UFO experience had indeed penetrated to the top levels of science and officialdom in a convincing way. Ever since mainland China came under communism, religion, astrology, mythology, sexology, and many other topics considered nonscientific or the degenerate products of capitalist culture were not allowed to be displayed or discussed in public. The entire nation lived in an environment of political dogmatism and materialistic philosophy. The thoughts and things of foreign cultures, especially the Western, were officially regarded as poisonous weeds or horrible spirits to be avoided, and thus they were prohibited. Even China's own ancient philosophies and cultural heritage were regarded as antagonistic to the thrust of the Cultural Revolution and were vigorously rooted out. America's moon landing was a scientific event of great world importance, but America was a capitalist country—so the official thinking in China ran—and therefore it did not matter whether the event was scientifically important or not, because it would appear to credit capitalism and discredit communism if it were publicly acknowledged in the Chinese media. Likewise, phenomena such as UFOs and ESP were not allowed recognition. The Gang of Four was especially emphatic in this regard. The whole nation was plunged into ignorance and scientific stagnation by the barriers erected in the name of political-philosophical dogmatism.

In 1976, when the Gang of Four was deposed, the political situation was very unsteady. People were afraid to make sudden changes and to show their interests and views openly. Gradually, however, the door was opened and decades of accumulated frustration were relieved. People were allowed to know of the outside world, within certain limits, and thereafter publications—both books and periodicals—poured into China from the United States, Japan, France, Hong Kong, and elsewhere. The Chinese people especially soaked up information about America and the Soviet Union conquering outer space.

In 1979 the Peking *People's Daily* published an article called "UFOs—A Puzzle to the World." The Chinese news service Hsin Hua transmitted it to Hong Kong, Macao, Southeast Asia, and Japan, and it immediately astonished many people. Just as amazing, in view of

China's all-too-recent history of news suppression concerning the paranormal, was the UFO coverage made by Peking's Central People's Broadcasting Bureau. Both native and overseas UFO cases were reported.

The *People's Daily* is a national newspaper run by the central government of China and hence is the mouthpiece of the Communist Party. Its commentary represents the government's sanction—or condemnation—of events. With the go-ahead sign so clearly given, *Guang Ming Daily* followed soon thereafter and published a second article on Chinese UFO cases. When the article appeared, it evoked many letters from readers who asked that such reports be continued; many also reported their own sightings. Within a year more than thirty newspapers and magazines published UFO articles and sighting reports. The most prestigious of these to carry such writings were *Aerospace Knowledge* and *Peking Evening News.*

But it was not to be a straightforward advance. Shortly after the media had been opened to news of UFOs, a researcher at Peking Observatory, Mr. Weng Shida, began a vigorous attack on the existence of UFOs. His article, "Peking Observatory's Science Workers Talk About UFO Matters" appeared in the *People's Daily* on February 22, 1979, and the essence of his position was contained in this statement: "According to the investigations by research groups and scientists, most UFO cases are merely astronomical and atmospheric phenomena. What have been called 'outer space ships' are mere imagination."

When Shida's article appeared, he was openly supported by many high-ranking scientists. Especially notable were the magazines *Science Experiment*, published by the National Science Academy, and *Knowledge Is Power,* under the management of the China National Science and Technics Association. The China National Labor Union and the Central Committee of the Chinese Communist Youth League even saw fit to agree with Shida's view by publishing articles that further attacked the reality of UFOs.

A scientific battle of epic proportions was being waged in the media, with the traditionalist-orthodox ranks of science arguing that there was no evidence for UFOs and that it was all superstition and fantasy, while the pro-UFO group kept giving sighting reports. The problem of evidence in this field is, of course, recognized worldwide. UFOs have been sighted for dozens of years in the modern age by thousands of people around the globe, yet hard evidence is rare, even with the advent of home video. Since a UFO has not yet landed on the White House lawn or at Tian An Men Square in Peking, Weng Shida and other critics argues that there was no case. (If one landed at Tian An Men, the news probably still would not be made known unless a busload of American tourists or other foreigners happened to pass by just then.)

Shida's article evoked fear in many editors who had been receptive to publishing articles about UFOs. The just-ended censorship and punishment for violating official views were all too recent in their minds. As a result, many articles on UFOs were put on hold, including one of my own. A 60,000-word manuscript of mine was to have been published by a Peking publisher, but the editor in chief, upon sensing that the political wind might be shifting, delayed publication. (Eventually the book appeared, becoming the first book on UFOs published in a Communist country. Its title: *Gossips on UFOs*, named after my 1980 article on UFOs in the *Guang Ming Daily* that brought me such attention in China.)

Upon receiving news clippings about the controversy from friends in China, I wrote to the *Guang Ming Daily*. Its science column editor replied, inviting me to write an article on UFOs. Thus my "Gossips on UFOs" article appeared. After its publication I learned that it was widely circulated and much appreciated by the editors, and that it generated a large number of reader letters, including many sighting reports.

The publication of my article coincided with a remarkable UFO sighting in China. Some time earlier the Outer Space General Commander had issued a call for assistance in understanding what UFOs were. People were alerted to search the skies. At 1 A.M. on June 20, 1980, Hsin Hwei County in Guang Dong Province was visited by several UFOs. The large "mother ship" was reported to be as big or bigger than a full moon and completely reddish. Next to it, two smaller UFOs could be seen, apparently attached to the large one. The small UFO on the right side was red; the one on the left was white. The mother ship flew from the east and remained motionless in the sky, while the two smaller craft circled.

This case silenced all the UFO critics who proposed to explain the phenomenon in terms of balloons, birds, man-made satellites, Venus, and moonlit clouds. The three UFOs produced a spectacular display during their few seconds' appearance, and then they flew southeast at extremely rapid speed. They emerged and disappeared in a fascinating manner. Because this case was so strange and no journalist was on the spot, newspapers and other media refused to publish reports for fear of being criticized as misleading people with "witchery words." A red "sun" emerging at midnight was strange enough, but who would believe that it was accompanied by a smaller "sun" and equally small "moon"? Although the incident was not

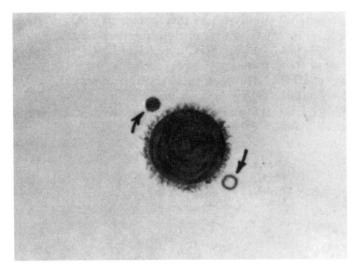

Figure 2.1 A large UFO mother ship and two "sons" appeared in Xin Hui County, Guang Dong Province, at 1 A.M. on June 20, 1980.

reported in the press, it nevertheless became known nationwide simply by word of mouth, so intense was the public's interest and so dramatic was the case.

During the last three years (1979–82), UFOs visited China all over, causing a writer in Peking to publish an article, "Do Flying Saucers Admire Foreign Countries?" By this he meant that UFOs were seen even more frequently outside China. In response to this assertion, an editor of the Hsin Hua news agency wrote an article, "Flying Saucers Are Not to Please Foreign Countries and Admire Them." This meant that Chinese sighting reports of UFOs are at least equal in number to those of other countries, and possibly more numerous. This exchange of shots in the press was ironic. From a time when news of UFOs was completely blocked, China had moved to a time when it was proudly and publicly comparing its UFO sighting reports with foreign ones and declaring itself to be of superior quality. Some of us quietly gave a sigh of weariness, thankful that the barrier was at last down and sadly mindful of how scientific research was subject to political control and philosophical dogma.

The public recognition of UFOs, along with other paranormal and unusual phenomena, had gone through its ups and downs—and will probably go through more. As my friend Zhang Jing Yun wrote, many barriers have been broken but others have been rebuilt.

The sheer weight of numbers of UFO sightings that became

known publicly was what finally broke the barrier to UFO research. In the last two years, by my count more than thirteen hundred such cases have been reported in mainland China. In addition, more than thirty books (most of them translated from foreign sources) and nine hundred articles on UFOs have been published. In a land covering nearly ten million square miles, with a population of one billion people who had been kept in the dark for decades, this breakthrough is a welcome bit of light.

3
Silencing
the UFO Critics

"Just as China had a 'Gang of Four' who played politics on the country, the U.S. has its 'Gang of Four' who play negativism on UFOs." A friend of mine made this ironic remark. Indeed, unlike the years of political upheaval, China's billion people recently produced a meager "Gang of One" to negate the existence of any unidentified flying objects. To give an idea of the pitiable position of this "Gang of One," it might not be pointless to paraphrase a passage from a reply sent by the *Mysteries of Nature*, in response to a letter I sent. In effect, the reply said:

"We are sorry to say that we consider it unfeasible to print your article. The table of contents in our first issue, which probably you have perused, contains numerous pieces concerning UFOs, of which Weng Shida's is the solitary one on the negative side. The same is so with the second issue. The minority should be treated fairly so as not to make his isolation too embarrassing."

A glance at the first issue of the *Mysteries of Nature* reveals that the pro-UFO articles run three to one; as many as seven affirmative articles appeared in the second issue, with none to the contrary. *The Journal of UFO Research*, which is published in Peking and of which I am an editor, has had only one article voicing anti-UFO opinion in its first seven issues. Such a situation by no means implies any "ignorance" on the part of Chinese UFO researchers; nor does it mean I have closed the publication to such articles. Rather, it indicates the extremely positive public attitude created by the persistence with which UFOs have haunted China over the past three years.

UFO enthusiasm, it is true, had been at low tide in the months following the publication of Weng Shida's comments by the *People's Daily*. During that period, *Aerospace Knowledge* magazine alone unflinchingly continued to print eyewitness reports. Its undaunted courage was lauded by Cha Leping, president of China UFO Research Organization, with the remark, "Only *Aerospace Knowledge* magazine has the guts to go against the tide." Weng Shida's interview, in fact, appeared in the *People's Daily* as if it were merely news reporting; no editorial comments accompanied it. Yet this did not hush up the public, who might have sensed trouble and chosen to be discreetly silent. With the power of visionary perception, *Aerospace Knowledge* magazine acted as trailblazer, touching off a fresh surge of UFO sighting reports. Most inspiring was an account by the noted poet Liu Shahe published in the *Science Literature* of Sichuan in 1981, which won popular acclaim for its humorous lightness. Here is the background.

In an article printed in the *Guang Ming Daily* in 1979, astronomer Weng Shida vigorously denied the existence of UFOs, claiming that a visitor from space is an outright impossibility, and that UFOs are nothing more than an illusion created by misperception of a balloon, an aircraft, a rocket, a cloud, a flock of birds, a swarm of winged insects, or a searchlight illuminating a cloud. As such judgment was much too arbitrary to deserve support, Liu Shahe was inspired to write the following widely circulated poem about UFOs:

> *Suddenly it appears,*
> *Mysteriously it vanishes,*
> *Flooding the sky with curiousity.*
> *Lights of green,*
> *Lights of orange,*
> *Dazzle man's eye.*
>
> *Flying disc?*
> *People beyond the earth?*
> *These are incredible.*
> *"Civilization is ours only," says he*
> *Out of conservatism and prejudice.*
>
> *What the naked eye has seen,*
> *What danced on radar screen,*
> *Was branded sheer illusion.*
> *Whereas stale dogmas*
> *are chanted as gospel.*

A visitor from another planet
On board a flying disc
Knocks at our door;
But we, frogs in the well,
Skulking in the bottom,
Dare not venture to answer.

As though to patronize him, Liu Shahe reported, a UFO swept over Chengtu at 1 A.M., June 29, 1980. To give the proper flavor of what follows, I will write as if the poet himself were speaking:

I was not yet in bed, working at my desk in a small room in the dormitory of Sichuan Federation of Literary and Arts Circles. Suddenly the fluorescent lamp went out. All was dark in the courtyard and a light rain was falling. My three neighbors had long since retired. A few minutes later a powerful light shone from outside on all the four windows of my room, which had been closed, for the duration of two to three seconds. I imagined someone flashing my windows with an electric torch, but on second thought I corrected myself, since what I had sighted was an even flood of whiteness, whereas the light spot of a torch would have been bright in the center, dimming away toward the periphery. Another few minutes passed and the illumination, a little weaker than the first, was repeated, this time lasting not more than a second. Neither could it have been lightning, which would have lasted much shorter, presumably not exceeding one hundredth of a second; besides, no thunder or any other subsequent sound reached my ears. The windows were brightened only in their lower halves, while the upper halves remained pitch dark. This indicated that the light had not come horizontally from any spot on the ground, but from somewhere midair in a slanting direction. But all this conjecture had been made afterwards: I was too scared to be analytical at the instant the sight occurred.

By next morning I returned to my dwelling in the second block of Dongfeng Road for breakfast. I was met by my son Yu Kun, who hurried to brief me in vivid terms on the appearance of a UFO before dawn, to the effect that a bright object had flown across the sky, that it was spherical in shape, its color blue at the circumference and red in the center, and that its rays illuminated the ground with a greenish tinge. Upon questioning him, he said he had been told the whole story. The sources were three persons living on the compound: Zhu Jiaqi, adult, male, editor of *Sichuan Music;* and Fang Xiaohua and Fang Xiaohan, adult sisters, daughters of another editor of the same magazine.

Not until a few days later did I have the leisure to visit the informants in person. Said Zhu Jiaqi: "I was sitting on my bed talking with my girl friend, when the fluorescent lamp on the desk reddened and dimmed, glimmered a couple of seconds, and went out. In a moment the window was lit up by a brilliant light from outside, its color white with red and blue tinges. The illumination lasted a few seconds."

Asked if he saw the shining object itself, he answered in the negative, adding that at that instant he had heard a sound from the air which was not the clicking of electric sparks, but rather like the buzzing from the wires or a massive transformer heard from beside a power pole, or the humming sound from an electric appliance when a short circuit occurred.

"Light and sound started and ended simultaneously," Zhu Jiaqi continued. "Suspecting an imminent earthquake, I jumped to open the door just as the illumination ended. I picked up the telephone and tried to contact a seismic department. I couldn't do it. The telephone didn't work. The courtyard was totally dark because all lights were out, and a light rain was falling. I came back in, shut the door, and sat on my bed, when the window was lit up again from without. The light was weaker and the duration shorter, just a second or two. No sound was heard, just like the first time. Shortly afterward the desk lamp lit up again. I looked at my wristwatch: 1:10 A.M."

His girl friend took over: "I am a worker at Number One Printing House in Chengdu. I went to work that morning when I heard my fellow workers' excited exchange of the news about a strong light sighted in the sky in the small hours. All witnesses are residents of the eastern city like us."

Stated Fang Xiaohua: "I was in bed when I saw a powerful light in the sky. My thought immediately turned to UFOs. I fear UFOs, so I put my hands on my eyes, but could still see the light between my fingers."

Said Fang Xiaohan: "I saw a very bright object in the sky which seemed to be red in the center and blue at the edges." I asked if she discerned the shape of the object. She said: "The whole sky was so bright it dazzled my eyes. I couldn't make out its shape."

Meanwhile Fang He, *Sichuan Literature* editor, said that he was amazed when the walls of his room were illuminated by a powerful light from outside. Other tenants described a dull sound they heard when the light occurred, something like the moving of heavy furniture in a room.

On the basis of these interviews I wrote a short report which I posted to Mr. Zhang Jingyun, a columnist in Hong Kong, also a UFO fan. He relayed the story to a science journal there, which printed it. Zhang himself wrote a short article entitled "UFOs in China." A few paragraphs follow:

"Not long ago a poet who resides in Chengdu, Sichuan, contacted me through a friend of mine in Hong Kong, asking me for a copy of *UFO— The Outer Space Visitor*, a book I wrote with coauthor Paul Dong, a resident in U.S. The United States has been a country where UFO enthusiasm has prevailed for many years, and for many years Paul Dong has engaged in amateur UFO study. I am a UFO fan myself. Coincidentally, I visited Australia last year at the time of the appearance of a UFO group (simultaneous with the disappearance of Valentich, a young New Zealand pilot, while flying his plane on October 21, 1978) which caused a sensation. It was then that I came to know that in addition to America and Europe, the UFO craze had spread to the continent of Oceania in the southern hemisphere. This is amazing."

"In the past twenty to thirty years, talk about UFOs and other mysteries in mainland China was branded groundless rumor and was taboo. With the recent lifting of the ban, UFO stories from abroad began to appear in Chinese press. More recently there was a report released through the news agency about a falling UFO sighted by civilians and soldiers in a mountainous area in Shansxi. This threw the first light on the matter."

In the early autumn of 1980 I made a long trip to Beidaihe to attend a poetry conference sponsored by Hebei Province. I brought the book *UFO—The Outer Space Visitor* with me to kill time on the journey and read it over not less than seven or eight times. While chattering about UFOs I was suddenly interrupted by Lang Po, a poet from Hebei.

"There's nothing new about that stuff of yours," he told me.

"Back in the late 1940s peasants in my native place (Xingtai, Hebei) knew well about UFOs. They said it was a traveling god who wore a straw hat, and that because the god had made himself invisible, people could only see the straw hat. The peasants claimed they had sighted the traveling god many times in the late 1940s. Another version, also from the villagers, said it was a ghost who did no harm to the people."

I was astonished indeed! A straw hat! I remembered the hosts of UFO pictures from abroad, especially those taken in the fifties. What else did they resemble, besides a straw hat!

Liu Shahe's account dealt a telling blow to Weng Shida's anti-UFO doctrine. The poet's great popularity must have made his victim feel awkward. Not willing to take his defeat lying down, Weng Shida continued to trumpet his views in a series of articles. But the more he wrote, the more conspicuous his weakness became. He lacked available data and, to quote a remark commenting on him by Cha Leping, president of China UFO Research Organization, he "could not go beyond cliché."

Then an article was written by Zhou Tijian, lecturer of physics at Peking University, entitled "Where Do UFOs Come From?" which he sent to *Astronomy Amateur*. The article served to support Weng Shida. However, the subsequent activity of UFOs and their countless witnesses made Zhou Tijian change his mind, leaving Weng Shida clinging alone to his tune of opposition.

As mentioned above, Weng lacked information to back his argument. To remedy this, he made desperate efforts at hunting up material from the Soviet Union. I was told that he took a few negative articles from Russia, which he had managed to procure, to a woman editor of the *Astronomy Amateur*, asking her to translate them. She declined, advising him to calm down and relinquish his obstinate view.

This endeavor frustrated, he racked his brains and cooked up another piece in question-and-answer form entitled "The Latest

Discourse About UFOs." Naturally, he found it difficult getting such trite stuff accepted by any journal. Finally it found its way into *Knowledge Is Power,* the solitary publication that offered help. But the shopworn "new" words on UFOs failed to apply to any UFO enthusiast or genuine researcher, for besides the lack of any authenticated background information, the article served only to demonstrate that no effort had been made by its author in the way of practical investigation, and that he had passed arbitrary judgment on UFOs after leafing through a few books or magazines he happened to lay his hands on. For this reason Zheng Wenguang, a science fiction writer who works at Peking Observatory, scoffed at Weng with a quotation from Mao Tse-tung: "No investigation and research, no right to speak."

In mainland China hardly any criticism by name is made in the press. Since his ascension to power, Premier Deng Xiaoping, stressing the need for solidarity, warned against press attacks on individuals. It has been common practice for editors to voice their own views, if need be, under an "editor's note." For this reason, any article upholding an affirmative position about UFOs would be preceded by an editor's note to the effect that no taboos should be imposed on the pursuit of science, that the UFO phenomenon must not be dismissed without adequate investigation, and that study and research on the subject should be encouraged. Such editors' notes apparently amounted to nothing short of merciless attacks on Weng Shida. Meanwhile, they helped to deepen the public's zeal for UFO study.

The majority of the population in mainland China wants unremitting efforts at UFO research, and this has received the support of more than half of the veteran press editors. These circumstances finally silenced Weng Shida. Coincidentally, perhaps, at this juncture he was removed from his post at Peking Observatory.

I know personally that there are a number of UFO fans among the Peking Observatory's staff; the same is the case with Yunnan Observatory. Another advocate of UFO study is an associate professor at Nanking University, while one third of the staff of the world-famous Purple Mountain Observatory in Nanking city is keen on the same subject of pursuit.

Nevertheless, it would be wrong to suppose that thinking is uniform among UFO proponents in China. True, opposition to merely considering the possibility of UFOs has given way in the face of widespread public acceptance based on numerous sightings that incontrovertibly demonstrate the reality of UFOs. However, demonstrating the reality of a phenomenon is not the same thing as *explaining* the phenomenon. The mystery of UFOs has not been solved by mainland China's scientists and researchers, any more than it has been by their counterparts in other countries. There are various schools of thought, ranging from the standard notion of extraterrestrial visitors from other planets to the view that at least some UFOs are living creatures, not craft, whose native state is akin to plasma or ball lightning.

Thus in mainland China the UFO mystery lives on, command-ing public attention and attracting researchers, after a hard struggle in the scientific community to accept the reality of what the rest of the world had accepted for decades. Progress is not always easy, but it is always worth the price, as I was to find out when I visited China in 1981 for the first time since I left it in 1947.

4
UFO Fever: My Observations During a Homecoming to Mainland China

In the summer of 1981 I visited China at the request of *The Journal of UFO Research* editorial board and the China UFO Research Organization (CURO). It was a very successful and gratifying trip, which I will describe here so the reader can see how China is now paying attention to UFOs.

When I arrived at the Peking airport and waited for my luggage to be checked, I saw through a glass wall that many people were waving in my direction. At first I thought their waves were intended for someone else, but then I saw one of my brothers, from whom I had separated long, long ago. He was holding a magazine opened to an inner page with my picture on it. He made a gesture and said, "All these folks are here to welcome you because they have seen your photo in the magazine."

When I was out of customs, many strangers came to shake hands with me and introduce themselves. The warmth of the welcome made me feel quite successful.

On the day after my arrival in Peking, I had an interview with all the editors from *The Journal of UFO Research*, the president and vice-president of Gansu People's Publishing Company, CURO chief executive Cha Leping, chief officials from the Peking chapter (the main office is in Wuhan), representatives from Peking Observatory, editors and reporters from seven magazines and newspapers in Peking, and all those UFO fans who heard about my visit. Throughout the whole day my quarters in "Friendship Hotel" were swarming with people who asked questions of all kinds.

The next day, I was invited by the Peking Ching Hua University student union to give a lecture on UFOs. The hall was fully packed. They wanted to know about the U.S. research on UFOs in the past; I told them all I could in that short time.

The third day it was arranged for me to deliver a talk on UFOs in the Peking Planetarium at 2 P.M. The auditorium there has 600 seats. Before 1:30 P.M. they were all occupied. Latecomers had to stand in the aisles and at the back of the hall. A friend of mine estimated that there were 750 people present.

Figure 4.1 The editorial board of The Journal of UFO Research.

On the fourth day I attended a discussion session on UFOs with the editorial board of *Astronomy Amateur, Aerospace Knowledge,* and staff members of "The Third Engineering Department." More than thirty people participated in this session. Later, *Aerospace Knowledge* and *Astronomy Amateur* reported on the discussion at great length.

I am a native of Canton. On the first day of my visit to Canton, the CURO Canton chapter requested me to give a seminar on UFOs. On the next day they arranged for me to give lectures in Canton

Figure 4.2 A UFO conference was held by the author, editors of Astronomy Amateur *and* Aerospace Knowledge, *and staff members of "The Third Engineering Department" at Friendship Hotel in Peking. This picture was taken after the meeting.*

Figure 4.3 The author after lecturing on UFOs in the Canton Science Museum. (In the front from left to right are Mr. Wen Kong Hua, director of the CURO Canton Branch; Mr. Liang Rong Lin, advisor of the Canton Branch and professor of physics department of Jinan University; the author.)

Jinan University. The morning session was attended by all the staff members, while the afternoon session was attended by all the students. On the following day I was invited by the Canton Science Museum to give a talk on UFOs.

During my six-week stay in China, I visited six cities—Peking, Canton, Shanghai, Hangchow, Suzhow, and Guilin. In every place I visited, I was invited to talk about UFOs. Because of limited time, I told them that I would do so on my next visit and that those who did not have the chance to come to my talks on UFOs could find them published in the coming issues of *The Journal of UFO Research.*

Figure 4.4 Hundreds of people attended a lecture on UFOs by the author in the Canton Science Museum.

The last city I visited was Guilin, a famous city of Guangxi Province. There is an old saying, "If you visit China without seeing Guilin, it is not a complete visit." Chinese people believe the Guilin scenery is best of all.

My three days in Guilin were very interesting. The first day I went to a mountain cave not far from the city. At one point I saw four soldiers and asked them, "Have you ever seen any UFOs in Guilin?"

"Yes," one of the soldiers replied.

"How many times have you seen UFOs? Are UFOs sighted in the Guilin area very often? Can you tell me about this?"

He looked at me in silence. I remembered that people told me soldiers are not allowed to talk to foreigners or anyone who is not a citizen of China, so I quickly presented a copy of *The Journal of UFO Research* to him and said, "I am one of the editors of this journal. It is published in China. We need UFO information. I would appreciate if you would tell me more about UFOs that you saw." He still maintained silence, however, and gave me no answer.

During the time I was in China, there were many border skirmishes between China and Vietnam. Many of the factories were moving out of Guangxi to the central region of China. Thus conversation with soldiers was a sensitive matter, and I attributed his silence to this.

Figure 4.5 A set of four UFO stamps issued by Grenada in 1977.

The second day in Guilin I went to a post office in the morning. I saw other soldiers talking to each other in front of the post office, so I walked over to see what they were doing. They were excited about obtaining a set of newly issued stamps. Seeing that they were philatelists, I pulled out a set of four UFO stamps (issued by Grenada in 1977) from my handbag and asked them, "Have you ever seen a set of UFO stamps?"

They immediately paid attention to the stamps and said, "We have seen UFOs, but never heard about UFO stamps."

"When did you see UFOs? What is the story?"

While they looked at each other, I said to them, "You are

welcome to have this set of stamps. Please tell me the story about the UFOs you've seen."

"Well," one of the soldiers said, "once we were training in the mountains. About midnight, the sky suddenly turned bright in the west and soon it turned red. We saw an object fly from the west to the north and keep changing its color from white to red. Once the object turned over and showed its other side." The soldiers kept looking at me and said, "Every one of us was surprised to see such an unknown object."

"It must have been a helicopter, wasn't it?"

"Of course not. We know helicopters very well."

I ceased my questions and gave the stamps to them in appreciation. I felt happy just to have gotten that much from the soldiers. I believe the story they told me is true, simply because Guangxi is one of the places UFOs are sighted most often.

During my stay in China, someone said that I was a bridge between America's and China's research on UFOs. I introduced many Chinese to the main UFO research organizations in the U.S.A. and their respective leaders. They are the Center for UFO Studies, the Mutual UFO Network (MUFON), the Aerial Phenomena Research Organization (APRO), the National Investigating Committee for Aerial Phenomena (NICAP) and several other research institutes, including the Fund for UFO Research. I hope that in the future I will still be the bridge between the U.S. and China, facilitating communications between the two countries.

Chinese UFO fans have asked me to deliver this message: They hope that American UFO experts will visit China to share their knowledge and UFO investigations. They are eager for such an exchange. And judging from my own experience, those who do go will be treated to a most enjoyable visit.

To properly describe UFO fever in China, I cannot avoid adding here some brief remarks about how the public almost literally rushed for copies of *The Journal of UFO Research*. Some readers may think I am just trying to get free advertising for the journal, but that is not the case. I only wish to show a true picture of the enthusiasm for UFO research in China.

In the People's Republic of China, all the newspapers and magazines are managed by the central government, either the provincial or the local government. *The Journal of UFO Research* is run under the People's Publishing House of Gansu Province. When UFO fever broke out, there were five provinces very eager to publish a magazine about UFOs. Because several editors of the Gansu People's Publishing House had similar (and favorable) views on the subject, they soon were smoothly producing the magazine.

From the very beginning, the publishing house did not think the magazine would be widely circulated. The first print order was only 100,000 copies. A great deal of money was spent advertising in *The People's Daily, Peking Evening News,* and *Guang Ming Daily.* When the first issue of *The Journal of UFO Research* came out and 10,000 copies were shipped to Peking, anxious readers rushed eagerly for them. Each reader bought two, five, ten, and even twenty copies. The editorial department stationed in Peking telephoned to Gansu immediately and asked for an additional 20,000 copies. Gansu could only afford to send 10,000 copies, which again were sold out immediately. For the third time Gansu was urged to send more copies, but the publishing house was unable to meet the request since it had no more copies at hand. But with orders rushing in from all over China, Gansu decided to print another 20,000 copies.

During the time from the first printing until the reprinting, Canton, with 4 million people, could only get 100 copies. Shanghai, with 12 million people, merely got 2,000 copies. Many students in Canton then went to the CURO branch in Canton to see if Mr. Wen Kong Hua, the director, could help. He himself was anxiously waiting for copies, so he cabled to Gansu several times to try to expedite things. He also wrote to me in America for help, but it was beyond my control. When the journal was reprinted, Canton only got 3,000 copies. They were sold out within twelve hours.

In the southern parts of China, such as Sichuan, Yunnan, and Shanxi, where UFOs frequently appeared, officials of UFO organizations also wrote to me to inquire about the insufficient distribution of the magazine in these provinces. They complained that only 4,000 copies were received. (Later another 20,000 copies were supplied.) I am sorry to say that one third of all China shared not even a single copy. Peking was the luckiest; it got 50,000 copies and sold every one. Peking has 8 million people, and, without a doubt, could have sold thousands more copies of *The Journal of UFO Research.*

As one of the editors of the magazine, I want to express my thanks to Dr. J. Allen Hynek and various other UFO experts who contributed their greetings to the magazine. We received many readers' letters indicating that they shared Dr. Hynek's views on UFOs. He is the most publicly recognized UFO authority both here and in China. Advertisements in the *People's Daily* by *The Journal of UFO Research* bore greetings from Dr. Hynek. During the time I personally observed the UFO fever in Peking, UFO fans asked many questions about Dr. Hynek. They were very interested in him.

At present, *The Journal of UFO Research* is circulated to nearly two dozen countries, including Japan, Korea, Canada, France, En-

Figure 4.6 Dr. J. Allen Hynek, left, and the author, at KGO radio station, San Francisco. (Photo courtesy of Shu Fen Dong)

gland, West Germany, Yugoslavia, the Soviet Union, Mexico, Spain, Italy, and, of course, the United States. It is a publishing success, and the reason for that is simple: UFO fever.

5
The Soviet Union's "Hungry Eagle Team"

The poem below was written in an attempt to capture the human dimension of an event involving a Soviet colonel in charge of what has come to be called in the intelligence community the "Hungry Eagle Team."

> *In voicing my worries, I cannot make sense,*
> *The punishment—changing my job—is undeserved;*
> *The "hungry vulture" laughs while I weep,*
> *The accusation against me is totally groundless;*
> *Better to get drunk with a cup of vodka,*
> *Heedless of joy or sorrow.*

The story behind the poem is most interesting; it explains the sorrow of the colonel. It came to me via my Chinese colleagues and was told like this:

In China there are hundreds of so-called "intelligence units" such as the Middle East Intelligence Office, the Latin America Intelligence Office, the Industries I.O., the Weaving and Spinning I.O., and so on almost ad infinitum. There is, as one would expect, a UFO Intelligence Office, and quite naturally it is especially concerned with collecting information about Soviet UFO cases and research. Since China and the Soviet Union have a long border in common, and since many UFO incidents have occurred along that border, the Chinese were naturally suspicious that UFOs were of Soviet origin. The UFO Intelligence Office was part of the Chinese response to what was perceived as a Soviet threat to China's military secrets and national security. In retrospect, one can see a subtle and ironic joke—a cosmic joke—in the situation. More on that in a moment.

When the UFO phenomenon gained worldwide recognition in the modern era, many of the incidents included Soviet sightings. This situation was disconcerting to the Soviet Defense Department. Therefore, it established the Hungry Eagle Team to protect itself against the possible UFO threat; intelligence gathering would reveal the true nature of the phenomenon and would allow the Soviet Union to monitor it. A colonel was assigned as head of the team. His mission: to investigate the sightings and, if any should be of a threatening nature, to smash the offending UFO by force.

One evening in the early 1960s a UFO with flashing red lights flew to a certain sensitive airspace over the USSR. The Hungry Eagle Team assigned two jet fighters to chase it. When the fighters were almost within firing range and the pilots prepared to launch missiles, the colonel stopped them because a civilian aircraft was passing by. Perhaps the colonel was concerned about the safety of a civilian plane; perhaps he simply wanted more time to take photographs of the UFO. In any case after the plane had passed, the UFO was still within firing range of the fighters, and the colonel gave the order to shoot. The pilots immediately launched rockets but incredibly, the UFO accelerated so quickly that it escaped without leaving a trace.

The pilots who had failed their mission were afraid of being reprimanded. They therefore blamed the colonel for the failure because he had ordered them to hold off firing rockets. Their defense worked; the colonel was reprimanded, not them, and was transferred to another post. In such a case, the actual punishment is more mental than physical, because there is no loss of rank or pay—only the stain of dishonor.

As it happened, the colonel felt he had been treated very unfairly. He was an enthusiastic UFO researcher, albeit a military one, and had tried his best to unravel the mystery of UFOs. To be censured for doing his job to the best of his ability, and possibly because he showed humane concern for a civilian aircraft, seemed to the colonel tremendously unjust. Very unhappy, he took to drinking. One night he was quite drunk, and, in his misery and inebriation, he wrote a poem on a napkin in a bar. When he left the bar, the napkin was salvaged by someone nearby who understood its meaning. It changed hands many times over the years, and the original words have been lost. The precise details of its travel have never been recorded, but the incident became widely known in China. I heard of it in 1981, while visiting there. It struck me as a poignant event, and I wrote the poem above to try to recapture the colonel's feelings.

The truth about UFOs is not easily obtained, and the situation is especially complicated because of the interest that the military forces of many countries have in UFOs. The Chinese and Russians are partly responsible for the uncertainty surrounding the nature of UFOs because they have deliberately introduced misinformation of false intelligence reports into the body of data collected by UFO researchers. For example, a recent report in the *Christian Science Monitor* (June 9, 1982, p. 2) begins by saying that flying saucers have not yet been proved to be visiting spaceships, but speculation that they are alien helps the Soviet Union to conceal secret military space shots. The article notes the conclusions of a UFO investigation team sponsored by the Committee for the Scientific Investigation of Claims of the Paranormal (CSICOP). Several world-famous UFO sightings in 1980 and 1981, the team says, were actually Soviet rockets launched from a secret spaceport. And although the Soviet government officially disapproves of speculation about alien space-ships, it wanted to keep the launches secret and thus did not discourage talk about the sightings being due to UFOs. James Oberg, a NASA employee and a member of CSICOP's UFO investigation team, said that such speculation provides a convenient cover for the Soviet's actual operations, some of which are illegal by international treaty and all of which are intended to be secret.

Soviet authorities often aid in sustaining the UFO image of their secret launches, the *Monitor* reported Oberg as saying. He adds that they conduct official investigations in which UFO witnesses are interviewed extensively, and sometimes Soviet Air Force planes are sent to investigate the "unknowns." Even the USSR Academy of Sciences has issued scientific papers on UFOs that conclude there is something mysterious to be investigated. The article comments that whether this is cynical deception or a reflection of academicians' ignorance of the launches is difficult to judge.

The CSICOP report is certain to be disputed by UFO research-ers, for it is quite certain that there have been numerous UFO sightings along the Russian-Chinese border in which both sides have scrambled fighter aircraft, thinking that the other side is responsi-ble for the strange lights in the sky. One rumor has it that China and the Soviet Union nearly went to war in 1970 over a confrontation that arose due to a UFO incident on the border, but that rumor is not true, even though it is widely repeated.

However, there is deep concern on both sides of the border to understand precisely what is happening with regard to UFOs. For even though the Soviets may encourage speculation about UFOs as a way of raising a smokescreen around their secret rocket launches, something is nevertheless happening that both sides recognize as transcending the technological capabilities of any nation of the world. It is ironic indeed—a cosmic joke—that China's current high interest in UFOs, and all its anxiety about them being Russian in origin, should derive from the time when the two countries were allies instead of enemies. In the early 1950s China and the Soviet Union called each other "brother." At that time, the UFO phenomenon was being popularized in the United States—their mutual enemy—and the Soviet Union shared with China whatever information it had on UFOs. The Chinese government kept the information more or less secret from its people, but the flame of widespread interest was kindled at that time. It continues today because of so many UFO sightings that obviously are not man-made rockets; what rocket can hover in midair, make a ninety-degree turn instantly around a pivot point, or reverse course while changing size? The UFO phenomenon seems almost to be mocking humans—Chinese, Russians, and Americans alike—in their efforts to penetrate the mystery of the nature of UFOs even while those same humans use the phenomenon as a cover for their more mundane and military goals.

The June 6, 1981, column of Jack Anderson provides a thought-provoking footnote with which to conclude this chapter. He reports that the U.S. and Red China are exchanging intelligence information informally for mutual interest. The U.S., he says, is primarily interested in air and radio activity the Chinese can pick up along their long border with the Soviet Union; the Chinese, on the other hand, are interested in U.S. satellite photographs of Soviet troop dispositions. But there's another subject the Chinese want information on: UFOs. Our Air Force gave up the search for UFOs ten years ago, Anderson notes, but the Chinese, he says, have reported recent sightings of glowing, dislike objects in the sky.

One can almost hear extraterrestrial laughter at "what fools these mortals be" in their efforts to solve a cosmic mystery.

6
UFO Sightings
That Shocked China

"Believe it or not"—that is an appropriate way to describe the UFO fever that has haunted China recently. In 1982 China's official units and the Kunming Film Studio coproduced a color education film called *UFOs Over China*. It would not surprise anybody if such film were shot in the United States or France. It did, however, amaze many people that a film like this was shot in China.

Those who find this unbelievable would change their minds if they were more familiar with the Chinese response to UFOs. They would, in fact, agree with the Chinese that the shooting of such a film is urgent. That is because the myth of the UFO has puzzled many of the Chinese people. Many of them have become frightened. Some believe that these unidentified flying objects might be secret weapons of Soviet Russia or the U.S.A., while other believe that they are visitors from other planets. Still others believe that they are a kind of omen. Thus it was necessary to produce a film in order to relieve the psychological tension of the confused, uncertain populace. The release of the film will inform people that UFOs are not an omen, nor are they secret weapons of the two "superpowers." UFOs are an age-old phenomenon, possibly craft from other planets.

In recent years, China has collected over three thousand UFO cases, both ancient and contemporary. I will refer to only a few cases that have happened since 1970. These cases, however, were enough to shock the Chinese people. For example, on July 24, 1981, between the hours of 10:30 and 11:30 P.M., thousands of people from twelve provinces saw a huge spiral object flying across the sky. The object looked like a moving dragon. It was estimated to be five times brighter than starlight. Shi Jun Sheng, a student of the Kunming Medical College, Yunnan province, used 7 × 50 binoculars to get a closer view of the object. He cried out, "It is a flying saucer! It has windows." His fellow students practically fought for the binoculars; all who saw the object believed it was a UFO. Later they drew what they had seen. According to their illustration, the main body of the object was a disc which produced blue and green light. On its upper half was a row of windows. The body was circled with six stripes of light which were golden-yellow in color. The body measured about four times the diameter of the full moon.

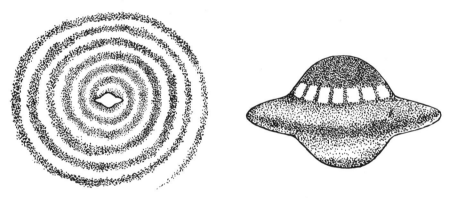

Figure 6.1 Eyewitness drawing of a huge spiral-shaped UFO that was observed almost simultaneously in twelve provinces at 10:30–11:30 P.M. on July 24, 1981. One observer, using 7 × 50 Zeiss binoculars, saw a row of windows on its top.

In Gui Zhou, a group of peasants described the object as being of immense size, about that of an airplane. Students in Sichuan drew a picture of it as "a dragon coiling up into the sky." They even took pictures of it. In Peking, astronomer Wan Sichao (who is also a consultant for *UFOs Over China*) emphasized that the object might be a visitor from outer space. The "huge lighted dragon" was seen in Hubei, Yunnan, Guizhow, Xinjiang, Ningxia, Anhui, Gansu, Shunsi, Inner Mongolia, Sichuan, Hebei, and Quinghai provinces by thousands of people. Even the cautious official New China News Agency dispatched news stories on August 5, September 4, and September 11 about this case in Chinese, English, and French. The longest new article contained some 1,200 words; such extensive coverage had never before been given in the news to UFOs. This particular case has been reported extensively by various American magazines.

是不是飞碟横空？

广东今全思潮 吴月珍 会员

"飞碟"这种传说中的外星人飞船，从前由于目击者不多，加上它神出鬼没，似有若无，因此怀疑者很多。今年七月二十四日晚在我国出现的UFO（不明飞行物）事件，其景象之奇特壮观，目击者范围之广，人数之多，都是前所未有的。人们于是更有理由提出问题：它是不是飞碟？这个不明飞行物体，是在晚上十时三十分左右出现的。当时月亮还未东升，在北方天空中突然出现一团似鸡蛋大小、呈椭圆形的皎白发光物，四周还带点晕雾。这团发光物逐渐变大，亮度则时明时暗，亮时如初升的月华。它一面作逆时针方向的旋转，一面向西飞行，随着旋转，它逐渐变小，并从核心

七月二十四日的空中奇景（画）

亮点处旋转出一道黄白色的明亮的螺旋状光带，光带的圈数愈来愈多，使它成为夜空中绚丽多彩和无与伦比的天象。经过五、六分钟无声的飞行后，这听不见它的声音。分析表明，这个不明飞行物的整个螺旋形光带的直径有一百多公里，真可谓之庞然大物。当中心发光体一面作逆时针方向旋转，一面向外喷射物质时，就形成一圈又一圈顺时针方向的螺旋形物质带，在阳光的照射下，成为光带。在六百多公里的高空，空气已非常稀薄，因此这一螺旋形光带不会被迎面的空气流吹散，从而能保持原状向前飞行。

人们不禁要问，这到底是什么东西呢？

从它的飞行高度和速度来看，它不能是一大群飞翔生物（例如昆虫），也不会是直升飞机的空中试验。因为在这

Figure 6.2 *This is the report of the July 24, 1981, sighting case published in a mainland China newspaper.*

UFO飞临成都上空

81.8.(川)长沙电报

科学之窗

UFO示意图

最近，本报陆续收到成都、什邡、郫县、蒲县、乐山、德阳、广汉等地群众来信，反映目击UFO（不明飞行物）情况。据目击报告称：七月二十四日晚十点四十分左右，一个不明飞行物突然出现。形状象一盘蚊香，呈反时针方向旋转，中心极亮。随着光环一圈一圈地逐渐减弱。光圈直径大约有一公尺左右，中心极亮都直径大约有十多公分。飞行高度和一般民航飞机飞行高度差不多。该飞行物最初出现在正北方向，并向西徐徐飞行，最后消失在北偏西的方向，前后飞行时间约几分钟。

据有关资料记载，一九七七年七月二十六日晚十点十分，成都上空也出现过UFO。时隔四年，两次UFO的出现，不仅时间基本相同，就其出现的空间位置、运动速度、方向，以及形态也都基本相同。这是偶然的巧合，还是太阳系不明天体有规律的运行，甚至有否可能是星外人的有意安排，这些都有待于作进一步的观察、研究。据记载，从一九四八年以来，世界各地有关UFO的目击报告有三万多例。据不完全统计，近年来，国内目击报告也超过三百例。随着人类科学技术飞速发展，神秘的UFO之谜终将被揭开。

（正华报寄摘自《成都日报》周末版）

Figure 6.3
The first officially recognized
photo of a UFO was taken in
mainland China at 4:08 A.M.,
August 24, 1980, in Chang-ping
County, Hebei Province, near
the Great Wall.

Another case that also attracted the interest of the U.S. media is one that was seen somewhere near the Great Wall. On the evening of August 24, 1980, three college students from the Peking Mineralogy School were camping in a valley near the Great Wall at Chang-ping County. At 4:08 in the morning, they saw something strange flying in the east sky. The object looked like a shining disc but was dim in the center part. It moved flutteringly in the sky for about half an hour. Then it flew suddenly toward the south, making an occasional dive, at amazing speed. It did not produce any sound at all.

The students took a photo of what they had seen. It was taken at f2 with a shutter speed of one-half second. They later wrote a letter to the science editor of the *Peking Evening News.* They said that since they did not have the experience of shooting pictures at night and since they did not bring a tripod with them, they did not know what the picture would look like. (They had not yet developed the negative.) The editor asked them to send the film to the *Peking Evening News* so that the newspaper could develop it for them.

As a result, China finally had its first UFO photo. When the photo appeared in the paper, it aroused great interest. Hundreds of letters from different UFO research societies came from everywhere in the world. Many of them requested a copy of the photo. A Miami correspondent stationed in Peking even offered to buy the photo for fifty dollars. According to Huang Tian Xiang, science editor of the *Peking Evening News,* the picture showed that the main body of the object was an oval-shaped structure.

Cases that involve a UFO "mother ship" have been reported all over the world. China is no exception. In June 1981, when I visited Peking, Hung Yun-fong, director of the editorial committee of *Astronomy Amateur*, showed me a report they received from a member of the Huan-ren Science Society in the Liaoning Province. The report, written by Xu Qi-guang, was sent to *Astronomy Amateur*, requesting that it be published. But the magazine has a rule not to publish any UFO reports. Thus Hung Yun-fong gave the report to me instead. The report said that at 7:20 P.M. on April 13, 1981, a huge fiery object as big as a basketball was seen in the southern sky of the Huan-ren County. The ball had red and white lights with a misty, cylindrical tail about two meters long. The fiery ball dispatched small fireballs continually. These small balls looked to be about the size of balls children play with. They were orange in color, and they followed the large fireball toward the northwest. After two minutes the whole array disappeared in the sky. It flew horizontally at about 10,000 meters altitude at the same speed as the jet plane.

I filed the report. Then, a month later, Mr. Shi Bo, assistant editor of *The Journal of UFO Research*, sent me an illustrated report about some UFO sightings. The date of the case, I noticed, was the same date as the report I had on file from Hung Yun-fong. When I studied the illustration, I could identify a "mother ship" image clearly.

Shih Bo had received seven reports that recorded direct encounter with the object on the same day. The reports recorded what was seen in Tianjin, Tangshan, Qinhuangdao (Hebei Province), Gai County, Hei Shan, Fushuen, and Qing Yuan County (all in Liaoning Province). In other words, the object flew from the north to the east, from Tianjin City to Qing Yuan County. It flew across two provinces and finally disappeared in Liaoning. The seven reports plus the one I had all seemed to refer to the same object. There was only twenty-six minutes difference between when the object was first seen and last seen. The timing was as follows:

- Tianjin City: 7:19 P.M.
- Tangshan City: 7:20 P.M.
- Qinhuangdao City: 7:20 P.M.
- Gai County: 7:23 P.M.
- Hei Shan City: 7:25 P.M.
- Fushuen City: 7:40 P.M.
- Qing Yuan County: 7:45 P.M.

The strange thing is that the object appeared to have different shapes when it was seen in different places.

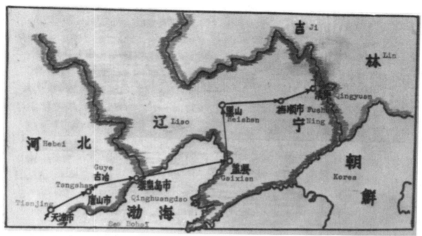

Figure 6.4 The map shows that the object flew over two provinces from Tangshan city of Hebei to Qing Yuan county of Liaoning.

On the map of Figure 6.4, the flying object flew over two provinces. Many of the UFO cases reported around the world have described UFOs having a similar shape.

Among the cases I have collected, there are two I call the "twin brothers." The first case, which occurred in the Hebei Province, described the body of the UFO as looking like a bullet or projectile with a ring around its body. That description matches exactly what was seen in the U.S.A., and earlier in Hong Kong. First I will tell you what was seen in China.

Gao Su-qiu, a primary school teacher at Tangshan (the city ruined by a disastrous earthquake in 1976) wrote a letter to Mr. Gin Tao, science editor of the *Guang Ming Daily*. She said she had seen an object at 3:55 in the morning on October 5, 1980—something very bright outside the window. At first she thought that it might be an "earth light"—an unusual phenomenon that sometimes precedes earthquakes. She woke her husband up immediately and both quietly watched what happened next. They then saw a cigarlike flying object flying toward the southeast. That object was about one meter long. It was a projectilelike structure pulling behind it a very striking light. The object was completely lighted with a shining ring in the center. It flew low at a fairly slow speed, and soon disappeared.

An investigation conducted later found that four youngsters who were fishing by the seashore that evening saw the same object too. They insisted that the flying object had a bright light which illuminated the beach. Mr. Gin Tao referred the story to *Mysteries of*

43

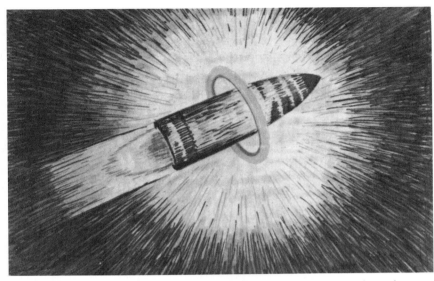

A

Figure 6.5 (A) Drawing of a cigar-shaped UFO with a ring seen flying above the sea near Dai Gang oil field, Tangshan City, about 3 A.M. on October 5, 1980. The shape is similar to a ringed UFO (B) seen the next month by a California pilot and reported in the February 1982 issue of MUFON UFO Journal *and the January 1982 issue of* International UFO Reporter. *(Figure B appeared in the first issue of* Natural Mysteries, *a Mainland China publication, 1981.)*

B

Nature, a quarterly published in Hebei Province. *Mysteries* published the report in its first issue and attracted many readers' interest.

A month after this happened, a pilot from California, Mr. Dennis, also saw the same kind of object while he was flying on a plane. The time was 8:45 P.M., November 5, 1980. He saw it a second time at 3 A.M. on the morning of April 8, 1981. The story of his sightings was published in the February 1982 issue of *MUFON UFO Journal* and the January 1982 issue of *International UFO Report* (published by the Center of UFO Studies).

One of the strangest and most shocking UFO cases—not just in China but in the world's entire record of more than 100,000 cases over the past 35 years—involved an unknown flying object that passed through a large crowd of people, though details are sketchy. This story was provided by Zhang Guang-yuan, editor of the New China News Agency. He said,

> Lin Bing Xiang, a doctor working in the Zhang-pu county hospital in Fujian, and Chen Cai-fa, an officer of the police department there, said that while they were watching a movie, *The Delta of River Danube*, at the stadium during the evening of July 7, 1977, at about 8:30 the audience suddenly screamed because they saw two unidentified objects flying toward them from the northwest corner. The objects were very bright. The audience was frightened and stampeded to clear a way for the objects to pass. Because of the confusion, there were injuries and even a death reported.

In China, people watching movies in open fields occasionally reported seeing unknown flying objects in the sky. Besides the instance above and the one described in Chapter 1, there was a similar case that happened in Tai Ning County, Fujian Province on December 7, 1976. A few hundred workers of He-cheng Chemistry Factory had gathered in the square to watch a movie. Half an hour after the movie began, a UFO appeared in the sky. Its strong white light made the square so bright that it looked just like daytime. People were amazed and scared.

I mentioned at the end of Chapter 1 that the Liberation Army had pursued an unknown flying object in Inner Mongolia by use of a motorcycle. Recently, Huang Tian Xiang of the *Peking Evening News* provided me with another such story. He said,

> In the evening of October 4, 1971, soldiers at Henan Province sighted a huge ball-like object moving low in the northern sky. The ball was twice the size of the full moon. It was orange in color and very bright. The army command there immediately ordered a car of soldiers to follow the object. When they arrived some thirty-five miles northwest

of Yu County, they met soldiers from another camp who were also tracking the object. But it had already disappeared.

It is difficult to get a clear picture from the brief report supplied by Tien-Hsing. Since whatever happened involved the military, it is understandable that details are sketchy. The incident is undoubtedly considered confidential.

Pursuing UFOs and attempts to encircle a UFO by the military are not new (see Chapter 1). I would like to add another story that involved the local militia. The story was supplied by an officer in the Finance Department in Hebei. He wrote the Peking *Guang Ming Daily* about what he had seen. One day in 1971, a bright, ringlike object appeared at night in the sky northwest of Hebei. The object moved in a spiral toward the ground. Many people saw it. The militia there thought it might be an enemy invasion, so a group of soldiers began searching for the object in the mountain, but after an exhausting night they found nothing.

Many of the UFO cases I've collected involve the military. This may be due to the fact that China has a huge armed force (about 4.2 million). One day in the spring of 1968, in Lushun city, the famous port in North China, citizens saw a flashing, golden oval-shaped UFO. Soon it landed on the shore. A sentry nearby immediately reported it to his commander. At the same time he fired his machine gun at the object. The object then flew away at once. Those who saw what happened all said that they were very scared.

Another instance happened in the autumn of 1975 (again, the details and the date are vague). One night two soldiers from a division saw a huge, saucerlike object overhead. The object had a soft reddish color. One of the soldiers rushed back to the camp to report what they had seen. The other remained there and kept a close watch on it. A few minutes later, the commander and ten armed soldiers hurried onto the scene. The soldier who was supposed to be there was not to be found. The whole division searched for him but they found no trace. A few hours later four soldiers heard someone groaning behind them. They turned around and found that the soldier had reappeared, but was unconscious. Amazingly, his eyebrows, beard, and hair had all grown long. When he awoke, he could not recall anything. He had lost memory of the event. His watch had also stopped. Investigation showed that his arm and watch bore weak magnetism.

Besides the army and the militia, the air force has also had its share of UFO experience, as mentioned in Chapter 1. The film *UFOs Over China* has a breathtaking instance that happened in 1980. It was reported that when five interceptors were flying in the evening, they saw a UFO appear not far away from them. Then they found that their communication with the ground base was gone. The pilots were very surprised and frightened. The event was observed by the ground crew, who confirmed the details given by the pilots. However, those details—like other military cases—are cloaked in secrecy.

Another instance happened on July 7, 1978, in the sky above a military base in Shanxi Province. A flying instructor, Sha Yong-kao, was resting in the observation tower. At about 9:40, he heard a report from a pilot in training who was flying above Xing-fen. The pilot said he had discovered a bright object flying in the sky. He was told to watch it closely. After a while he reported again that the unknown object was about at 3,000 meters altitude (about 900 meters above the plane). The object made two circles above the plane and then flew to the north. After investigation it was found that during that time no other plane had been flying that area. Moreover, no airplane would have its entire body illuminated.

To say that "China has two suns" may not be an exaggeration. During the last 12 years more than 160 reports of a UFO that rivaled the sun in brightness have been recorded. In all these cases, a huge red object has been seen to ascend in the sky and travel extensively. Here are a few of those cases.

Toward the end of May in 1980, Li Rong, a resident of Dailian (a famous port in North China near the city of Lu Shun) saw a huge red sunlike object moving from the west to the east. The time was about 8:00 P.M. The UFO was not going very fast. It also appeared to drag a red and yellow tail. The object lighted Li Rong's yard with reddish light. After two minutes, it disappeared.

Another report—very sketchy—reads like this:

> In the midsummer of 1974, between 7 and 8 P.M., the sky above Lanchou city (Gansu Province) was clear. After dinner Chen Guang Hua and his friends were at the stadium. Suddenly a red disc rose above the northwest corner of the stadium. At first it looked like the sun was rising. The disc was very big—bigger than a basketball. Then it became smaller in size. When it ascended the sky, it reduced its size till it looked like a small star and finally disappeared. It all happened within a minute.

A chemist, Lin Ya-Bo, of Xiang Xin city in Hunan Province reported that one day in May 1978, he saw a big round wheel in the sky. It was about the same size as a truck wheel. The center of the wheel was dark red. The color became lighter toward the wheel's edge. It flew from the east toward the west, in a clockwise direction. According to Lin, the object looked like the rising sun in the morning but it was much bigger, more transparent, and its light was less painful to look at. He said many other people also saw the object that evening, "The strange happening impressed me very much but to this day I have not found an answer in any book. It remains a mystery to me."

A student, Shen Su Wen, from the Hongzhou No. 3 Secondary School, also reported, "On July 16, 1977, I was washing my feet as usual on the balcony of my house. The time was 10:48 P.M. The moon was hanging in the blue sky and the stars were shining bright." When Shen had finished washing and was ready to go to bed, he saw a very bright red object flying from the northeast toward the south at steady speed.

"The object I saw was circular in shape. It was the size of a rice bowl. It had strong light and dragged a tail. The tail was twice as long as the body."

A similar report made on September 11, 1976, stated that Ma Bai Kong saw a red flying object. Ma was an officer in the geology department at Tie Li County, Heilongjiang Province. His colleagues also saw the same object that night. It looked as big as a bicycle wheel, and was reddish in the center. It flew from the north toward the south. It was about 7,000-8,000 meters above the ground. The militia in the area saw it also.

UFOs shaped like Saturn (with its well-known rings) have been seen in many places around the world, including China. A report by Professor Tu Deng-feng of the Jiangsu Mineralogy School, published in the second issue of *Mysteries of Nature* (1981), said that at 8:05 P.M. on June 17, 1980, the sky was clear and he and four colleagues were talking in the yard. At this time two machine shop teachers, Jiang Zong Li and his wife, ran to the group and cried out, "Look, look! Flying saucer, flying saucer!" Tu looked toward the northwest where they pointed. Not far away from a star was a flying object five times brighter than the star. Tu said it was flying from the northwest to the southeast, spinning in a clockwise direction. It had a clear ring around it that looked like the ring of Saturn. It stayed in the sky for about two minutes until it was obscured by clouds. But after ten seconds they saw the body of the object again. It was expanding slowly, but the light, however, became weaker. After five minutes it disappeared. Later, two lecturers returning from a walk said they had also seen the same object.

Cases reporting UFOs making sharp right-angle turns are also recorded in China. In Kunming, Yunnan Province, Wang Li-zheng, a member of the China UFO Research Organization (and a consultant for the film *UFOs Over China*), said that on the evening of November 26, 1980, he saw a UFO turn sharply at a ninety-degree angle:

I saw the object flying the sky one evening. Six other workers saw it too. The sky was clear and the visibility was unrestricted. The object was one-fourth as wide in diameter as a full moon and flew at half the speed of an ordinary jet plane. It was about 10,000 meters above us and flew quietly. The object was red in color and every three seconds it blinked once. As it blinked, it looked like a fire ball with flaming lights. Suddenly, it made a ninety-degree turn. Then it disappeared behind the mountain. The time was then 7:41.

Another report came from Guilin, Guangxi province, by Zhou Hou-zhu. He sent a letter to the *Journal of UFO Research* which said that at 8:30 P.M. on December 4, 1980, he saw a red lighted spot flying from north to south. It was 70-85 degrees from the horizon. It was as bright as a star. Its flying speed was not very fast. However, when it reached the top of the sky it made a 90-degree turn and then disappeared in the sky.

There are 72,000 square kilometers of desert area in China—7.2 percent of China's vast (9,600,000 square kilometers) land. The huge expanse of desert includes five provinces: Inner Mongolia, Xin Jiang, Gansu, Qing Hai, and Ning Xia. Here are some UFO cases that occurred in the Gobi Desert. UFO reports from Gobi make up 6.5 percent of the total 3,000 cases on file with the China UFO Research Organization. Thus some people believe that the desert may be a base for UFOs.

A geologist who worked in Xin Jiang Province during the last eight years said that several times a year he saw UFOs landing in the desert. Another youth from Peking who now resides in Xin Jiang also said that one summer night he and his friends saw a UFO flying across the sky of the Gobi Desert. In 1978 a worker of the Karamay oil field headquarters reported that he saw an oval-shaped object, silver in color, moving up and down the grassland of the desert. It did not make any sound and it emitted no smoke. The oil field headquarters believed that it might be some form of enemy attack, so they notified the army division stationed nearby. Soon a group of soldiers armed with antiaircraft weapons arrived. They moved at high speed toward the grassland, hoping to capture the object. When they arrived, they found it still there. The soldiers and the armed oil field workers then encircled it. But when they came near the object, it suddenly took off and disappeared into the sky.

The Gobi Desert region was the site of a shocking incident involving a famous scientist, Peng Jin Mu, from Shanghai, who mysteriously disappeared in the desert. Peng was a research fellow at the Science Academy of Shanghai and the vice-president of the Xin Jiang Science Institute. In 1980 he led a research team deep into the Gobi; one day he went out to look for water and never returned to the camp. The government and the air force sent airplanes and soldiers to search for him. The search thoroughly covered the area within a radius of three hundred kilometers. However, the only thing they found was Peng's footprint and a few candy wrapping papers at a spot where he took a rest. The government finally decided that Peng might have been buried by a sandstorm. This is a plausible conclusion. However, some people suggest that Peng might have been kidnapped by a UFO. If Peng was buried by a sandstorm, there must have been signs left showing that he had been struggling. Moreover, the search was carried out immediately half a day later when Peng failed to report to the camp. Within half a day Peng could at most walk no farther than thirty kilometers. If he was lost in a sandstorm, it would probably have been seen by people in the camp, but they saw nothing.

These UFO cases are only a few of the three thousand cases on file with CURO. You may think that the cases I have mentioned are the most extraordinary ones—but they may not be. The most interesting and exciting cases could be those recorded by the observatories and by the military. However, all those are kept secret for reasons of "national security," and I have no way to get access to them. Huang Tien-hsing, science editor of the *Peking Evening News*, has been warned that he cannot disclose any cases about UFOs that are related to the country's security. Xie Chu, a UFO expert and editor of *Aerospace Knowledge*, had published a science fiction story about UFOs in his magazine. The story, entitled "Encounter in the Night Sky," described how the Chinese Air Force used missiles to attack a flying saucer. Might the exciting story reflect some actual happenings that are kept secret? After all, Xie is an official and he knows some UFO secrets.

Without even considering the confidential cases gathered by the military units, the three thousand cases that the UFO Research Organization has collected are enough to make the majority of Chinese people believe that UFOs are a fact. In China today there are twenty-eight research societies pursuing research on UFOs. More interesting is that many primary and secondary schools frequently hold forums on UFOs. For example, the Xinyang Road Primary School in Guangxi has had a monthly lecture on UFOs since May 1981. Many secondary schools in Canton city also set up lecture groups on UFOs. The groups are led by some one hundred staff people from different schools. The lectures are given once a week. In addition, many engineering and aerial organizations have also set up similar UFO study groups. All this is due to the UFO fever generated by many shocking cases, widely observed, of UFOs passing silently across the skies of China.

7
UFOs in Taiwan: The Cases and the Debate

UFOs are a puzzle whose reality is debated worldwide. Whenever the topic surfaces in public, there is vigorous, often heated, discussion and argument among the learned. Taiwan is no exception.

The debate over UFOs in Taiwan always involves four people: Dr. Shen Jun Shan, San Mao, Cai Zhang Xian, and Lu Ying Zhong. Cai Zhang Xian, who may be constrained by his position as the director of the official observatory, never participates in open discussions. Nevertheless, people all know that Director Cai believes that UFOs do exist. As for the others, the story is this.

If you are in Taiwan, Hong Kong, Japan, or Southeast Asia and ask who San Mao is, people will say that she is a famous writer. San Mao travels widely to many parts of the world, especially Africa and Spain. She is an intelligent, experienced journalist whose articles are published in prominent newspapers and magazines throughout the Orient. Once a Hong Kong columnist wrote about her: "... last year a group of writers, reporters and editors visited Singapore and Malaysia. Among the members of the group were well-known editors, authors and reporters. But everyone's attention was on her. It seemed she was a shining star."

Except, that is, to Dr. Shen Jun Shan, a physicist who challenges San Mao in debate and who disagrees that UFOs are real. Shen is a celebrity in Taiwan. He has studied physics at the State University of New York. Presently he is a physics professor of Qing Hua University, and concurrently is the director of Taiwan Astronomy Association and a member of the editorial committee of the *Taiwan Science Monthly*. He wrote a bestseller there, *Informal Talks on Astronomy*. When the Science Commission was founded in Taiwan in 1980, he became one of its directors. In 1979 he and Cai Zhang Xian, who is director of Taiwan's Yuan Shan Observatory, participated in the 17th International Astronomy Union (IAU) convention in Montreal, Canada. Thousands of Taiwan college and high school students know who Shen is.

So San Mao and Shen Jun Shan are formidable opponents, each capable of presenting the viewpoint he or she supports with force and authority. San Mao has openly declared that UFOs exist. The reason is simple: She has seen them personally. "I have seen UFOs twice," she said, "once about six years ago and again about five years ago in the Sahara Desert of Africa."

In an article written by San Mao, she said, "It was about 6 o'clock in the evening, when I was on my honeymoon in a small town. I was unaware of the arrival of the UFO, which came without sound or noise. But the electric power went out and the whole town plunged into darkness." At that moment, she wanted to go out and see what had happened, but she was unable to start the car. At the same time, she saw a huge ball-shaped object hanging above the sky. It did not look like a saucer, as people generally describe it, but rather like a transparent ball. Its color was somewhat between white and gray. She could not see clearly what was inside it. It was huge, hanging silently about thirty stories high. She thought it could be an air balloon, but quickly realized that the wind was strong in the desert and no balloon could stay there steadily without moving. However, she was not scared. The people of the whole town gathered around, watching it. When she and her husband were ready to leave, suddenly the UFO turned a ninety-degree angle and flew away fast, disappearing without a sound.

Shen Jun Shan is a well-known opponent of UFOs in Taiwan. He argues that the idea "seeing is believing" may not be correct. "People have different opinions about strange phenomena. The UFO is one of this kind of phenomena," Shen said. "What San Mao saw was not a UFO. What she saw was most probably a mirage." Shen is a professor of physics. He believes that only with enough evidence can facts be established; short of that, discussion and declarations are insufficient, if not useless.

"If we had direct evidence—for example, if we caught a flying saucer and put it on display here—we would have to accept it as a fact," Shen said. True enough, but the question is, if a flying saucer were captured by the Taiwan or American government, would they display it—or even disclose it? There are UFO researchers who feel that the U.S. government has indeed obtained a crashed flying saucer and is keeping the fact hidden behind a cloak of secrecy labeled "national security." So Shen's objection is not an ironclad argument. Nevertheless, he persists in his position that UFOs are "a beautiful story to tell at night under shining stars."

Once Shen wrote in a newspaper:

> The U.S. and the Soviet Union both have space observation stations with sensitive instruments. These man-made satellites are so sensitive that no human eyes can be compared with them. If some unknown objects were sighted, both the American and the Soviet space stations would have reported them. Nevertheless, there have never been any records on these sensitive instruments of what has been seen by some people in recent years.

I must repeat what I said above: If the U.S. and the Soviet Union do observe UFOs, will they disclose the news? Shen never seems to consider this question. He also stated in his article that "American and European countries have spent large amounts of money to investigate UFO reports. Most of the cases investigated can be explained one way or another. The mirage theory mentioned above is one of the explanations."

San Mao steadfastly opposed Shen's viewpoint. She has often said that "the scientific knowledge of mankind is still very limited. There might be another world—not in outer space, not in the physical universe, but in our very environment, unexplainable, unproven, but existing among us."

I wrote to San Mao asking for her comments on Shen. Her reply was thought-provoking. In the letter she said, in effect: "I believe UFOs are real. It is ridiculous for Shen to say what I saw was a 'mirage.' As I lived in the Sahara Desert for two years, of course I have seen mirages. But they are quite different from UFOs."

San Mao's point is well taken: She found Shen's explanation that the UFO was a mirage to be naive.

San Mao was staying at an island about one hundred miles from the Sahara when the UFO appeared. She felt that since there are fewer people on a desert, that could be the reason for UFOs to come there often. Among her friends there was a Spanish couple; the husband is the postmaster of the post office there. They were the first to have been informed about the coming of a UFO. Then they saw it. In another case, San Mao said, some people were even taken away by UFOs to Tenerife Island and have "lost" time for two hours.

She told me in her letter that she has not taken photos of any UFOs. What she saw that time in the Sahara was a transparent ball-shaped thing, very big, but not very tall. It was silent and did not move. During the time of its presence, the whole city lost electricity. Cars could not be started. The time was around seven or eight o'clock in the evening, not yet dark. The place was Villa Cinero, and the date was about July 16, 1974. (The date could be a bit off, but the month and year were correct, she said, because she was married on July 9, and went to the small town near the desert for her honeymoon.)

Due to the fact that she was completely fear-free, without any tension at all, San Mao said, she watched the UFO silently and without thoughts for thirty minutes. She did not go to get her camera. Later on she became tired of watching and left. When she looked back, the UFO made a right-angle turn and flew away without a trace. During the whole event, her mind was very clear, she commented, and afterward, she did not think about it very much.

Another UFO occurence happened to her in the desert one night at midnight. An orange-colored flying object appeared in the sky, she said, and seemed to fire out small bullets, like a mother plane shooting out small planes flying around it. She was scared and lay down facing the ground. It was a tense moment. But she also felt funny and not sure of herself. There were some local people with her, whose presence made the happening very real—definitely not a hallucination.

Yes, San Mao believes in UFOs because, as she often tells her friends: "When someone has seen a UFO, it is hard for them not to believe it."

In her letter to me, San Mao objects very much to the word "mirage" used by Shen Jun Shan in describing what she saw on the desert. In all his articles on UFOs, Shen uses the concept of mirages to deny the existence of UFOs. In fact, he uses the word so often that it irritated pro-UFO Taiwanese. They ask, since a mirage is supposed to appear in deserts, oceans, and lakes, then how do we explain the mirage appearing over Taipei City? In one case, six Taiwan Air Force fighter planes chased a UFO in the sky over the Taiwan Strait. How do we explain that? Director Cai of Yuan Shan Observatory in Taipei, who has been there for thirty-six years, has seen UFOs three times with his own eyes. Are these all "mirages"?

Dr. Shen has no explanations for these questions. All that he can say is: "All the UFO phenomena can be explained in terms of physics." That is too much of a generalization. How would he explain them in terms of physics? How much has he explained? Has he ever made physics experiments on UFOs? What are the results? Shen has no answer to any of these questions. This has made those who are pro-UFO repudiate Shen's loose talk all the more.

No one in Taiwan has any doubt about Shen's academic achievement and his qualifications for his position. Nevertheless, the fact is that he has never studied the problems of UFOs. "No investigation and research; no right to speak out." This is his weak point, which is also the weakness of those who criticize UFOs based on their subjective view and intuition to judge UFOs. I have made a study of people who do not believe in UFOs, and found out that once they go deeper into investigating and researching the subject, most of them change their original view. The reason is simple: UFOs are real. Of course, UFOs are not necessarily visitors from outer space. They may be some natural phenomenon present since ancient times. But the point is, there is something *real* there.

Figure 7.1
Professor Lu Ying Zhong in his Cosmos *magazine office.*

Lu Ying Zhong, editor of *Cosmos* magazine and director of the Taiwan UFO Research Organization, watches closely the publications and speeches on UFOs by Shen. Zhong was formerly a section chief of the Atomic Energy Commmission of Taiwan; he is presently a professor at Cultural University. Any time Shen attacks the UFO phenomenon, Lu rebuts him.

Lu's position, prestige, and public speaking ability are not comparable to that of Dr. Shen. But Lu knows Shen's weak point— his lack of knowledge about UFOs. Several times Lu has requested Shen to have a person-to-person open debate on television. Shen always keeps silent about Lu's requests. I understand that Director Cai of Yuan Shan Observatory supports Lu. Shen's authoritative image should not be allowed to overshadow the prestige Cai deserves. Cai has seen UFOs several times, while Shen has no such experience. Cai often tells people about the existence of UFOs, although he cannot really explain the nature of the phenomena.

The first time Director Cai saw a UFO was on March 5, 1956. He saw a shining object south of the constellation Leo to the east, moving slowly toward the north. Its color was dark red, but very bright. When it moved past the polestar to the north, its brightness dulled a little. Later it moved to the west of Ursa Major; its speed slowed down, then it stopped for a while. Then it turned toward the east and suddenly turned back at a faster speed. At this point, Cai raised his telescope, but was too late to see it clearly because the brightness of the UFO became weak. When the UFO reached the Canes Venatici constellation, it looked almost like a dim star. Gradually it disappeared. Cai points out that this UFO was visible for about thirty-five minutes. It was silent, thus it was impossible that it was an airplane. If it were an airplane, it should not have been so bright when flying 10,000 to 20,000 feet above the earth. Cai said that from the way it moved, this UFO must be a controlled flying object.

The second time he saw a UFO was on September 5, 1959, when Cai discovered one near the North Star. The position of the UFO was even higher in elevation angle than that of the polestar. It flew around the North Star in thirty minutes. In Cai's estimation, if it were an airplane, it would have made the circle in two to three minutes.

The last time Cai saw a UFO was June 28, 1967, when he saw a shining UFO appear near the Pegasus constellation. At first, he thought it was a new star. He rushed into his office to take out a star map for comparison. However, when he came back with the map in less than two minutes, the shining flying object had already become very dim and had flown around the Pegasus constellation, straight toward the northeast. After about thirty minutes, it disappeared into the night.

Judging from its flight time, Cai says, it could not be an airplane, and judging from its straight flight to the northeast, it could not be a balloon, because balloons travel erratically. Obviously it could not be a star because a star doesn't change its position in relation to other stars. Judging from its flight halfway around the Pegasus constellation, it could not be a man-made satellite because a satellite travels in a straight line.

Cai not only often suggests the existence of UFOs, but also supports their study. The *Astronomy Newsletter* he edits often publishes eyewitness reports of UFOs. Yuan Shan Observatory, of which he is the director, frequently had discussion meetings on UFOs. He invited me to give a lecture on UFOs at Yuan Shan Observatory, which I did on July 2, 1979. The small auditorium was full. Many people came in vain and had to leave because there were no seats for them. It was hot in July in Taiwan. There was no air conditioning in the auditorium, only electric fans. I lectured for three hours, and no one left. Afterward Cai took me to a restaurant. While we sat at the table, he told me that he was very much interested in UFOs, and we talked at length about our mutual interest.

Nearly two months after I returned to the United States from Taiwan, on October 29 there was a big headline in *The United Press* (which has the largest circulation in Taiwan) entitled "UFO Visited Taiwan." The story said that about 10:30 in the evening of October 28, a huge saucer-shaped object appeared in the sky over Taipei City. There were many small holes around the edge of the saucer from which red lights beamed out. It stayed relatively low in the sky for one or two minutes. Many Taipei residents were alarmed and called the police, the observatory, and the newspapers. When Director Cai received the phone calls, he rushed to the rooftop of his observatory, but the UFO had flown away. Only stars were shining in the sky.

Although Cai had not seen the UFO, several hundred Taipei residents saw it. A student of the police academy surnamed Ma wrote a letter to the *China Times*, in which he described the event vividly. He said that at 12:13 on the morning of October 29, he saw a shining, round, flying object about two thirds the size of a book desk. It constantly changed its degree of brightness. At first it stopped to the west of the school. After half a minute, it started moving to the west and disappeared. Two minutes later, the object appeared again. This time it was shining like the flames of an oil refinery. When the flame was dim, a row of silver-colored windows could be seen.

Every time a UFO is seen in the sky over Taiwan, people call the observatory. Since there is only one observatory in Taiwan, it records all UFO cases in the area. Here are three of the best cases.

The first happened on the evening of August 1, 1973. At 11:47, a high school student in Taipei named Chi Zhong Jie was on the third floor of his house, looking at the sky. Suddenly he noticed two huge, double-shaped flying objects in the sky moving from the west to the north. They stopped there. At that moment, he rushed downstairs to get his camera and take a picture. About twenty seconds later, these objects shot back to the west like two shooting meteors and disappeared. Chi said that the objects were silent. At that time a cool wind was blowing. Only the moon was in the sky. The two objects looked silver-white, like streetlights.

Chi's photo is the first UFO photo taken in China. Another UFO photo was taken on August 24, 1980, near the Great Wall in Mainland China, and the *Peking Evening News* announced that it was "the first

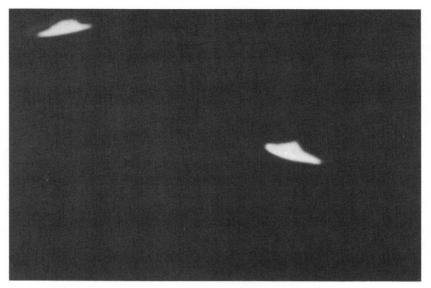

Figure 7.2 This is actually the first photo of two huge double-shaped UFOs taken on August 1, 1973, at 11:47 in Taipei City of Taiwan, by a high school student, Chi Zhong Jie. This is the first UFO photo taken in China and published in a Taiwan magazine in 1978.

UFO photo of China." However, since Peking considers Taiwan to be part of the People's Republic of China, I have written to *Peking Evening News* to correct its error.

To obtain Chi Zhong Jie's UFO photo, I asked Director Cai to contact him on my behalf, which he did. Some time later Chi mailed me the negative and told me about the event:

> It was 1973 when I saw the double-shaped UFO. I thought it was something else—perhaps a mirage. As I was not sure, I did not publish an account until 1977. A teacher of mine knew a reporter, who sent my report of this event to the paper. The reporter, however, added inaccurate material to it, saying that I was superstitious and foolish. As a result of all this, I was falsely accused of an inaccurate report by the observatory.

The second UFO case in Taiwan happened on January 3, 1975. It was 9:35 in the evening when Sun Yuan Jian, an experienced member of the Taiwan Astronomy Association, was in Wai Shwang Xi District of Taipei County (near Don Hu University) observing the planet Saturn. Suddenly he saw a shining object in the northern sky between the Boötes and Gemini constellations. Luckily, he had a

Figure 7.3 Double white-and-red UFOs rotating around each other were observed by Sun Yuan Jian with 12 × 30 binoculars at 9:35 P.M. on January 3, 1975. Sun is a member of the Taiwan Astronomy Organization.

telescope with which he could see clearly. The shining UFO seemed to consist of two connected objects, one with a white light and the other with a red light. At first the white and the red lights were shining separately. Later, the red light gradually became orange in color, and then the white light also became orange, all the while revolving around each other. Moments later, they slowly rose up higher and higher. Soon they reached the elevation angle of the Cepheus constellation. Then suddenly they made a ninety-degree turn and flew toward the southwest, gliding downward. Meanwhile, they reduced speed intermittently. It was one minute from the time the UFO was discovered to the time it disappeared.

Sun wrote a report on the incident, which was published in the *Astronomy Newsletter*. He listed four points that led him to believe the object was a UFO:

1. Judging from their shining beams, the two forms were not airplanes; if they were, they would not be silent; their sounds should have been heard.
2. Since an airplane flies very fast, generally it cannot make an abrupt ninety-degree turn, but instead must bank slowly to turn.

3. Their shining lights were different from those of an ordinary airplane, and airplanes cannot fly revolving around each other as these objects did.

4. It was after nine-thirty in the evening when they were discovered. Thus it was impossible that they were man-made satellites.

I asked an artist to draw a picture of the event, and then I showed it to Yuan Shan Observatory personnel for their study. They could not explain the phenomenon.

The third UFO case over Taiwan happened at about 5:10 A.M. on June 13, 1981. On that day a farmer named Chen Kang Tong and his wife went to work on their farm in Chia Li Town, Tainan County. On the way, they heard a strange noise above them. They looked up and were scared. They saw a spinning, shining object falling down. Chen later told the police that the object was about three feet in diameter, transparent like a diamond, in the shape of a cone, with a flat top and a pointed bottom. A light beam came out from the top and another from the bottom. The two beams turned on and off alternately. Through the transparent shell, many instruments could be seen, which astonished the farmer and his wife.

The farmer said, "The UFO slowly landed at the back of a tree and continued spinning like a toy. It shot out thin fog like a screen. About ten minutes later, the UFO flew away without a trace. At first it flew to the north, but later on it turned toward the south and disappeared very fast."

Afterward the farmer took a reporter to a fruit tree, and said that the UFO had slowly glided down from above his head and landed near the tree. It looked somewhat like a conch shell and continued spinning slowly. When its pointed bottom touched the ground, it made very little noise. It did not leave any trace on the ground soil. It stayed there about ten minutes, then suddenly took off fast from the ground, throwing up dust, first shooting up high toward the north, and then turning toward the southeast, where it soon disappeared.

This UFO incident was sketchily reported by Dr. Hynek's *CUFOS Associate Newsletter* (July 1981).

With a population of 17 million, Taiwan has two UFO research organizations. One is the Taiwan UFO Research Organization, led by Lu Ying Zhong. The other is Chung Hua UFO Research Center, led by Chung Dunn, a dentist. The former has five hundred members, the latter about two hundred. The two jointly sponsored UFO research exhibitions in 1980 and 1982, which attracted more than two thousand visitors. In 1981, Chung Hua Television of Taiwan produced a one-hour TV show about UFOs, entitled *Visitors from Space*. I am told that the program enjoyed a high viewing rate.

All in all, the enthusiasm about UFOs in Taiwan is second only to that of mainland China. Taiwan newspapers and the television station frequently talk about UFOs. It seems that Dr. Shen Jun Shan is the only one who denies the existence of UFOs. Obviously, he does not have many followers, just like the situation for the anti-UFO forces in Mainland China. There as well as in Taiwan and their neighbors—Japan, South Korea, Hong Kong, Macao—UFO studies are popular. The enthusiasm of the United States for ufological research has spread to the Orient, and thus in still another area, East is meeting West.

8
UFO Research and Cases in Hong Kong and Macao

Hong Kong is a small city, three by eighteen kilometers in area, situated close by the province of Guangdong. Separated from Hong Kong by a narrow strip of water is Kowloon, similar in size. The Chinese regard Hong Kong and Kowloon as one city and call it Kong-Kow (Hong Kong-Kowloon). The two cities combined have an area about that of San Francisco, and yet enjoy a prosperity unequalled by any of the cities of the world. This is because Hong Kong is a free port, with a harbor deep enough to accommodate large mercantile and war vessels and with a modern airport. Each year more than a million tourists (not including visitors from Mainland China) come to Hong Kong from different parts of the world. Large numbers of American and British military men came here on furlough during the Korean and Vietnam wars. There are bars and nightclubs galore, catering to the needs of seamen, tourists, merchants, and British troops in Hong Kong. It was here that the story of *The World of Suzie Wong* takes place.

There is an old Chinese saying: "The sparrow may be small, but it has all the vital organs." Though small, Hong Kong has almost everything that exists in the world. It is a mercantile kingdom, with a quasi-autonomous government, a local currency, and a police force of several thousand, in addition to the symbolic presence of a British garrison force. The best products of America, Britain, France, and Japan are available in Hong Kong—and what is more, often at lower prices than at their places of origin. The press and the financial market in Hong Kong are among the world's most sensitive; they respond promptly to anything of importance that may happen elsewhere in the world. New French fashions and the latest Hollywood hairstyle become popular in no more than a few days among Hong Kong's ladies. Can anyone imagine that something as sensational as UFOs would be an exception?

The film *Close Encounters of the Third Kind* was a box office hit in Hong Kong, but it was not responsible for the UFO fever that, as in the mainland, rages there. In fact, as far back as the 1950s, at the time of the film *The Day the Earth Stood Still*, UFOs had already drawn the attention of the Hong Kong public. A friend in Hong Kong told me that one summer night during the Korean War (he couldn't give me the exact year), a giant cigar-shaped UFO appeared over the bay of Hong Kong. Surrounded by a white mist, the object emitted red light every few seconds, giving the mist a reddish hue. Flying very slowly, it made no noise and finally disappeared with abruptly accelerated speed, leaving behind a long white streak which remained undispersed for quite some time. The strange spectacle was witnessed by many who happened to be strolling or enjoying the cool air near the beach that night.

Though a small city, Hong Kong has had a population of 5 million since 1973. There were about a dozen newspapers and about forty magazines of various kinds. Any news about UFOs was always a welcome item for all these periodicals. In particular, the widely circulated *The World of Science* carried a spate of reports about UFOs. In 1979 there was a letter to the editor of a newspaper from two citizens, Liang Minghui and Chen Minghui:

> We were eyewitnesses of a UFO on two consecutive days, July 9 and 10, 1979. The location was over Kowloon across from Hong Kong. At 1:15 P.M. on July 9, we saw a white UFO moving at a very low speed. At first circular in shape, it later became a single line, then a cross and finally resumed its circular shape before gradually diminishing in size and vanishing in the sky.
>
> At 1:45 P.M. on July 10, at the same spot, the object reappeared. At first it was white and circular, but later it became two circles, blue on one side and red on the other with white in the middle. It was moving very slowly, and just as on the previous occasion it diminished in size and finally disappeared.

Later that year the same newspaper carried an even more interesting letter to the editor. It said that at about 9:45 P.M. on the night of August 5, 1979, the writer of the letter happened to be on the balcony in his home at Shangxui (about ten kilometers from the center of Hong Kong) and saw in the northern sky a spot of yellow light, something like a star, yet larger, brighter, and yellower than a star. He thought it very odd. Then the yellow object began to twinkle, and a red and a green lantern were lit on either side with something like an arc seemingly linking them up. It was so dark that the outline of the object was not clearly visible.

The UFO flew from north to south across the shantytown and the writer's building, and once it was past the building, he and his family, who were also present, were unable to see it anymore. The UFO's appearance lasted about half a minute; it was seen by every member of his family.

The writer's father thought that it was a military helicopter (because helicopters frequently fly past there in daytime), but the writer didn't agree with him because the object gave no noise and a faraway helicopter can always be heard even in daytime, let alone on a still night like that evening was.

I have collected more than thirty cases of UFOs that have been observed in Hong Kong, and there is one case which, being of the same type as one reported in the United States, has stuck in my memory, for I have always taken a particular interest in any UFO case the like of which has been reported in two different countries.

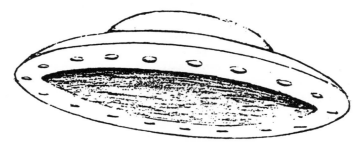

Figure 8.1 The same type of UFO has been reported in the United States. This drawing appeared in the December 1979 issue of MUFON UFO Journal *(No. 142), page 4. (Courtesy Mutual)*

The case happened on the night of September 9, 1979, and was one that caused the greatest sensation even in Hong Kong. Many residents called and wrote on that day to the observatory, the police department, and the newspapers to report the UFO.

One reader wrote to a newspaper that he had just gotten out of his car at 10:20 on the night of September 9, when he saw a star flitting across the sky with a trail of white smoke. The spectacle was most impressive.

Three other readers calling themselves members of an amateur photography club enclosed a drawing of a saucer-shaped object in their report to a newspaper. They were photographing in the neighborhood of Long Chiang Street at 11 P.M., September 9, they wrote, when they suddenly saw a moving white spot high above in the sky. At first they thought it was a meteor and did not pay much attention to it. A few minutes later, the white spot came closer and remained stationary in midair. They saw clearly that it was of circular shape, with rings of light flashing on its bottom; no sound was heard. They promptly took pictures of it. A few seconds later the circular object flashed with white light and for a while they could see nothing. When they regained their vision, the flashing flying object had gone.

Another reader described the object as "something like a glittering diamond, giving out intense light, and when the light was dimming, it appeared as a saucer which then turned into something like a comet, approximately as large as two airplanes."

The Hong Kong Amateur Astronomical Society, the "Zuo Jing Club," *The World of Science,* and the Hong Kong Space Museum have collected UFO cases over the years, but they did little more than collect them without attaching much importance or showing much enthusiasm to research, except for *The World of Science,* which frequently held observational activities of stars and UFOs. Owing to the impact of the UFO craze of recent years on the mainland, a Hong Kong University physics junior, Zheng Qingyun, has organized the Hong Kong UFO Research Organization to establish direct contact with the Canton UFO Research Organization. At present, the Hong Kong organization has scores of members.

Macao, separated from Zhong Shan County of Guangdong Province on the mainland by a stream, is of even smaller size than Hong Kong and has a population of several hundred thousand. Few foreigners would go on a tour to Macao, which takes only an hour and twenty minutes to reach by boat from Hong Kong. Macao depends on Hong Kong commerce, Hong Kong tourists, and overseas Chinese visitors, as well as its gambling trade, for its very existence. Yet surprisingly enough, this small city was also frequented by UFOs. There is also a twenty-five member UFO Society headed by a painter, Mr. Pan Lungshan. Mr. Pan is fond of writing and makes frequent comments on the UFO phenomenon. He is a determined believer in UFOs. In 1979, when I was in Hong Kong, he paid me a special visit, bringing me a large amount of information, mostly stories about UFOs over the years as reported in local newspapers such as the *Macao Daily* and *Oversea Chinese Daily.*

For instance, on July 6, 1978, a student of Hong Kong University coming to Macao from Hong Kong on a pleasure tour witnessed an unidentified object at an altitude of about 10,000 feet in the northeastern corner of the sky at 9:05 in the evening. The object rhythmically flashed in three colors—white, red, and orange. There were seven white flashes followed by two red flashes, then turning to orange, reverting after one flash to white again, and repeating the cycle for about three minutes. The student reported what he saw to the Macao Weather Bureau because there is no observatory in Macao, but the bureau offered no explanation.

Five days later, on July 11, when people gathered on the west beach to watch a conjunction of Venus and Saturn, a UFO appeared—apparently the same UFO, by coincidence—flashing as previously the three colors: red, orange, and white. But this time there was also blue light. Among the eyewitnesses were reporters of *Oversea Chinese Daily*. They came to the conclusion that the object was neither a man-made satellite nor a meteor, for neither could change its color; nor could it be an airplane, for it was moving many times faster than an airplane, and besides, it was noiseless.

At 8:45 on the evening of July 13, a similar or perhaps the same object reappeared. This time the color changed from white to green, then to red, and the flashing UFO abruptly shook itself before dashing upward and then coming to a stop while continuing to flash. About five minutes later another UFO emerged somewhere in the neighborhood, flashing in a similar manner and also remaining stationary. Moments later a third one appeared with similar flashes, but moving slowly. It then turned around to fly at high speed toward the larger of the other two UFOs, and on approaching it, suddenly vanished.   Then the second UFO followed suit and also vanished while approaching the first UFO. Thus the three seemed to have combined into one.

Because the "strange objects" had appeared again and again, a group of astronomers and UFO fans flocked to the seaside with telescopes to await their chance to see it. As expected, a·UFO was again seen, this time by three young men at 8:00 on August 16. Using their telescopes, they found the object to be oblong in shape and dazzlingly bright, brighter even than the moon. The objects's appearance lasted about twenty seconds.

At 7:17 P.M. on September 1, the three young men again found several flying objects as large as Venus in the southeastern sky. With telescopes, they saw that the objects were composed of several light spots of orange, white, and red. The objects continued to appear and disappear alternately eleven times in a row. When they appeared, some were found flying, others remaining stationary, with their lights varying in intensity. One of them, which was originally the size of Venus, later suddenly became several times larger without changing its distance from the observers.

UFOs usually make their appearances at night. But once on

July 15, 1978, a silver-white dazzling UFO suddenly appeared in daytime over Macao. When the news spread, people from homes, offices, and shops went into the streets to watch. The next day the event was reported in the *Oversea Chinese Daily* by saying that UFOs had once again become the talk of the town. Hundreds of residents had rushed to the streets to watch the flying object that made its appearance in the sky, the article stated. It went on to say that the object first appeared in the sky over a neighboring area of Taishan and flew in a southwesterly direction from the northeast. The time was between 2:00 and 2:40 P.M. Its distance made the object look very small; it appeared circular in shape. It was seen at a position northeast of the sun and seemed close to it, though one could still see it flashing with silvery light. It was flying not so fast as an airplane but faster than a helicopter. At times hidden by the clouds, it emerged now and then. People standing in the streets looked at it with heads raised and went about spreading the news. Many turned out from homes, offices, and shops onto the streets, talking with animated gestures. For a time traffic was blocked. The *Daily's* reporter, upon learning the news, rushed to the scene and saw for himself the object emerging twice from behind the clouds. The newspaper staff nearby turned out in full strength to watch the spectacle along with everyone else. People who were too late to catch a sight of the spectacle felt quite sorry about it. For days there had been plenty of news about UFOs in the sky, but it was the first time in recent years that a mysterious object in the sky was ever observed in daytime.

According to Pan Lungshan, one of the eyewitnesses of the two UFO incidents in Macao, both cases cannot be explained away as airplanes, helicopters, meteors, balloons, man-made satellites, and so on. The reporters of the *Macao Daily* and *Oversea Chinese Daily* who were also among the eyewitnesses agreed that UFOs belonged to the inexplicable.

At present, the study of UFOs in Hong Kong, Macao, and the mainland is closely related, and the researchers keep in close touch. Only Taiwan and the mainland have been prevented from establishing official contacts for political reasons.

9
UFOs
in Ancient China

UFO researchers the world over have been seeking evidence from ancient records for further proof of the existence of UFOs. In various parts of the globe there are mysterious traces and relics suggestive of UFOs and extraterrestrial contact. Likewise, in ancient books, including even the Bible, similar suggestive indications can also be found. UFO researchers in China firmly believe that a vast country with such a long history as China must have in its ancient books and records an immense wealth of data about UFOs. They have indeed found some evidence in this regard which suffices to prove the existence of UFOs in ancient China, though it falls short of establishing that flying saucers from an outer space ever visited the planet. So far UFO experts in China have found more than sixty such mentions of ancient books. Some are very brief passages consisting of only a few sentences; others run as long as several pages. To be sure, some of the records are ambiguous, explainable either as astronomical or atmospheric phenomena or as UFOs; but there are also some accounts so vivid that they seem to describe a craft from another planet before our very eyes.

For example, there is an astounding account in *Dong Tien Ji (Peeping on the Sky)* of the Tang Dynasty (618–907):

> In the Tang Dynasty a celestial ship, over fifty feet long, was found and placed in the Ling De Hall. The ship gave out a metallic sound when struck, and was of very hard material which was rustproof. Li Deyu,

the Tang Prime Minister, cut over a foot of a slender long stick of the ship and carved it into a figure of a Taoist priest. The Taoist figurine flew away and then returned. In the years of Emperor Daoming, the figurine disappeared and the ship also flew away.

Judging this account in light of modern scientific knowledge, the so-called "celestial ship" may well have been either a spaceship carrying a visitor from outer space or an instrument of exploration under remote control. "It gave out a metallic sound when struck, and was of very hard material which was rust proof" apparently indicates that it was made of a high quality substance. The slender long stick would seem to be an appurtenant instrument. Notice that when dismantled and carved into a figure, it could also "fly away and return again." This seems to suggest that it was carrying out some kind of survey under remote control. In the year 800, in the reign of Emperor Guangming, the spaceship appeared to have concluded its mission of investigation and so left. It seems improbable that the record giving the exact time, place, and name of the person involved could be a mere cock-and-bull story.

Professor Zhang Longqiao of the Chinese department of Peking Teachers College published an article entitled "Could It Be That a Visitor from Outer Space Visited China Long Long Ago?" in Peking's *Guang Ming Daily* of February 18, 1979. The article has drawn the attention of UFO enthusiasts and the intellectual world, and has been reprinted in Japan, Taiwan, and Hong Kong. A brief translation of the article has also appeared in an American magazine.

Zhang discovered this vivid account of a UFO from the ancient book *Meng Qi Bi Tan* (Essays Of The Meng Hall) by Shen Kua of the Song Dynasty (960–1127). He described himself when discovering the story as being "pleasantly surprised and immensely intrigued"; he was "inclined to think that this might in a big way supply a clue that a flying craft from some other planet once landed somewhere near Yangzhou in China."

According to an account given under "Strange Happenings" (a chapter of *Meng Qi Bi Tan),*

> In the years of Emperor Jiayou (1056–1064), a UFO as bright as a pearl often made its appearance over the prospering city of Yangzhou of Jiangsu Province, particularly at night. At first the object was seen on a lake in Tienzhang County in eastern Anhui and later on the Pishe Lake northwest of Gaoyou County in Jiangsu. Subsequently it was often seen by the local inhabitants near the Xingkai Lake. One night, a man living by the lakeside found a shining pearl close by while studying outdoors. The object opened its door and a flood of intense light like sunbeams darted out of it, then the outer shell opened up,

Figure 9.1 The portrait of Shen Kua, a great scholar of Song Dynasty
(A.D. *960–1127).*

appearing as large as a bed with a big pearl the size of a fist illuminating the interior in silvery white. The intense silver-white light, shot from the interior, was too strong for human eyes to behold; it cast shadows of every tree within a radius of ten miles. The spectacle was like the rising sun, lighting up the distant sky and woods in red. Then all of a sudden, the object took off at a tremendous speed and descended upon the lake like the sun setting.

Yibo, a poet of Gaoyou and a frequent eyewitness of the moonlike pearl, wrote a poem about it, but after some years the moonlike pearl disappeared.

As the pearl often made its appearance in the town of Fanliang in Yangzhou, the local inhabitants, who had seen it frequently, built a wayside pavilion and named it "The Pearl Pavilion." Inquisitive people

70

often came from afar by boat, waiting for a chance to see the unpredictable pearl.

In the opinion of Professor Zhang, the account, so clear as it is, cannot be based on dream imagery, hallucinations, ghosts, or religious visions, and it is further supported by being "seen often by the local inhabitants." He added that there are in nature creatures that illuminate themselves, such as fireflies, certain fish, and so on, but nothing like that was described as being "as large as half a bed and too bright to behold with naked eyes." So far no bioluminescent living body of such a magnitude has ever been found.

Zhang then went on to say that the object described as a pearl was exactly like the illuminating and semitransparent UFO that is often seen; the description given of the light inside the pearl as being "as large as a fist and too dazzlingly bright to behold with naked eyes" is similar to the description of the intense light from the lighting equipment of UFOs. He added that the light that shot out from the body as intense as sunbeams and reaching as far as ten miles away showed that the lighting technology far surpassed the level achieved by people even today.

Had it been from a layman, this ancient account of a UFO might be incredible. But coming from the celebrated scientist of ancient China, Shen Kua, it deserves serious study. Chinese history describes Shen Kua as a versatile scholar who made outstanding contributions in the fields of astronomy, mathematics, physics, geology, and medicine. As "Imperial Astronomer," he had taken part in astronomical observations and calendar making. Excelling particularly in astronomy, he had spent three months observing and locating the position of the Polaris with his self-made instrument, the "peeping tube." He plotted the position of the Polaris as observed in early, mid, and late nights on a graph. After a careful study of the more than two hundred graphs he had drawn, he concluded that Polaris was three degrees off the North Pole—a conclusion that modern science supports.

As far back as the last year of East Han Dynasty (25–220), the great Chinese astronomer Zhang Heng gave a theoretical scientific explanation of the illumination and the waxing and waning of the moon. In his book *Meng Qi Bi Tan*, Shen Kua elaborated on the theories of his predecessor. He held that the moon, like a silver pellet, did not illuminate by itself; it only reflected light when the sun shone upon it. At the beginning of a month (lunar calendar), the sun is seen to be on the side of the moon, and the moon, thus lit up on one side, looks like a crescent. At the middle of the month, the sun being at an increasingly greater angle from the moon casts its light obliquely, making the moon look fuller. Suppose you paint one side of a pellet white, Shen Kua said. The painted part will look like a crescent when viewed from the side and like a full circle when viewed from its front. This explanation which he offered may be said to be closest at the time to a scientific explanation of lunation and was made easily comprehensible by the pellet analogy.

Shen Kua also offered a correct explanation of the rainbow and atmospheric refraction. He held that the position of the rainbow was opposite to that of the sun, hence an evening rainbow always appeared in the east. He quoted the theory advanced by another scientist at the time, Sun Yanxian, that "a rainbow happens as the sun shines on the raindrops in the air." Shen Kua's explanation that the rainbow is a phenomenon of atmospheric refraction is basically in accord with modern scientific principles.

Shen Kua also found that sun rays refract in the atmosphere before reaching the earth's surface; he thus came to the conclusion that the sun, as he observed by people on the earth's surface, is not in exactly the same position as the actual sun, and the altitude of the sun as observed by human eyes is higher than the actual altitude of the sun. At the time, this discovery was remarkably original.

There were many books written by Shen Kua; *Men Qi Bi Ji* was one of his later works. This famous book has remained in circulation in its entirety up to the present. Twenty-six volumes in all, it was expanded by the addition of another three volumes of "Supplement" and one volume of "Continuation." There are 609 chapters, one third of which are concerned with natural science, dealing with a wide variety of subjects and containing a wealth of information. "Strange Happenings" are accounts given in Chapter 21.

It is a fact that there were UFOs in ancient times, and their appearance in China is well recorded. Here is still further evidence of their existence before this century.

At the end of last century (about 1890), the famous painter Wu You Ru of Qing Dynasty (1644–1911) witnessed at the Zhu Que Bridge in Nanking, along with hundreds of other passersby, a fireball radiating red light in all directions in the sky. The spectacle was painted by Wu in his "Red Flames in the Sky." He dated the work, and in 190 Chinese characters on the painting, he described what he saw. His words run as follows:

> It was about eight o'clock in the evening, September 28. In the southern sky of Nanking City appeared a fireball, egg-shaped, red without light. It floated in the air, slowly eastward. As the twilight sky was cloudy and dusky, its appearance was conspicuous. And on the Zhu-Que Bridge gathered a crowd of several hundreds, standing on tip-

*Figure 9.2 The famous painter Wu You Ru of the Qing Dynasty (1644–1911)
witnessed a UFO, along with hundreds of other people, about the year 1890. His
famous work "Red Flames in the Sky" is kept as a treasure in Bi Yuan
Publishing House in Shanghai.*

toe, craning their necks upward. It lingered for a period of a meal's
time, fading into the distance little by little. Some said it was a meteor
passing by. But a meteor took but an instance to slip away, while this
ball's movement, from its first appearance in the near sky to the final
disappearance in the distance, was quite stagnant. So it cannot be a
meteor. Others said it was a lantern-kite that children flew. But the
wind blew north that evening, while the ball turned eastward. So it
cannot be a lantern-kite either. For a time everybody spoke, but none
could solve the mystery. An old man said, "When it first arose, there
was a slight noise which was hardly audible, like the buzzing approach
of men darting across the South Gate."

This famous work by Wu Youru has been kept as a treasure in the Bi
Yuan Publishing House in Shanghai. But as the people of the time
had no idea what a UFO was, the painting was kept for its value due
to the painter's name rather than the strange object it depicted. Wu
died in 1893 (his year of birth remains unknown). According to

73

Chinese UFO researchers, the painting was presumably done between 1890 and 1892.

Wu made many paintings in his lifetime. A *Collected Treasures of Wu Youru's Paintings* was published later, with the "Red Flames in the Sky" printed on page 11 of the first volume of his *Collected Paintings No. 12*. It was discovered by UFO researchers only in recent years when UFO study became popular in China. Because of its value and authenticity, it was included in the section dealing with ancient UFOs in the film *UFOs Over China* made in China in 1982.

With a history of over five thousand years and with countless volumes of ancient books, China undoubtedly has far more than sixty items of UFO records from ancient times. More are bound to be found in the future. The three accounts of UFO cases I've described here are among the most remarkable of the sixty thus far found in ancient Chinese records, but I dare say that other equally breathtaking examples will come to light.

The Second Mystery: Psychic Phenomena

10

Tong Yu:
The Discovery
of a Prodigy

Often I ask people, "Do you believe in the possibility of exceptional human functions, such as the ability to read with your ears, or telepathy, or the ability to see through a solid wall, or to move objects by sheer mind power?" Usually the answer is, "I would if I saw it with my own eyes." However, some people still do not believe it even after they have seen it!

Why? The reason is that these kinds of extraordinary phenomena, resulting from human potential brought into full play, deviate from normal human behavior so much that they contradict conventional concepts and traditional knowledge. The witness, because he does not understand what he observes, decides that it is just a trick, sleight-of-hand, not real. He prefers to remain with what is known and therefore comfortable to his peace of mind, rather than admitting there are mysteries in the universe. Therefore the saying "Seeing is believing" may apply to the young who are simple, naive, and curious, but to an older person, cautious and close-minded, who only follows tradition and the bounds of conventional knowledge, such phenomena simply cannot be acknowledged as real. To do so would be detrimental to his reputation and social status. Dogmatism wins over scientific honesty. Thus arises the phrase, "old diehard."

I have a story that counters the saying, "Seeing is believing." It concerns a report by a most uncommon person, Qian Wei Chang, one of the so-called "Three Qians of China." The term refers to the three most famous contemporary Chinese scientists. Because they have the same surname, Qian, they are referred to collectively this way. First is Qian Xue Sen, the "Father of the Missile" in China. (I will tell more about him in the next chapter.) Second is a physical mathematician, Qian San Qiang. Third is Qian Wei Chang, a specialist in elastic force. It was reported that on May 19, 1981, Qian Wei Chang revealed the following:

In March 1981 four children from Kunming, Yunnan Province, who were said to possess the power of moving objects at a distance (psychokinesis) and through a wall (dematerialization) were taken to Peking to give public demonstrations. Qian tested them personally. Tearing a button from his coat, he put it on the table and covered it with his cap. The children quickly caused the button to "fly" into the next room.   Also present on the occasion were two other distinguished scientists, Zhou Peiyuan, formerly Peking University president and now chairman of the Chinese Science and Technology Association, and Professor Mao Yishent, an expert bridge engineer. The performance was so impressive that these two men felt it necessary to make their own personal trials. Zhou asked the children if they could "fly" a flower from the garden into his covered teacup. In a moment he found a flower in his cup. This was the much-publicized sensation of 1981 in China referred to as "a flower in the teacup." The story, however, did not appear in the popular press; it was carried by the *Reference News*, a newspaper of smaller page size which outsells the *People's Daily* by 3 million copies (11 million copies are printed and sold per day, while *People's Daily* sells 8 million). Unavailable on the market, *Reference News* furnishes China's several dozen million government cadres with inside stories. Many foreigners arriving in China try in vain to get copies of it. A foreign correspondent chanced to come by a copy of the paper in the street on a rainy day. He picked it up in elation, hurried back to his hotel, and dried it over a ventilator. (The paper also often carries UFO reports from Taiwan.) In my six weeks' tour of China I managed to procure just one copy of *Reference News*. While it would be exaggeration to compare it to a confidential document, it may justifiably be called "the small secret newspaper." Once publicized, "a flower in the teacup," naturally, reached an audience far in excess of 11 million. Presuming that each reader tells it to ten acquaintances, then the story must have been known to 110 million or more people. Zhou Peiyuan, chairman of the Science and Technology Association, proved to be an old diehard materialist. In a subsequent interview with *Exceptional Human Functions: Investigation Data,* a newly launched journal aimed specially at negating the validity of such reports, Zhou said that as an effort at popularizing science, the publicity of exceptional human functions has not been free from falsehood. A scientific attitude should be a prudent one, he emphasized. His attendance at an exceptional human functions performance found its way into the press with the assertion that he believed it. Later he was contacted by *People's Daily* by telephone and asked if it was true and whether he believed it. His answer was in the negative, because it was against the law of nature. He found it necessary to make some explanation. He was watching a show by four children from Yunnan, he said, when one of them mumbled something and then a flower was found in the teacup. It was not a flower from Peking, and it was neatly cut and trimmed. How could it be possible for a flower to travel into the cup, he wondered. He was in the company of other scientists and they, like him, refused to believe it was true.

Rather than venturing any commentary on great scientists being "fooled" by children, I have instead told this story because it shows that the saying "Seeing is believing" simply means nothing to one whose mind is set in doctrinaire concrete. I also recounted the story because it explains why, after he had been discovered, Tong Yu underwent the adversities he was to experience. It is no fun to be a prodigy. The boy's story has been the cause of the enthusiasm throughout China for the study of exceptional human functions; it likewise touched off a heated debate between two camps of scientists.

The controversy stemmed from the appearance of Tong Yu in Sichuan Province. *Sichuan Daily* printed a report on March 11, 1979, about a boy in Dazu County, Sichuan, who was able to read with his ears, and research departments began probing into the matter. The boy, Tong Yu, age twelve, immediately received publicity under "Science Tidbits" or "Latest Discovery of Science" in provincial, regional, and municipal newspapers and most scientific journals. He was also covered in publications by industrial enterprises and railway and army units. Besides reproducing the *Sichuan Daily* story, some scientific journals backed it with reports about individuals having similar capabilities.

The manner in which Tong Yu came into public notice was interesting. One day in October 1978, while walking with another boy, Chen, Tong casually scraped his ear on Chen's coat pocket. He visualized immediately in his mind's eye a pack of cigarettes bearing the trademark of a flying swan. "There is a pack of flying swan cigarettes in your pocket, isn't there?" he asked, to the surprise of his companion. The latter, however, did not take it to heart, dismissing it as a random guess. Two months later some workers were

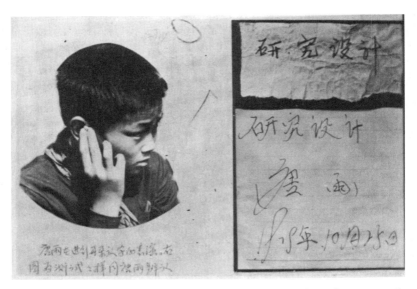

Figure 10.1 Tong Yu is able to read with his ears. At right is the test sample and the result of his "reading." (Photo courtesy of Zheng Jia Sheng and He Qi Fu).

playing riddle guessing when Tong, who was watching, suddenly said: "I can guess the characters. You may write anything on a piece of paper and wrap it up for me to guess." One wrote the character "fang" which means "house," crumpled the paper into a ball, and handed it to Tong Yu. The boy put the paper ball against his ear and correctly pronounced the word. Others tested him with the characters meaning pig, cow, horse, sheep, and dog, and they produced the same effect. News spread quickly about the boy's ability to "read" by ear. To confirm the reports, the county's Science Commission and Bureau of Education and Culture send fact-finding teams to investigate, and it was proved that in addition to his ability to read characters, Tong Yu could discern the color of ink in which they were written. The news of this soon reached the regional government, whose leaders reported the matter to the Provincial Party Committee. This alerted the media, who rushed to the boy's home, testing him with such characters as Zhongguo (China), Sichuansheng (Sichuan Province), Anding Tuanjie (peace and solidarity), and others written in different colors. In a few minutes Tong Yu pronounced the characters and their color accurately. They then tried English letters. Not knowing English and therefore unable to "read" them, Tong took a pen and drew the letters correctly, based on what he saw in his mind. All spectators were amazed.

Tong Yu explained that he felt as though his hands were charged with electricity, so that the moment he picked up the paper ball the vision of a character emerged in his mind. When he held the paper to his ear, the character would spread out as a movie screen. The "mental picture," he said, was very clear when his mood was good and when there were no interfering noises.

Later, Tong Yu gave a show in Chengdu in early March that left Sichuan Party Committee officials awestruck with his ear reading.

But things do not always go smoothly. From March 13 to 20, not long after *Sichuan Daily* featured the story, an investigation team was dispatched to Dazu by Sichuan Medical College. After a week's observation, the team concluded that the boy's ears were incapable of "reading," that being auditory organs his ears could only receive messages carried by sound waves and not those expressed in written characters. "Tong Yu is deft in tricks of fraud," claimed the medical group. "What he did was essentially a juggler's job."

On April 19, when Jiang Yan, a girl said to possess similar EHF abilities, was put to test at the Science Academy's Psychology Research Institute, a picture was taken showing her stealing a look at the test object. Strict measures were taken against possible fraud. First, three folded paper slips enclosed glass fibers which would fall out if the paper was unfolded. After the girl gave the answer, which was correct, to a test slip bearing the character Mi (riddle), some fibers were found on the floor and picked up by an examiner on the spot. When she tried with two other paper slips, she said, "I don't see any characters," and returned them unopened. Next a test paper bearing the figure 0.5, was given to her. It enclosed some white powder. To this Jiang gave the correct answer, but some of the powder was spotted on the leg of her trousers, which betrayed her having opened the package there. Last of all, some of the papers were sealed with glue, and the girl failed to "read" any of them. In addition, the Research Institute people also asked her to close her eyes and put the test paper to her ear. The result was utter failure for the girl.

Press commentary took over. On May 5 *People's Daily* carried an article by Zu Jia entitled " From 'smelling words' to 'reading with ears.' "Another was by Ye Shangtao, headlined "On press reporting of reading by the ear." Both authors charged that such reports have been irresponsibly flippant. Thereupon *Sichuan Daily* and officials of the provincial government involved in the matter came out with self-criticism. This was followed by proclamations of repentance by some newspapers which had published similar stories. Critical commentary then appeared in such periodicals as *News Front, Knowledge Is Power, Social Science Front, Guangzhou Daily,* and

Wen Wei Daily. This was the first round of attacks suffered by the press for publicizing "auditory reading."

However, believers in Tong Yu's exceptional functions refused to give in. They reasoned that the boy might have lost his functions temporarily due to nervousness or other reasons and that he was sure to regain them. To check up on the Sichuan Medical College report, Tong was put to another test on September 14, 1979, by a new investigation team. The team was jointly organized by Dazu County's Science Commission, Propaganda Department, and Education Culture Bureau, some hospitals, and a teachers' training school. It arrived at this conclusion: "Tong Yu is found capable of differentiating colors and characters with his ears. This is an objective reality, an unimpeachable truth. None can deny it." On October 1 the boy's father and elder brother addressed letters to interested journals, in which they stated that they had taken the boy to Chengdu, where he was strictly examined by research units. Under close scrutiny, the boy could differentiate colors and characters accurately with his ears. Hard facts proved that, far from being any trick of jugglery, Tong Yu's capacity of auditory reading was the result of an exceptional physical instinct, the letters said.

A report was made by the Science Commission of Jiangjin Regional Government, which has jurisdiction over Dazu County. Entitled "Latest Report on Tong Yu's Capacity of Ear-Reading," the article stated that the commission, in coordination with the regional government's Propaganda Department and the Regional People's Hospital, delegated a special fact-finding team to conduct an on-the-spot investigation in Dazu. The result produced was identical with that of similar tests undertaken by Dazu County Science Commission and other units, namely, that Tong Yu actually possesses such functions.

In response to a call from *Sichuan Daily's* readers voicing "ardent appeal for clarification of the controversy so as to promote scientific research," further coordinated investigations were undertaken by the editorial office of both *Red Scarf* in Chengdu and of *Sichuan Daily*, in conjunction with the Science Commission of Jiangjin Regional Government and the Science Commission of Dazu County. The investigation, which lasted from October 24 to 26, 1979, produced the "Report on a Child's Capacity of Telling Colors and Characters by the Ear." It said that strong testimonies had been offered by the public in Dazu to the truth of the boy's functions, and that they voiced indignation against the boy's critics, who, they charged, had reversed the facts and passed a wrong verdict on a problem of science. "Taking practice as the only criterion of truth," said the report, "and starting from the spirit of responsibility to the Party and the people, we observed the boy's behavior closely seven times in the course of three days. We found the boy's said functions to be objective reality. They are connected with profound scientific problems to be explored by further research."

The report had wide publication in the press, including locally distributed newspapers and scientific journals. For example, it was printed in full by *Tianjin Daily* on December 9, while *Gansu Daily* backed the news with a commentary headlined "No Arbitrary Conclusions for Unexplored Realms of Science."

Figure 10.2 Famous writer Xiao Jun and his wife examining the EHF of Wang Qiang (left) and Wang Bin. The photo was taken after the examination. (Photo courtesy of Zhou Wen Bin)

Besides Jiang Yan, two other Peking girls, Wang Qiang, thirteen, and Wang Bin, eleven, who are sisters, were found to be endowed with similar EHF capabilities. The young girls were observed by more than a thousand witnesses in succession between mid-April and early June of 1979. A person who had long studied the sisters' exceptional functions said that in the course of more than four months he gave twenty-nine practical tests, each lasting about two hours, the longest lasting six hours. From four to twenty-five slips of paper were used each time, each slip bearing one to five characters or figures. The tests had been very strict, claimed the experimenter.

In August 1979 further tests were given to the sisters by professors from the biology, radio, and electronics departments of Peking University. The results were affirmative. A professor working at Peking University's office of natural science explained that the sisters' manner of functioning, unlike those of vision or hearing, did not produce sensation the moment a stimulus was received. The sisters' psychological state strongly affected the result of the test; when they were happy and active, the test was successful, but the result was bad when the sisters were placed among strange people, when spectators were numerous, or when the examiners were tired or hungry.

Later, enthusiasts in ear reading investigated Jiang Yan in her home. They found that the girl's exceptional functions were strong from March to April 1980, and they began to decline in late April when she was upset with disturbances, till at the time of the interview she had lost her EHF for two months. Said a member of the visiting team: "We don't deny that Jiang Yan did commit some falsehood; but the question is, hasn't she ever been honest? How could a girl of eight understand the solemn demands of science! She just knew that she was to 'listen' while she could, and to look when her 'hearing' failed her."

In the opinion of the Peking University professors, Jiang Yan's temporary loss of exceptional functions had been the result of the upsetting effect of certain disturbances in her life, and something could be done to restore them. They said: "We are considering the possibility of motivating Jiang Yan's functions by testing the Wang sisters." One of the professors paid a visit to Jiang in the rain on August 11. "Ear reading is a reality," he insisted. "Jiang Yan's functions don't work, it's true; but they can be restored." Jiang Yan was invited to attend a testing performance by Wang Qiang and Wang Bin conducted by the Peking University professor on August 19 at the No. 9 Middle School of Peking, in cooperation with seven or eight editors of *Peking Steel Works Journal*. During the examination, Jiang Yan was seated between the two sisters. When Wang Qiang and Wang Bin went on describing with accuracy the characters and figures placed under their arms or into their ears, Jiang began to regain her confidence. "Let me have a try," she said. The professor folded up the prepared test paper and handed it to her, and she held it against her ear. "I got it," Jiang exclaimed with elation, "it's red." The audience was taken by excitement and all eyes were focused on her. "Three horizontal strokes," she announced, batting her eyes. "Tell it, quick!" shouted one from the audience. "Just a minute. Don't talk," replied the girls with composure. A deep silence prevailed. Presently she made a loud proclamation: "It's the character Wang." The professor unfolded the paper. Spread before the spectators was the character in red ink. The audience burst into applause.

A detailed description of the occasion was given by one of the attendants in a report headlined "Jiang Yan Recovers Her Exceptional Functions: Spurred by Wang Sisters." It was an impressive story.

Henceforward reports about exceptional human functions in children, especially Tong Yu, swept across the whole county.

11
Nature Magazine and EHF Research

Nature Magazine was first published by the Shanghai Science and Technology Publication Company after the downfall of the Gang of Four. At that time, China was promoting the Four Modernizations program, which included defense, science, industry, and agriculture. The magazine was born under these circumstances. Its contents are intended for college students, teachers, and people in scientific and technological fields. It ranks third among the important magazines of China, comparable to *Scientific American* and *Science* in the United States. However, the circulation of *Nature Magazine* is only forty thousand, a relatively small number compared with the circulation of the other magazines in China. Nevertheless, it has firmly established itself and has won the respect of scientists throughout the country. Its editor in chief is He Chong Yin, who is well known in the Shanghai scientific community. Among the members of the editorial board under Yin is an editor named Li Shun Qi, a member of the China UFO Research Organization. Li is also the editor who published an article of mine, "The UFO Phenomenon As I See It," published in *Nature Magazine* in the January 1981 issue. When I visited China in June 1981, I went to Shanghai to see Rao Zhong Hua of *Science Pictorial*, a sister magazine of *Nature Magazine*. In its editorial office, I met Li Shun Qi, its editor, who said to me that he highly commended "UFO Over Chengdu" as an extraordinarily interesting article by a famous Chinese poet, Liu Shahe (I described it in Chapter 3, "Silencing the UFO Critics"). Since then *Nature Magazine* has continually published source materials and research reports on exceptional human functions under the editorial management of Zhu Yi-yi, who is about thirty and a college graduate who majored in biology.

Since the discovery of Tong Yu in Sichuan Province, many newspapers and magazines publish news about him. *Nature Magazine* is the most enthusiastic supporter of Tong Yu. This resulted in criticism, led by *Wen Wei Daily*, accusing *Nature Magazine* of being an irresponsible publication of unscientific information. To answer the criticism, *Nature Magazine* published in its February 1980 issue an article, "Believe Your Own Eyes," by Zhou Wen Bin, a famous reporter from the Peking *Guang Ming Daily*. It contained an editorial footnote saying in effect: To clarify the matter and correct the wrong media reports, our magazine again publishes this factual report by comrade Zhou Wen-Bin of *Guang Ming Daily*. Please excuse us for not answering individual letters.

Zhou's is an excellent report. In short, it says that at first Zhou himself could not believe the reports about Tong Yu. However, after Zhou personally gave Tong Yu several tests which proved that Tong Yu is able to use his ears to read letters, Zhou could not "disbelieve his own eyes."

Nature Magazine firmly believes that the human body has the potential for exceptional functions. This viewpoint has the support of Qian Xue Sen, the Father of the Missile in China, and other scientists as well. And it is said that it has the tacit support of the present Prime Minister Zhao Ziyang. In every issue it prints not only news about EHF, but also one to four research articles on them. In the April 1980 issue, this magazine printed on its cover photos of fourteen psychic children from all over the country, with a large photo of Tong Yu at the bottom right corner. This is their editorial statement: "We believe in Tong Yu, and EHF is a fact."

There is a reason for *Nature Magazine* to have won the support of Premier Zhao Ziyang, who used to be the first secretary of Guangdong Province. After the downfall of the Gang of Four, Zhao was promoted to governor of Sichuan Province. During his rule of Sichuan, he made extraordinary achievements in economic development. At that time, there was a popular saying, "Hungry? See Zhao Ziyang." Before he was promoted to prime minister, he once received Tong Yu while in Sichuan. After he became premier, it is understandable that he cannot openly support the research of EHF; it is simply being politically sensitive in matters of statecraft and diplomacy to avoid such controversial and unconventional topics.

At the beginning of 1980, EHF research in China met a wave of opposition. The spearhead of the opposition was pointed against

Figure 11.1 Professor Qian Xue Sen (fourth from left in the front row) talked to the media in Peking, July 1980, on the importance of studying EHF. The photo was taken after the conference. (Photo courtesy of Zhou Wen Bin)

Nature Magazine. To counter it, Dr. Qian Xue Sen visited the editorial board of *Nature Magazine* on the morning of June 4, 1980. He is one of the most highly respected scientists on mainland China. He is the head of the College of Machinery in Peking, a member of many important scientific institutions, and closely involved in atomic projects. Even during the stormy Cultural Revolution, his prestige was undamaged. He had a photo taken together with all the editors to show his support. The photo was printed in the magazine with the caption: "Comrade Qian Xue Sen visited the editorial board of the *Nature Magazine* and had a warm talk with the editors for more than one hour." Moreover, the conversation with Qian was very interesting. He said that a magazine should have its own area of specialization.

You have published many research articles on qi gong science, and many other articles on exceptional human functions, like using ears to read letters. You also had a conference on the science of exceptional human functions. This is the way that you established the special characteristics of your magazine. My recent articles in *Studies of Philosophy* also touched these subjects, using dialectical naturalism to study human potential. No one has ever taken the initiative to discover the potentials of the human body. From now on, we should use modern science and technology to study these subjects, attempting to discover human potential. Therefore, we should study Chinese medical theories, qi gong, exceptional human functions, and so on. In the final analysis, all this will result in developing exceptional human functions. You have studied all these areas. This is the special field of your magazine.

He commented further, saying

> There is a lot of opposition to the integration of Western and Chinese medicines, including qi gong and EHF. It is all right to have different research approaches on the same subject. There are many natural phenomena that science cannot explain. A new scientific study almost always faces opposing ideas. Many examples of this can be found in the history of science. In science, we always need a leader who is strong enough to face critics. *Nature Magazine* is a leader in its field. That is the reason why I have come to visit and show my respect.

Then he highly praised the speech, "Exploring the Mysteries of the Science of the Human Life," made by He Chong Yin, the editor in chief of the magazine, at the opening of the first conference on the scientific study of EHF. By his open support of EHF, Qian said to all China, "Continue your good work, I support you."

Six months later, Qian published a long article of about ten thousand words, "System Science, Thought Science, and Human Body Science" in the January 1981 issue of *Nature Magazine*. In the July 1981 issue he published an article entitled "Opening the Basic Studies of Human Body Science." As a result of the positive attitudes of the Father of the Missile and *Nature Magazine* toward the study of

Figure 11.2 Editor in Chief He Chong Yin of Nature Magazine, *a strong supporter of EHF research, meets three psychic children. (Photo courtesy of Zhou Wen Bin)*

human body science, the criticisms of EHF and EHF research were swept away, and a new wave of EHF research has started. Many EHF study groups have been formed all over the country. There are EHF study groups in provincial science and technology units, schools of higher learning, medical schools, and physics and biology institutes. Many newspapers, magazines, and publishing companies previously controlled by the oppositon started publishing news and reports on the study of EHF.

The wave of enthusiasm for EHF is not limited to mainland China. Publications in Hong Kong, Japan, and even Taiwan now report EHF research news from mainland China. So eager are the Chinese for knowledge of this mystery that I even received letters from college students in chemistry and physics from Peking and Shanghai who wrote to me asking for information on overseas study of EHF. When I visited China in June 1981, I saw and heard enthusiastic discussions about UFOs and EHF all over the country. Professor Liang Rong Lin of Ji Nan University told me that he believed more in EHF than in UFOs.

To understand the overwhelming influence of Qian Xue Sen in the study of EHF, we must first know his background. In 1935 Qian went to America to study, enrolling at Massachusetts Institute of Technology with a major in aeronautical engineering. Later he transferred to California Institute of Technology and completed his Ph.D. During World War II he was the head of the missile unit of the advisory committee of the U.S. National Defense Sciences. After the war he headed a group of experts who went to Germany to investigate German missile developments and to interview imprisoned German scientists. He was highly thought of by the U.S. government. Later he was appointed the Goddard professor of jet propulsion at Cal Tech. (Robert Goddard, 1892-1945, was the American scientist who is considered the father of modern rocketry.) Meanwhile, the Shanghai Jiao Tong University was considering appointing Qian as president, but the minister of education of the nationalist government vetoed the idea because at thirty-four, Qian was thought to be too young to be a university president.

Qian Xue Sen petitioned to become an American citizen, but was turned down because a U.S. security unit accused him of once being a member of a Communist cell in Los Angeles. This accusation was never proven, but it affected Qian's feelings and his career. In 1950 Qian wanted to return to mainland China, but his voyage was blocked by the U.S. government because he knew a lot of American secret defense information.

The U.S. government had considered allowing him to participate in atomic research, but this was also denied him for the same reason. As a result, he switched to theoretical study of the possibility of sending a man to the moon. Finally, Qian returned to Peking in 1955. The U.S. government let him go in exchange for eleven American pilots taken prisoner in the Korean War. A U.S. Defense Department official objected to this deal, saying, "The exchange is like four American tank divisions for eleven pilots." When China successfully tested atomic bombs and missiles, some said with regret that the exchange was like *forty* tank divisions for eleven pilots. It is fortunate that China was underdeveloped. If Qian were working in a China as technologically advanced as the United States, the Chinese would probably have been the first the reach the moon. It is rumored that when Qian was teaching at Cal Tech, he tried to improve some of the textbooks because they were too elementary.

In April 1970, China successfully launched its first satellite. In the next twelve years, it sent up a total of twelve satellites. In September 1981, China for the first time launched three satellites simultaneously. In October 1966, China successfully tested an atomic warhead launched on a guided missile to a distance of 644 kilometers.

Between May and June 1980, China, under the direction of Qian, fired an intercontinental ballistic missile a distance of 10,000 kilometers, which attracted the attention of the whole world. The missile developed under Qian's guidance uses liquid oxygen as fuel, and the technique is more advanced than that of the Soviets. This is an honor attributed to him. An American newspaper commented that "the success of firing an ICBM to the South Pacific by Communist China is the victory of a former American Air Force colonel." (Qian was an American Air Force colonel during World War II.) I would say rather that it is the personal victory of Qian Xue Sen, who is praised by the Chinese as the Father of the Missile.

On October 12, 1982, China successfully tested a guided missile fired from a submarine in the ocean north of Taiwan. Thus China became the fifth nation—along with the U.S., the Soviet Union, Great Britain, and France—to have the capability of launching guided missiles from submarines.

This led an American rocket shuttle flight pilot, Colonel Chuck Loosma, of the *Columbia*, to say two months later, "There is no power that can stop China from becoming the third nation that can send men into space." His words were reported in the news on December 9, 1982. Perhaps before the publication of this book, China will already have sent up the first non-Occidental astronauts.

In light of the above, it should be clear why the study of EHF in

China has been so enthusiastically pursued. The encouragement and influence of Qian Xue Sen is equivalent to that of Einstein backing the atomic bomb during World War II. There is no doubt that the current critics of the study of EHF are against *Nature Magazine* directly and Qian indirectly, and it seems safe to say that they, like the opponents of UFO research, will soon wither away in the face of overwhelming public and scientific support.

12

"EHF Fever": The Dramatic Public Interest in Psychic Phenomena

From 1979, when Tong Yu was discovered, to 1981, more than thirty children were found in various parts of China who proved to possess extraordinary psychophysical functions. For the record, their names, age at the time of their discovery, and their functions are given in this table:

- ☐ Tong Yu (male, 13; functions: reading and color perception by ear)
- ☐ Wang Qiang (female, 13; functions: reading and color perception by ear and armpit, telepathy)
- ☐ Wang Bin (female, 11; functions: reading and color perception by ear and armpit, telepathy)
- ☐ Jiang Yin (female, 9; function: ear reading)
- ☐ Li Yonghui (male, 9; functions: moving objects and breaking twigs by power of thought)
- ☐ Dong Haojin (male, 4; function: moving objects by thought)
- ☐ Xu Qian (female, 14; function: seeing clairvoyantly through walls)
- ☐ Xie Chao Hui (male, 11; functions: seeing clairvoyantly through human bodies and iron boxes)
- ☐ Li Zhong (female, 13; functions: moving objects and breaking twigs by power of thought)
- ☐ Zhu Jiu (female, 9; functions: opening locks and breaking twigs by power of thought)
- ☐ Shen Kegong (male, 11; function: performing mental arithmetic faster than a calculator)

Figure 12.1
Fourteen psychic children
gathered in Shanghai City.
This picture was taken after
the conference. From right in
front: Xie Chao Hui, Huang
Hong Wu, Wang Bin, Tiang
Yan, Zhang Xue Mei. From
right in back row: Mou Feng
Qin, Xu Qian, Yu Rui Hua,
Xiong Jie, Wang Qiang, Hu
Lian, He Xiao Qin, Zheng
Hong. (Photo courtesy of Zhou
Wen Bin)

- Zhang Lei (female, 13; functions: sensing another individual's thoughts, moving objects by thought, remote viewing)
- Yu Rui Hua (female, 15; functions: clairvoyant vision, remote viewing)
- Wei Rouyang (male, 11; functions: numerous— ear reading, clairvoyant vision, magnifying objects by sight, transporting objects by thought, signal storing—literally photographic memory)
- Dong Changjiang (male, 4.5; function: telepathy)
- Zhang Xue Mei (female; functions: reading by fingers and scalp)
- Xiong Jie (female, 11; functions: transporting objects by thought, seeing clairvoyantly through walls)
- Zhao Hong (female, 12; functions: clairvoyant vision, reading by palms)
- Huang Hong Wu (male, 12; function: seeing clairvoyantly through human bodies)
- Mou Feng Gin (male, 20; functions: clairvoyant vision, remote viewing)
- Liu Dong (male, 20; functions: seeing clairvoyantly through human bodies, magnifying objects by sight)
- Wang Xiaodong (male, 12; functions: breaking twigs by power of thought, clairvoyant vision)
- Sun Liping (female, 12; functions: clairvoyant vision, moving objects and breaking twigs by power of thought) She was the one who "flew" a

flower from the garden into a covered teacup (see Chapter 10).

- ☐ Li Xiaoyan (female, 11; function: clairvoyant vision)
- ☐ Shao Hongyan (female, 12; functions: clairvoyant vision, moving objects and breaking twigs by power of thought, adjusting watches from a distance). She was the one who "flew" a button into the next room (see Chapter 10).
- ☐ Li Songmei (female, 11; function: clairvoyant vision)
- ☐ Li Chengyu (male, 9; function: clairvoyant vision)
- ☐ Liu Lisha (female, 10; function: clairvoyant vision)
- ☐ Zhao Guimin (female, 11; functions: clairvoyant vision, sensing another individual's thoughts)
- ☐ Song Ji (male, 10; function: ear reading)
- ☐ Zhang Li (female, 9; function: reading by palm and armpit)
- ☐ Wu Nianqing (female, 10; function: reading by ear and armpit)
- ☐ Feng Xianu (female, 7; functions: remote viewing, performing mental arithmetic faster than a calculator, breaking twigs by power of thought)
- ☐ Chen Xin (female, 10; function; clairvoyant vision)
- ☐ Di Rong (female, 13; function: seeing clairvoyantly through human bodies)
- ☐ Zou Huiping (female, 12; functions: clairvoyant vision, telepathy)
- ☐ Wu Ming (female, 11; functions: seeing clairvoyantly through human bodies, transporting objects by power of thought)

In addition to these children, there are several hundred others who have less conspicuous exceptional functions. Also, a number of children and young people have temporarily displayed exceptional functions after being encouraged or after induction of EHF abilities was done by qi gong or acupuncture. For example, in Chapter 10, I cited the case of Jiang Yan, who once lost her special functions but recovered them when asked to observe a demonstration of similar functions by two other girls, Wang Qiang and Wang Bin.

Experiments have proved that qi gong can help to bring out potential abilities of the human body. Acupuncture also plays its role, for among the 949 acupuncture points (of which 361 are commonly chosen for treatment), a few can be stimulated to produce the effect of adjusting the muscles and thereby releasing dormant psychophysical functions.

As I mentioned earlier, several hundred children have been found to possess exceptional bodily functions. However, this is a conservative figure, and undoubtedly more are still to be identified. An elderly Chinese doctor practicing in traditional herbal medicine,

Feng Hua, who made an analysis based on factors such as China's history, climate, environment, mode of life, population, and the physical characteristics of the Chinese, concluded that such specially gifted children are quite numerous. He estimated the proportion at two in every million, which would bring the total to two-thousand in China's population of one billion. This more than doubles the number already discovered. There would seem to be a rich field of research subjects still to be discovered.

The gifted children mentioned above are not uniform in their capability. Some are stronger than others. Some display a function only when they are in a cheerful mood; others remain inactive unless stimulated or induced. The three dozen nationally famous exceptional children are outstanding among the hundreds of similarly gifted, and a few elite are expected to emerge from the well-known three dozen. This is suggested by the records of China's history. In the past, a few exceptional individuals appeared in each century who astonished their contemporaries with what was considered to be superhuman abilities. An example was Bian Que of the Warring States period (403-221 B.C.), who, according to Sima Qian in his *Records of the Historian*, "could see a person on the other side of the wall."

In the age of the Three Kingdoms (220-280), Hua Tuo, a famous physician, could see his patient's internal organs. Once he diagnosed a sick woman as having a stillborn fetus. Neither the patient nor her family believed it, for she had just had a baby. But when she took the medicine Hua Tuo prescribed, a dead fetus was delivered, and the patient was cured.

In the reign of Emperor Wu of Han, a man named Dongfang Shuo was known as capable of doing strange things. According to *Chronicle of Han Dynasty (Han Shu)*, Dongfang Shuo could see through opaque objects. When the emperor learned about it, he was very curious and summoned Dongfang Shuo for tests. The man was asked to tell the contents of some sealed boxes; he complied faultlessly. The emperor was much impressed and awarded him ten rolls of silk. A chamberlain, Guo, refused to believe it, claimed that Dongfang was a bluff, dismissed his success as sheer luck, and offered to compete with him. Another test was held, and Guo ended up a complete failure. The emperor ordered him to be lashed.

In the latter period of Sui dynasty (581-618), an army officer lived who could shoot a bow and arrow accurately with his eyes closed. A commentary in *Miscellaneous Notes of Taiping (Taiping Guangji*, Volume 227, p. 1744) said that when he concentrated mentally, he was a better shot than with his eyes open.

During the Tang dynasty (618-907), a man named Quan Shi could see through the ground and "often helped people to excavate objects from underground" *(Miscellaneous Notes of Taiping,* Volume 227, p. 505).

During the Song dynasty (960-1279), Cai Tie could tell the sex of the owner of things by smelling them. He could also tell if the person was dead.

The *Chronicle of Nanhai County,* Guangdong Province, tells of two unusual men in the country who lived during the Qing dynasty. One, Liang Zhuangshi, a fortune-teller by profession, could tell fortunes without a single mistake. Another, Chen Qiyuan, could differentiate colors in the dark. He was also skilled at wood carving, and could engrave one hundred Chinese characters on a wooden seal one inch in diameter. Once, on a trip to Hong Kong, he gazed at some vessels at sea miles away from the summit of Mount Taiping and accurately pronounced the name of each ship.

This reminds me of a case told to me by Zou Xinyan, a science editor of Central People's Broadcasting Station, whom I interviewed in July 1981. The story was about a Chinese astronomer in the Warring States period, Gan De, who discovered some satellites of Jupiter with his naked eye. *Kaiyuan Classics of Divination (Kaiyuan Zhanjing),* an astronomy book composed in Tang dynasty, quotes Gan De's observatory notes as saying that "Jupiter, which is big and luminous, seems to have small gloomy stars around it. I call them the planet's allies" (by which he means satellites). The discovery was made two thousand years before that of Galileo (1564-1642). The accuracy of this ancient account was confirmed by the Peking Observatory, which reported that a ten-man observing team organized in 1981 by the Chinese Institute of Natural History made unaided observations of Jupiter and duplicated Gan De's astounding feat.

Highly interested, I pressed for more details. "Why," asked I, "has such a record, so clear-cut and significant, been ignored by Chinese astronomers?"

Mr. Zou replied by quoting Mr. Xi Zezong, a noted Chinese astronomer and deputy director of Natural Science History Institute, Chinese Academy of Sciences, who said: "I noticed the record twenty years ago and discussed it with some comrades. They were of the opinion that since Jupiter's satellite was found by Galileo through the telescope, its observation with the naked eye would have been an impossibility. Consequently the note about Gan De was ignored."

What terrible prejudice! Because history says that Galileo

found Jupiter's satellite by telescope, and this "history" is taken as "common sense," even "gospel," the same discovery by naked eye would be a violation of all these and hence must be ignored! This is indeed sheer ignorance.

"If we confine ourselves to what had happened in history," Zou said, "or to any individual's experience, or to what is accepted as common sense, then we would be bound hand and foot, while shutting our eyes on the chances of discovering new truth. We would stay forever where we are."

Lighting a cigarette, Zou continued: "Fortunately, after the lapse of twenty years, Xi Zezong has outgrown stale, prejudiced ideas and made public this episode of history, giving the great ancient astronomer his due."

Zou quoted Xi in conclusion: "Clearly, a new approach must be adopted toward historical records. Anything which seems to be unintelligible must not be arbitrarily labeled as 'blind faith' or 'superstition.' "

A member of the Chinese Society of Natural Mystery, Zou quoted the above remark of Xi as an explicit criticism of a handful of scientists who posed themselves against the study of exceptional human functions in 1981, the year that saw an unprecedented increase in the discovery of such interesting cases.

Besides, the above story tells us unequivocally that Gan De, who lived two thousand years ago, was gifted with the function of remote viewing. Whether it was remarkable ocular vision or true clairvoyance cannot be determined at this time.

The famous Chinese classical novel, *Romance of Three Kingdoms*, which is available in American libraries, features the character of Zhuge Liang (nicknamed Kongming), a brilliant strategist whose name is known to China's one billion people. He apparently possessed exceptional physical functions.

For generations China has produced people who were capable of doing curious things, and whose names figure in historical classics. They proved to have special functions that are in many ways analogous to those of the EHF children, such as the ability to see through a wall, cause some object to disappear suddenly or move to a distant place, remove an object from a sealed box, and so forth.

While in Guangzhou I met Mr. Liang Rong Lin, a professor of physics at Jinan University, who told me emphatically: "It looks now as if people ought not to be surprised at the behavior of Jiang Yan, Tong Yu, and their like. Ear reading and thought transference are not uncommon phenomena any more. I hope explanations can be made on the basis of physical science to show how a person under close

Figure 12.2 Professor Liang Rong Lin (middle) of Jinan University.

observation can cause an object to vanish suddenly from sight and move to another place unnoticed."

"This still cannot be called exceptional," Professor Liang continued in excitement. "What would you say to a living animal being brought out uninjured through a hole many times smaller than itself? This reminds me," he went on, "of the mystery of UFOs, which apparently are free from the restrictions of time, space, and the qualities of matter. But I cannot give explanations...."

"Professor Liang," I interrupted, "have you witnessed any performance by EHF children?"

"I have not only seen them twice on television, but observed their public display with my own eyes," he answered. "What I witnessed had been only ear reading, thought transference, and the like, which have been facts beyond any doubt. As to the capacity of observing through a wall or causing an object to disappear by the power of thought, these events have been witnessed by prestigious persons, and I see no reason to doubt their validity."

"What would you say about the outcome of the investigations?" I asked.

"That would be the concern of scientists and the government," he said. "In Guangdong, the provincial government plans to include the exceptional function display in entertainment programs for foreign visitors. Besides foreign exchange earnings, the purpose of such performances will be to demonstrate the existence of exceptional human functions so that the world knows about them."

He paused and then continued: "The plans are that each visitor will be charged a fee to cover three days' lodging, some demonstrations of the functions, and a guided sightseeing tour of Canton."

Professor Liang is about fifty, his hair gray. He has excellent health and a friendly, expansive personality. The China UFO Research Organization chose him as the right man for their top advisory position. He has also been advisor to the scientific film, *UFOs Over China.*

When I visited Canton in 1981, Professor Liang arranged my lecture on UFOs at Jinan University, which was very successful, thanks to his help. In my contacts with him he impressed me as a very competent person. As I write this, he is under consideration for the presidency of the board of the China UFO Research Organization. The first president, Mr. Cha Leping, has sent in his resignation after being criticized for incompetence.

What Professor Liang told me makes it clear that the study of exceptional human functions in China has not only drawn public attention, but it has also become the subject of significant scientific investigation across the country. EHF research bodies have mushroomed in many provinces as scientific, medical, and educational departments assigned part of their staff to engage in this field of study. These provinces are: Guangdong, Sichuan, Fujian, Hubei, Hebei, Yunan, Gansu, Anhui, Ningxia, Jilin, and Zhejiang—eleven in all. The names of establishments undertaking the study of the subject are:

- China Society for EHF Research (an organization of national scale which plays the leading role)
- Shanghai Laser Technique Research Institute
- Physics department, Peking Teachers' College
- Peking University
- Acoustics Institute, Chinese Academy of Sciences
- High-Energy Physics Institute, Chinese Academy of Sciences
- Yunnan University
- Yunnan College of Chinese Traditional Medicine
- Lanzhou University
- Changchun College of Chinese Traditional Medicine
- Hangzhou University
- Anhui Normal University

- Jilin Normal University
- Jiamusi Medical College
- Bethune University of Medicine
- Hubei College of Chinese Traditional Medicine
- Changchun College of Chinese Traditional Medicine
- Chungking Medical College
- Chungking University
- Chungking Laser Research Institute
- Qinghua University, Peking
- No. 507 Institute, Commission in Charge of Science, Technology and Industry for National Defense
- Zhangshan University
- Sichuan University
- Sichuan Medical College

Also engaged in EHF research are numerous minor organizations in the counties, whose primary fields of research include physics, biology, physiology, psychology, medicine, education, and defense.

This widespread interest has been paralleled in the media, which has widely publicized the subject of exceptional human functions. A partial list of the newspapers and magazines covering EHF includes:

- *Peking Wanbao (Peking Evening News)* (Peking)
- *Guang Ming Ribao (Guang Ming Daily)* (Peking)
- *Shoudu Steel Plant Bulletin* (Peking)
- *Peking Science and Technology News* (Peking)
- *Chuncheng Evening News* (Kunming)
- *Gansu Daily* (Gansu)
- *Sichuan Daily* (Sichuan)
- *Yangcheng Evening News* (Canton)
- *Ningxia Daily* (Ningxia)
- *Ganzi Daily* (Gansu)
- *Zhoushan Daily* (Zhoushan Islands)
- *Xi'an Daily* (Xi'an)
- *Changjiang Daily* (Wuhan)
- *Changjiang Science and Technology News* (Wuhan)
- *Shenyang Daily* (Shenyang)
- *Tianjin Daily* (Tianjin)

- □ *Nature Magazine* (plays a leading role) (Shanghai)
- □ *Xinguancha (New Observer,* monthly) (Peking)
- □ *Kexue Yuandi (Fields of Science,* monthly) (Peking)
- □ *Science and Future* (monthly) (Peking-Hong Kong)
- □ *Science Life* (monthly) (Shanghai)
- □ *Science Pictorial* (monthly) (Shanghai)
- □ *Spring for Science* (monthly) (Canton)
- □ *Kexue Langhua (Spray of Science,* monthly) (Tianjin)
- □ *Mysteries of Nature* (quarterly) (Hubei)
- □ *Science Fiction* (quarterly) (Hubei)
- □ *Wenzhai (Digest,* weekly) (Peking)
- □ *Hubei Pictorial* (Hubei)
- □ *Hubei Health* (Hubei)
- □ *Wuhan Children* (Wuhan)

Nature Magazine, one of the periodicals most devoted to reporting exceptional human functions, started a small-size newspaper, *EHF Report,* which was launched October 15, 1980, for the sole purpose of reporting and publicizing research on the subject. Its contents include the discovery of children having EHF, progress of research in this field, results of tests and experiments, historic records about EHF, academic activities in the field, and related reports from abroad. Its column "Letters from Readers" has been especially colorful because it provides EHF enthusiasts unlimited chances to speak up. From its first issue the paper aroused the interest of readers across the country, and it almost replaced *Nature Magazine* in its role of carrying EHF reports. So from then on *Nature Magazine* resumed its former role, leaving the matter to be handled completely by *EHF Report.* The purpose was to give the paper full play in publicizing the discovery of cases and promoting their research.

In the meantime *Nature Magazine,* though confining itself largely to its original field of coverage, continued to carry EHF stories, but with emphasis on more technical articles about experiments and research. The following list of articles which it published serves to indicate the shift in the magazine's editorial stance before and after the launching of *EHF Report* on October 15, 1980. The article titles are not always elegant due to their technical nature.

- □ Observation report on "distinguishing images by nonvisual organs" (September 1979)
- □ Inquiry into image perception by non-visual organs and the human body's mechanism of electro-magnetic inductio (October 1979)

□ The ability to see with the hand (October 1979)

□ Investigation report on an exceptional function of the human body (November 1979)

□ Investigation report on the ear's ability to read and distinguish colors (November 1979)

□ Preliminary conclusion of observing Xie Zhaohui's performance of reading and image perception by ear (December 1979)

□ Investigation report on Ton Yu's ability to read and distinguish colors by ears (December 1979)

□ Decline and recovery of Jiang Yan's extraordinary sense functions (December 1979)

□ Believe our own eyes (February 1980)

□ Mysteries experienced in France (March 1980)

□ Probing into secrets of science of life (April 1980)

□ Abide by truth and inquire into it (April 1980)

□ Pay attention to EHF research (April 1980)

□ Non-ocular reading as I see it (April 1980)

□ Universality of exceptional human functions (May 1980)

□ Tests on the ability of perceiving colors by non-visual organs (May 1980)

□ Process of image manifestation (June 1980)

□ Recent progress of research on EHF (August 1980)

□ More on universality of EHF (September 1980)

□ A case of EHF and direction distinguishing (October 1980)

□ System science, thought science and human body science (January 1981)

□ Magnetism and EHF (February 1981)

□ Preliminary observation of cerebral blood circulation chart of EHF individuals (March 1981)

□ Result of preliminary test of human body's capacity to magnify objects by sight (March 1981)

□ Process of distinguishing multi-layer overlapped objects by EHF (April 1981)

□ A case of EHF and direction distinguishing (April 1981)

□ Preliminary observation of color-perception by color-blind children through EHF (April 1981)

□ Preliminary experiment on mechanical effect of EHF (May 1981)

□ Dependence of non-ocular image perception ability on neurological channel transduction (June 1981)

□ EHF and neurological channel phenomena (June 1981)

□ Preliminary study of neurological channel transduction characteristics of EHF individuals (June 1981)

- □ Preparatory Committee for Chinese Association of Science of Human Body founded (June 1981)
- □ Launch the fundamental study of the science of the human body (July 1981)
- □ Promote the study of the science of the human body (July 1981)
- □ Progress of past year's EHF study and its outlook (July 1981)
- □ Abnormal phenomena of EHF under light-sensitive research (August 1981)
- □ Experiment with biological detector for study of the physics of human body radiation (August 1981)
- □ Some experiments of moving objects by EHF (September 1981)

The year 1981 saw the surge of nationwide enthusiasm in EHF as a result of continued publicity by *Nature Magazine, EHF Report,* and dozens of other newspapers and periodicals. At the public's request for a film to be made on the subject, the Central Newsreel and Documentary Film Studio started work on the film *Do You Believe It?* on July 7, 1981. Four EHF children, Mou Feng Qin, Yu Duanhua, Xu Qian, and Xiong Jie, were enlisted in the cast, and an editor of *Nature Magazine,* Zhu Runlong, was made advisor. The film was supervised by Wang Jiuwen, an editor of the film studio.

At 2 P.M. on July 7, 1981, shooting began. The first segment began with the four children introducing themselves. Then Xu Qian was seated on one side of a wooden screen, and the other three were placed on the other side, seated in a triangle facing outward. Then an assistant, Dou Qichun, took Xu Qian's hand and had him write in chalk on a black slate:

$$3 \times 5 = 18?$$

Next, Zhu Runlong, the advisor, asked the three children on the other side of the screen to write out what they had "felt" on paper. In one minute they were asked to show their answers, which were identical to the smallest detail, not even missing the question mark at the end. This "reading through the wall" brought huge applause from the viewing public whenever the film was shown.

This success was immediately followed by the launching of another film *Image Perception by Non-visual Organs,* at the Shanghai Scientific Educational Film Studio. Several EHF children, notably Tong Yu, were featured. Although the title of the film is hardly one that Hollywood or American box office would choose, the news caused a sensation among Shanghai's 12 million people.

How do things stand today? Numerous radio and television stations, newspapers, and magazines, as well as the scientific and educational communities are surging with enthusiasm for EHF research. There are two reasons for this. First, it is truly a remarkable subject, indicating untapped potential for higher human development. Second, it is a protest against information about and research into psychic phenomena, both earlier in China itself and even now in other parts of the world. "EHF fever" may be moderated in China in years to come, as the subject becomes more familiar and eventually commonplace, but the reality of Exceptional Human Function and the legitimacy of research into it is now firmly established within the borders of that ancient land.

13
Proving It Real: Dramatic EHF Cases

What fanned up the nationwide mania for exceptional human functions? The answer is simple: Their existence has received scientific recognition. People are curious by nature. When an incredible thing is proved to be valid, it is bound to draw public attention. EHF is for real.

Why, then, has recognition of EHF not occurred through the centuries of Chinese history? Why did EHF not come to the fore until now? There are two reasons. First, like other cultures, the ancient Chinese were superstitious; they frequently attributed to supernatural powers anything they could not understand, lacking the power of science to seek an explanation. Second, despite the rapid progress of modern science, it still fails to furnish explanations for many natural mysteries—as this book demonstrates vividly. Consequently, even what a competent observer-scientist has seen with his own eyes might be dismissed by others as fraud or poor observation. This has happened in China and in the West alike.

A fuse is needed to ignite a major blast. The "fuse" in this case is patient research in the face of great difficulties. For example, when Person A sees someone capable of reading with his ears, he thinks it funny or nonsense and ignores the matter. But when Person B sees someone who can read with his ears, he becomes curious and inquires into it. Sooner or later, the matter draws attention. Others ask to see it and test it. If the phenomenon is real, it cannot be ignored or suppressed forever. Then the news spreads, scientists take over, experiment, and conclude that instead of trickery or illusion, it is—in the case of EHF—a potent function of the human body. So the public is convinced, EHF research societies are set up, further tests are made, and new cases are discovered. More tests, then more discoveries...'

Are EHF illusions or tricks? "No!" was the unanimous answer of twenty officers from Peking.

"What more do you want to see?"

"No more, thank you. We give in."

The story about the "giving in" took place on April 14, 1980, when a group of Party members from Peking, including a woman from the Propaganda Department of the Party's Central Committee, were in Harbin, Heilongjiang Province, to watch a performance by five EHF children. To prove the validity of the alleged mysterious functions, the woman pointed to her own abdomen and asked eleven-year-old Hu Ming if there was anything peculiar inside. After a few moments' gaze, the child pointed to the right side of the woman's body and declared: "There is a round thing in here," adding with a gesture, "It is about that big." This astonished the woman, who knew that she had a tumor in that part of her belly. Then a similar test was administered by a woman from the arts department of the *People's Daily*, who pointed at her own head and asked Hu Ming what was in there. The child gazed a moment and answered, "There is something the size of a fingertip behind your head." The questioner testified to the truth of the reply. One person after another from the audience came forward with similar tests, which the child performed without a single failure. The spectators were so excited that none felt the cold of the August night of Harbin. This event was the subject of an interesting report written by a correspondent covering the visit.

There are now so many recorded instances of seeing into opaque objects, including the human body, that this EHF is known as "X-ray vision" or "penetrating vision." (Westerners would call it "clairvoyance.") Chinese doctors pointed out that though machine X rays can be harmful, X-ray vision by EHF is perfectly safe.

Xie Zhaohui, an eleven-year-old boy of Wuhan, Hubei Province, was found to possess EHF in April 1979, and was given a year's special training at the Hubei Hospital of Traditional Chinese Medicine. Afterward he was asked to examine 105 patients; there were 50 cases of liver disease, 40 were pregnant women, 11 had bone fractures, and 4 others whose conditions were not specified in the report I have. However, the report says that nearly all cases were diagnosed correctly; there were only 12 misjudgments. The 24 medical staff who took part in the tests agreed on these four points:

1. The patients prefer EHF examination to X rays.
2. Penetrating vision by EHF is real.
3. EHF is inferior to X rays in accuracy.
4. The accuracy of EHF can be raised by a process of training and encouragement.

Their experimental procedure was this: Considering that Xie Zhaohui was only eleven years old, and therefore devoid of any medical knowledge, he was first asked to examine a mannequin to get some understanding of human anatomy. Then, working on the patient, he was made to go part by part. Prior to actual examination he was tested with written characters on slips of paper. If he identified them successfully, it showed that his functions were normal at the time and could work on the patient. If not, the work had to wait. Only two to three patients were examined at a time. The child viewed them from a distance of two to three feet, and could report the result after focusing his gaze for a few minutes.

Another child, Huang Hong Wu, a thirteen-year-old boy of Wuhu County, Anhui Province, was able to see through the human body. A hospital arranged for him to come there twice a week to check the fetus position of pregnant women. The boy's rate of accuracy reached 95 percent.

Statistics show that in China's twenty-six provinces, cities, and autonomous regions, children found to be capable of penetrating vision account for 37 percent of the total number of EHF children.

Wei Ruoyang, eleven, of Gansu Province, who was in Peking for his part in the film *Do You Believe It?* being produced at the Central Newsreel and Documentary Film Studio, was met by an engineer from the municipal engineering bureau. The engineer asked the boy to look underground and tell the location of the buried pipelines. The boy complied, with the engineer checking his account against the blueprints. The boy was correct almost to the last detail, as if he was looking at them through something transparent.

Chinese scientists believe that if such penetrating or clairvoyant visual function can be trained to increase its efficiency and accuracy, it could be put to practical use in mineral prospecting, road building, construction, and other engineering tasks.

Another EHF child is Zhue Mei, a third grade pupil at the primary school attached to Shanghai Jiaotong University. Her functions were discovered in 1981 when she was nine. She possesses the curious ability of opening a lock of psychic power. As reported by Xiao Xia, correspondent of Shanghai's *Science and Life* magazine, who interviewed the girl on April 16, 1981, Zhue Mei is from a family of intellectuals, her father being lecturer of ship dynamics at Jiaotong University, and her mother an assistant engineer at Yanan Chemical Works. Both parents vigorously confirmed the authenticity of Zhue Mei's special functions, so the correspondent took her to the magazine's editorial office to be tested.

The testing began with Zhue Mei's ability to read without using her eyes. A slip of paper with some characters written on it was placed in her sleeve. While her examiner was looking at her watch to check the time, the girl proclaimed: "Aunt, don't bother about the watch. I know it already. There are two characters, one is Da ("big") in red, and the other is Zheng ("upright") in blue." She was right both in the characters and their color. One of the editors, a man in his sixties, was incredulous. He tested her personally, asking her to tell the character on the corner of page 3 of a closed magazine. She did it with perfect accuracy.

Another editor wanted to test her with a picture. "Pictures are even easier," said Zhue Mei with a smile. "I'll show you something more difficult."

"What is it?"

"I can open a lock." The girl lifted her face with pride.

A padlock was quickly obtained. It was fastened, then put in a cardboard box and sealed with tape. The key was enclosed in another sealed box. Then both boxes were put in Zhue Mei's hands, while dozens of eyes focused on her. After a moment she declared, "The lock is opened." The boxes were unsealed, and to the amazement of all, the lock was open, with the key in its hole.

Zhue Mei, who was in a very cheerful mood, whispered into the ear of an editor, "Many other children in China can do the character and picture reading, and some can also do the lock opening. These are not strange," she said with a playful grin, "but I can get the beans out of that bottle."

"Can you do that for us now?"

"Yes."

A plastic bottle was soon found and filled with red beans. Then it was corked, placed in a cardboard box, and the box was sealed up with adhesive tape. Zhue Mei took the box in her hands, her face very calm. Her mother, who was by her side, spoke for a few minutes, explaining, "This is a more difficult job. It must be done in three steps: Open the bottle, take out the beans, and cover the bottle again. It takes more time."

"But it doesn't," said the girl in protest, returning the box to the table. It was immediately opened. The bottle remained covered, but the beans were out. Barely five minutes had passed. The girl's successful performance was greeted with warm applause.

Spectators asked Zhue Mei about what her feelings had been when she did all this. Zhue Mei replied, "I can't tell exactly. There seemed to be something on my hands. At first they felt a little numb, then it went up slowly to my head, and came like television to…" and she pointed at her forehead.

Finally, the editors administered a test of "flower blossoming." A flower bud was placed in the girl's hand, which she held gently as she released her psychic power. In ten minutes the flower was in full bloom, to the amazement and applause of the spectators.

The wonders of exceptional human functions soon became a recognized fact in China. However, some scientists insisted on seeing them with their own eyes. Accordingly, public tests on EHF children were given at many science units, including the High-Energy Physics Institute, Atomic Energy Institute, Chemical Engineering Institute, and Biological Physics Institute of the Chinese Academy of Sciences, Military Medical College, Science and Technology Association, and a number of major universities. For example, on the night of February 8, 1980, a famous EHF girl, Yu Rui Hua, gave a show at a Shanghai science seminar. The event was sponsored by the Atomic Energy Institute. A lead tank used for storing radioactive elements, 20 kilograms in weight, was placed before the girl. A test paper was

Figure 13.1 (Left to right) Wang Qing, Wang Tong, and Dong Hao Jun, all of Peking, experimenting with "ear reading" at the High Energy Physics Institute of the Chinese Academy of Sciences. (Photo courtesy of Han Xiao Hua)

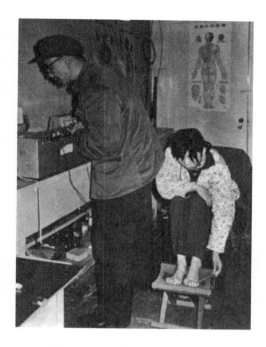

Figure 13.2
Liu Yongxun, at High Energy Physics Institute, testing the voltage of certain points in Wang Qiang's body where nerve centers are supposed to be located. (Photo courtesy of Han Xiao Hua)

placed inside and then the tank thoroughly sealed. Yu Rui Hua put her hands on the tank and concentrated. Fourteen minutes passed and her face was flushed. Seeing she was tired, the attendants suggested a rest, but she refused, saying: "I feel the signals already. I must catch them." By the eighteenth minute she asked to have the light turned off. Then she joyfully exclaimed, "I've got it! I've got it! Turn on the lights, quick!" Everyone was pleased and urged her to tell the result. Cheerfully she proclaimed: "It's a little man with a head, two outstretched hands, a pair of legs, his feet raised high. His head is red, and the body blue. And there is a circle beside his feet."

When the tank was opened and the test paper shown, the audience saw that Rui Hua was correct in every detail. The "circle"she saw was an apple.

On April 17 another test was arranged for Yu Rui Hua in Shijiazhuang, Hebei Province. The audience consisted of seven security men, a group of reporters, and some scientists. One of the security men said to her, "One of us is armed. Can you pick him out?" The girl gazed a moment from a distance and pointed to two of them, saying: "Either of you." Then another asked: "Can you be more exact? Locate the gun and take it out."

"All right. Please turn out the lights." In less than a minute she asked for lights, then said with a smile, "I'll get the gun out, okay?"

Figure 13.3 Yu Rui Hua (middle in front row) and three other girls (left to right): Hu Lian, Mou Feng Qin, and Xiang Jie. The girls demonstrated EHF by distinguishing a target object inside a lead tank. (Photo courtesy of Han Xiao Hua)

She walked up to the two officers in the middle, put her hand to the left side of one and pulled out a gun. All seven officers stood aghast.

On July 20 a test was held at Peking Military College of Medicine on five children having special functions: Yu Rui Hua, Wei Ruoyang, Dong Changjiang, Wang Qiang, and Wang Bin. The show

*Figure 13.4
Mou Feng Qin, age twenty, demonstrates EHF, distinguishing a target object in a lead tank at the Shanghai Atomic Energy Institute. (Photo courtesy of Zhou Wen Bin)*

had an audience of several dozen scholars who were heads of colleges and research institutes, experts, professors, scientists of various specialties, and a large group of journalists from major newspapers.

The program began with Yu Rui Hua making an X-ray vision examination of Professor Liu Yongxun of the Military College of Medical Science. The two were seated face to face. Gazing a minute at the professor's chest, the girl declared, "There is a scar of a long cut on your right side. The upper part of your right lung is missing." Then Professor Liu undid his clothes to prove that she was right. He had had an operation for partial excision of his right lung.

Next Yu Rui Hua used her penetrating vision on the three layers of clothing of a woman staff member of Hebei Provincial Science Commission. Then she did the same on a woman journalist from *Hebei Daily*, telling how many pieces of clothing she was wearing and their colors.

The second event involved the boy Wei Ruoyang working similarly on Xing Zhulin, advisor at the Military College of Medical Science, and Wang Daojian, director of the Second Research Institute. The boy proclaimed that there was also a scalpel mark on Xing's body, while Wang had a tumor on his lower left rib. Both scientists undressed to prove the validity of the judgment.

Next came Dong Changjiang, whose special function is "reading by head." Two equations were written on the spot by Professor Zhou Tingchong. One was $1 + 4 = 3$; the other $^{15}/_3 + 9 = 8$. Then the paper was placed on the boy's head. In a moment Dong Changjiang wrote out both equations with perfect accuracy.

The fourth demonstration was "psychic transduction," performed by the girl Wang Bin and also by Dong Changjiang. A journalist wrote "3" on a piece of paper and handed it to Wang Bin, asking her to communicate it to Dong Changjiang by psychic signal. Within a minute, Dong wrote out the same figure.

Item number five was Wang Qiang's performance of "penetrating reading by armpit." A character, Hao ("good"), was written in red by Deputy Political Commissar Li Si of the Military Academy of Medical Science. He folded up the paper, placed it in a camera film tube, screwed on the lid, and handed it to Wang Qiang. The girl shoved the tube into her clothes under her armpit. In about a quarter of an hour she pronounced the word and told that it was written in red.

Prodigies of mental arithmetic have been reported in various parts of the world, including Hong Kong, with a population of 5 million, and Taiwan, with 17 million. Could not a billion people produce a greater prodigy? Undoubtedly, yes. That is the case in

Figure 13.5 China's "supercomputer": Shen Kegong, a thirteen-year-old prodigy who takes twenty seconds to give an answer to $625^9 = 14,551,915,228,366,851,806,640,625$.

mainland China. The boy's name is Sheng Kegong; he has been nicknamed "Supercomputer." He was discovered a few months after Tong Yu.

It happened in the spring of 1979; word of it soon spread like wildfire. A math examination had been given to all sixth-year primary school pupils of Xiaxian prefecture, Shanxi, to which the schools delegated their best pupils. The exam was held at the communes in which the schools were located. In the examination room of Dalu commune, the proctor-teacher found a boy asleep at his desk soon after the papers were distributed. Shaking his head in disapproval, the teacher approached him and found, to his surprise, that the boy had already finished the test and had dozed off because it was against the rule to hand in the paper before the end of the session. The boy was Sheng Kegong. Even more remarkable things were to happen.

In September 1980 an all-Shanxi abacus contest was held, in which Sheng Kegong took part in mental arithmetic competition against 1,200 finance and accounting personnel. With astonishing speed and accuracy, the boy performed many problems of multidigit integer, decimal, and fractional arithmetic, as well as squares and square roots. For instance, he resolved $639 \times 33 + \sqrt[3]{884736}$ and gave the result 21183 in 3.4 seconds, a speed that beat the electronic calculator. His talent aroused an admiring stir among the participants. He was awarded the title of Special-Class Mental Arithmetician, and received a certificate of merit conferred in person by Pan Ruizheng, a vice provincial governor.

Responding to invitations, Sheng came to Peking on October 3 and there gave performances at the China Abacus Association, China Science Association, and the Central Television Station.

At the first performance, sponsored by Central Finance and Economics College and China Abacus Association, the hall was filled to capacity. People were standing in the aisles. Under the gaze of an audience of hundreds, Sheng Kegong answered twenty questions in a row with perfect accuracy and astonishing speed, at times writing out the answer before the examiner had finished copying the question. For instance, for 4,789,240 ÷ 45, he wrote down the answer, 106,427.5555... in 1.6 seconds, and in 1.8 seconds calculated 35 × 45 × 25 to be 39,375, each time evoking warm applause. As the last item, he asked Huang Tianxiang, a science editor of *Peking Evening News*, to pose a problem which was given as 169^3 × $\sqrt[3]{59319}$. For this he gave the answer 188,245,551 in two minutes. Curiously, this had one more digit 5 than the examiner's own answer. When the latter claimed him wrong, Sheng protested vigorously, insisting that he was right. He was seconded by Shi Shenshou, another boy having similar capability, who was present at the scene. So Huang had to have it checked on the calculator, and the result showed that Sheng was right. The fact was, Huang had inadvertently left out a 5 in copying the prepared answer. This again set the audience astir in long cheers and applause.

More spectacular was his exhibition of skill at the China Agricultural Bank, when he took twenty seconds to give an answer to 625^9 as

$$14,551,915,228,366,851,806,640,625$$

The mental calculation of the twenty-six-digit number with such speed and accuracy left the audience speechless with astonishment.

Sheng Hairong, Sheng Kegong's father, told a journalist that in the past the family had not paid much attention to the boy's extraordinary talent. However, he said, he could recall some interesting episodes. Once Sheng's mother took him out shopping. When she was about to pay for her purchases, the boy claimed that the assistant had been wrong in the total. Rechecking proved Sheng right. He was then of preschool age. His father worked as accountant for the production brigade, and often did calculations with the abacus while murmuring the numbers he worked on. Once, while this process was going on, Sheng Kegong, who was playing nearby, put in, "Papa, you are mistaken." At this his father snapped, "Go play and don't be naughty." To his surprise, however, he *was* wrong in the calculation, as was proved later.

Through innumerable tests and examinations, Chinese scientists have proved beyond a shadow of doubt that exceptional human functions do exist. This has also aroused the interest of psychologists and psychic researchers in the United States. *Nature Magazine*, enthused about the situation, did something for the first time: It put up an advertisement in *Guang Ming Daily*, the number-two major newspaper in Peking, which consisted of a passage quoted from Dr. Qian Xuesen, noted physicist:

Figure 13.6 The first national Scientific Conference on EHF was held in Shanghai City. (Photo courtesy of Zhou Wen Bin)

In the period between the first National Scientific Conference on EHF in Shanghai and the second one in Chungking, the rate of development has been increasing, and there has been progress in every passing day. The prevailing enthusiasm reminds one of the appearance of the law of relativity and quantum mechanics in the arena of modern science before the sixties. The difference is that then the arena was western Europe, but now it is people's China. Isn't it gratifying!

(The quotation was from Qian Xuesen's "Develop the Research of EHF," published in *Nature Magazine* in July 1981.)

What is the significance of the advertisement? It has the following purposes:

1. To announce the validity of EHF;
2. To continue *Nature Magazine*'s support for EHF research;
3. To increase *Nature Magazine*'s readership;
4. ·To voice the support of *Nature Magazine* for Dr. Qian's views of science;
5. Naturally, to declare a degree of triumph.

Enthusiasm in EHF has not only spread over the mainland, but has drawn the attention of newspapers and a parapsychological society in Taiwan. As to the United States, closer press coverage has continued on the developments of EHF in China. By now more than one third of the countries the world over have reported the news, including the Soviet Union and especially Japan.

Speaking personally, I have been enthusiastic about the study of both UFOs and EHF, for the simple reason that I have seen a UFO with my own eyes. As for EHF, after a month of self-training, I was able, strictly through mind power, to cause a string with a tiny bell suspended at the end to revolve around a circle drawn on a piece of paper. With three more months of training I could lift my left hand effortlessly with mind power while lying in bed.

I began to train my mind's psychic potential in 1979 following a trip to Hong Kong for neurasthenic treatment. Early that year, a friend of mine, Mr. Mok, introduced me to a noted Hong Kong hypnotist who can cure neurasthenia with qi gong and mind power. Mok had been a serious neurasthenia victim, and had complete recovery with the hyponotist's help. I had five sessions with the hypnotist during my ten-day stay in Hong Kong. Upon my return to the United States, I kept up the exercise earnestly for three months, and it proved effective.

Since I could develop psychic energy with my own effort, why should I not believe in children gifted with such power by nature, I thought. Although I accepted the idea in theory, nonetheless I still hoped to meet some such children myself. In 1981, when I was in Canton, I asked Mr. Wen Konghua, director of the Canton Branch of China UFO Research Organization, to arrange an interview for me with one or two EHF children.

"No need to seek elsewhere," he said. "In my hometown there is a boy who can submit to a test, though his function is slightly inferior."

"What are 'slightly inferior' functions?"

"He cannot do ear reading or X-ray vision. But his eyes can magnify."

At this I was immediately reminded of the study about the

discovery of Jupiter's satellite by Gan De. Before I spoke, Mr. Wen added, "Curiously enough, he can read very tiny characters which are invisible to many, and read them out without missing a single one."

"Good!" I exclaimed. "Let me meet this boy gifted with magnifying vision." I was quite excited because, as I explained to Mr. Wen, magnifying ability suggests the ability of remote vision.

"Do you mean he can see distant things?" Mr. Wen asked in wonder.

"Why, don't you know the boy is capable of remote vision?" I asked in return, adding, "Magnifying vision always goes with remote vision."

It was a lucky chance. I have been wondering how the human eye could reach great distances. Now I might have a chance to prove the possibility of Gan De's discovery of Jupiter's satellite.

So we traveled to Mr. Wen's hometown. The test was done at his house. Due to the limited electrical supply, in the common villager's house each room is lighted by a twenty-five watt bulb. Because of this, the average man over forty-five cannot read the small characters in the newspaper without spectacles. But Xiao Ming, the twelve-year-old boy, could read every one of the smallest characters at a distance of six feet. This suggested the likelihood of Gan De having discovered Jupiter's third satellite two thousand years ahead of Galileo.

If anyone still refuses to believe in remote vision, let us come back to Yu Rui Hua, whose feats I described earlier. Once when she had just finished her performance, a journalist started writing his story while sitting some ten paces from her. Someone asked the girl if she could read the manuscript from the distance, and she answered in the affirmative. Then she started to read aloud what had been written. She kept reading till the spectators applauded.

In Hong Kong, where scarcely two minutes are needed for any occurrence on the mainland to be known throughout the city, the inhabitants remained skeptical after EHF enthusiasm had reigned for a year on the mainland. This was because they had never seen any EHF activity, and could only speculate on press reports.

In June 1980, Ms. Tan Feng, editor in chief of Hong Kong's *Science and Future* magazine, visited Peking with two correspondents. She called on a professor of Qinghua University, where she met a member of Peking University's EHF research team. A Shanghai EHF girl, Zhang Lei, happened to be on Qinghua campus, so a test was undertaken the same day. The observers included Zhang Zugi of Peking University's biology department; Xiao Jianxiang, popular science writer; Tao Dejian of Qinghua's architecture department, and Tan Feng, who presided over the test.

Tan took a little picture book and chose three colored pictures from it. She cut down the first and placed it in a dark blue cloth bag. Then she asked Zhang Lei to put her hand in the bag to feel the picture. A minute later she declared the picture as yellow background with three little black ants, and she was right. Then the second picture was put in the bag for her to feel with her fingers, and again she told correctly that it was red in background with watermelon in the center. The came the third picture. The girl touched it with her fingers and announced, "Light green, with two eggs." This time she was mistaken about the background color, which was light blue. This was a test of finger reading, the results being 98 percent correct. Not bad!

In China today, scientists, doctors, technicians, professors, editors, writers, and others agree widely on the reality of EHF. In making this report, I am not propagandizing for EHF. The facts can be verified by others. My wish is to offer unbiased information, but I offer it with a sense of hope that the unjust ridicule and rejection of psychic and paranormal phenomena seen in various parts of the world will finally cease, even as it is now dying down in China.

Acceptance of EHF and other extraordinary events has not come easily behind the Bamboo Curtain, however. The next chapter describes some of the opposition.

14
The Conservative Scientists Attack EHF

Soon after Tan Feng tested the EHF children, four Hong Kong students—three majoring in physics and one in social sciences—visited mainland China under sponsorship of the university authorities. The four students came to Peking first, where they were welcomed by the physics students of Peking University and then brought into a discussion meeting. The Peking students stated that EHF is real, although at first they too had not believed it. After several tests, however, EHF was proven to be a fact.

Peking University itself had started the study of EHF several years earlier. However, the researchers concluded that the extraordinary phenomena of the human body they witnessed are not paranormal, but rather are normal—but latent, or only poorly developed—human abilities. Every human being has these functions, they said. The difference is that some people have them strongly, while in others they are very weak. Children usually have these functions more strongly than adults do, which is why the the people who have been discovered with EHF are almost all youngsters.

The day after meeting with the Peking students, the four Hong Kong students went to Shanghai to visit the office of *Nature Magazine*. They were welcomed by Zhu Yi Yi, the editor responsible for reporting EHF research. At the same time, Zhang Lei returned to Shanghai from Peking and was immediately scheduled by Zhu to be tested by the four visiting students. At the test, Zhu described how Zhang Lei's EHF was discovered:

On February 26, 1980, Zhang Lei's father bought a booklet on magic card games and showed his daughter how to perform them. Having watched her father's performance, she said, "That was no big deal; I can do it too." Then the father picked up a card and told her to make a guess. Continuously she made twenty correct guesses. By then the father realized that he had a daughter with EHF.

The test was carried out in the sitting room of *Nature Magazine* office. Ten demonstrations were made. The results of six of them were totally correct. Two were partially right; the other two failed.

The two partially correct tests happened in this way. In the seventh demonstration, the student visitors wrote on a small piece of paper the character *tian* (⊞), a cross within a square, meaning farmland. Then they put it in a tin box for Zhang Lei to try to read. She gazed at the tin box for six minutes and twenty-four seconds, and then wrote down ⊏⊐ and then ⊏⊐ . Some of the testers considered her answer partially correct because she had not been able to put ⊏⊐ on top of ⊟ to make ⊞ , while others took her answer as correct, saying, "It's truly wonderful to be able to see through a tin box. Why fuss?"

In the sixth demonstration, the testers outside the testing room wrote "people" on a small piece of paper and twisted it into a small paper ball. They returned to the room and put it into Zhang Lei's ear for her to read. After ten minutes she saw, or rather "heard," the word "people." Her answer was correct.

More than half the youngsters tested have this kind of nonocular vision, which includes reading with an ear, finger, crown of the head, armpit, bottom of the foot, and abdomen. A word written on a piece of paper and put in a tin box can be seen, or read, by youngsters with their nonocular vision. This is amazing enough to scientists. Even more amazing is that words on a piece of paper twisted into a paper ball or cut into small pieces can still be "read" correctly by youngsters with EHF. According to the explanation of Bei Shi Zhang, director of the Institute of Biology and Physics of Academia Sinica,

> Ocular vision is better than nonocular vision, but nonocular vision has its peculiar advantage—view expansion. With it, the person, can, in his mind, make the twisted or cut-up piece of paper with words on it return to its original shape and become intelligible. The person also has the ability of seeing through metal and plastic to read words on twisted or cut up pieces of paper. All this cannot be accomplished by normal ocular vision.

Bei Shi Zhang also said that both ocular and nonocular vision are human biological functions for transmitting information through space. Each has to consume energy. Therefore each causes fatigue and reduces its function to a lower energy level. Nonocular vision has aroused the interest of many scientists, whose approach to this phenomenon starts with study of the change of the energy levels, the frequency of the changes, and the transmission of energy in space.

Now let's examine how the eighth demonstration was carried out. The testers outside the testing room wrote on a piece of paper the first line of an ancient four-line Chinese poem by the well-known poet, Li Pai. The poem reads:

In front of my bedside I see moonlight.
It looks like frost on the ground.
Looking up, I watch the shining moon.
Deep down, I feel homesick.

The paper was folded a few times and put into a tin box. The group thought that even if Zhang Lei could see through the tin box, she could not possibly see a complete sentence on a folded piece of paper. Surprisingly, after nine minutes, she read out the sentence completely correctly. Everyone in the room was amazed.

According to Zhang Lei, in the process of "reading" words on a piece of paper in a tin box, the shape of each of the Chinese characters "pops up" in her mind one by one, or part by part. As soon as the character is completely formed, this popping-up process stops momentarily. Then the process starts again until another character is completed. For example, in the case of reading the first line of this poem, the shape of the top part of the Chinese characters for "light" popped up in her mind first (丷), followed by the bottom part of it (兀) to form the whole character for "light" (光). Then the two characters for "shining moon" appeared, and last of all the two characters for "bedside." In other words, the last character for "light" appeared in her mind first, and then the characters for "shining moon" and "bedside" followed.

When the four Hong Kong University students finished watching the demonstrations, they felt that although science and technology have made wonderful progress, there are still innumerable mysterious phenomena that scientists cannot possibly explain.

Although Hong Kong and mainland China are separated only by a little water, due to China's closed door policy in the past, Hong Kong and China seemed for generations to be far apart. Now that China has adopted the open door policy, visitors from Hong Kong find everything in China somewhat strange. However, they do feel the warmth of their fellow countrymen. They found Zhang Lei to be a nice girl with EHF. One of the four students was deeply moved. He copied the following poem, which is popular among Hong Kong students, and presented it to Zhang Lei:

Mountains may fall,
Oceans may go dry,
Friends may forget you,
But never shall I.

It is a beautiful picture, with science, friendship, and warm feelings among compatriots blended together. Nevertheless, in the eyes of certain conservative scientists, this charming picture would become one of ugly, shameless cheating and fakery.

The leader of the conservative scientists is Yu Guang Yuan, the vice-chairman of the Chinese Academy of Sciences, vice-director of the Academia Sinica's Science and Technology Committee, and director of the Institute of Marxism, Leninism and Thoughts of Mao Tse-tung. From his authoritative position, he directs the attack on the study of EHF. His verdict: EHF is not real—only a bit of trickery and delusion. His rationale is that eyes are for seeing, ears for hearing, the nose for breathing and smelling, and anything contrary to these biological functions is contrary to science and truth. Since he considered EHF "unworthy of attention" when he learned of it, he and other conservative scientists have refused to even look at it personally. It is said that Yu, highly trained in science, cannot understand that science has not yet explained all the mysteries of nature.

Be that as it may, while EHF is being widely studied in mainland China, a group of highly positioned conservative scientists, newspaper editors, and politicians cannot restrain their dislike of EHF, and they let Yu Guang Yuan take the lead in attacking EHF. He began by writing seven long articles, 7,000 to 10,000 words each, and published them in the authoritative monthly, *Knowledge Is Power*. The first article appeared in October 1981. The titles of the seven articles are :

1. "Criticism of the Propaganda for 'Reading With Ear' in the Past Two Years"
2. "The Propaganda Is Not New and Not Limited to Our Country"
3. "The Much Publicized EHF Is Not a Fact, But a Magic Game"
4. "Articles Attacking 'Reading with Ears' Have No Opportunity to Be Published"
5. "Disclosing to More People the Falsehoods of these Magic Games. It Would Be All Right to Test EHF Once More. But It Must Be a Truly Scientific Test."

6. "The Problem Must Be Resolved on the Basis of Philosophy—We Are Against the Theory of Experience."
7. "Now Is the Time to Stop this Propaganda. But the Propaganda Has Its Roots, Which Cannot Be Eradicated All at Once."

Only three of the series have been published; the rest are scheduled for publication within a year. What did Yu say in "The Propaganda of 'Reading With Ears' in the Past Two Years"? Essentially, he says that it is improper for newspapers and magazines to publish propaganda for EHF because it contradicts the principles of dialectical materialism, and that he is sorry that *People's Daily* has been singled out for criticism.

People's Daily is the leading paper of China. It is published by the Central Political Committee, and is the voice of the government. Historically it has been that *People's Daily* can criticize other newspapers, but other papers do not dare to criticize its viewpoint.

Yu admitted in his article that during the previous two years, criticism against "reading with ear" received many complaints. For example, one newspaper wrote that a recent report in *Sichuan Daily* stated that a youngster was able to read and see colors with his ears and the *Daily* later reported a student named Jiang Yan, age eight of Mo Shih Ko Elementary School had the same function. Word spread all over the capital city and in a few days, the *Daily* said, about one thousand people from near and far came to watch the demonstrations of EHF abilities by Jiang Yan. They generally considered EHF an important discovery in the research of the mysteries of the human body.

However, soon afterward, a reporter for the *People's Daily* named Zu Jin started writing articles attacking EHF. The first article was entitled "From Sniffing Words with Nose to Reading with Ears." In it he emphasized that "reading with ears" is contrary to common sense, unscientific, ridiculous, and a shell game. The article accused parents of EHF youngsters of playing a con game. As a result, those researchers concerned with this intriguing discovery were by implication being duped and deserved to become laughingstocks.

Other newspapers responded in defense. They even used the authority of some famous people to make threats. For a while, the waves they made created new misunderstandings about EHF. One wrote:

> Those who write newspaper articles attacking reading with ear...put on a disciplinary air like that of the religious judges of the Middle Ages. The kind of attitude of "bending with the wind" and "twisting of facts" was common during the time of the Gang of Four. But three

years after the Gang of Four collapsed, this kind of false accusation is no longer tolerable.

This was in the October 19, 1979, issue of *Peking Steel Works Journal*. Other papers, such as the *Shanghai Liberation Daily*, also strongly criticized *People's Daily*.

The situation has also been reported by foreign news media. For example, the Agency France reported (December 21, 1979, from Peking) that *Shanghai Liberation Daily* wrote that "some youngsters can read words and pictures with their ears and armpits, and some newspapers made implied attacks on *People's Daily*, which published reports in May denying the existence of youngsters with EHF and warned Chinese reporters to be careful in their reports on this subject." *Liberation Daily* also reported that "this kind of thing is difficult to believe. Nevertheless, since so many scientists saw EHF in action with their own eyes, we should believe it to be true."

This reaction of *Liberation Daily* to the denial of EHF by *People's Daily* pointed out that

> Some comrades have made a "subject judgment," which lacks sensitivity and is narrow minded. Observers say that *People's Daily* almost never accepts attacks on it by other papers. However, many newspapers and magazines openly or implicitly criticized *People's Daily* for its stand on the subject of EHF, and *People's Daily* kept silent. Unlike other newspapers, *People's Daily* has never changed its attitude towards EHF, which antagonized those who propagandize "reading with ears."

In his second article, Yu pointed out that extrasensory perception (ESP) has a long history. It is an "ancient superstition" which later became necromancy, sorcery, and divination for cheating people. It can be traced back to the history of hypnotism at the end of the eighteenth century, he said. Hypnotism itself is a method of healing by suggestion developed by Franz Anton Mesmer, an eighteenth century Frenchman. Marxists do not deny hypnotism. Engels himself had successfully experimented with it, and discovered that under hypnosis, a person goes into a condition of overexcitement associated with a passive will. The person has no mysterious relationship with the hypnotist, however. Any other person can do it the same way, Engels said. But Mesmer wrongly explained hypnosis as "human magnetism." And many people, Yu pointed out, mystified it so that it became forerunner of spiritualism, a religion that believes in communication with the spirits of the dead. Since the mid-nineteenth century, Yu said, some people practiced this kind of superstitious trick for money.

Besides loudly declaring ESP to be "ancient superstition," Yu also banished psychokinesis, EHF, parapsychology, spiritualism, and psychical research as pseudosciences. When a friend of his wrote a book containing a chapter titled, "Don't Let Spiritualism Be Disguised as Science," the publisher deleted the chapter, saying the subject was too controversial to print. Yu considered the act unfair to the author.

It is true that at a time when two thirds of the 470 newspapers of China were enthusiastically reporting news on EHF, any objection to EHF would be considered ignorant of the facts. Most news media supported EHF. Indeed, for a while some of the news media against EHF seemed to be prevailing. But now they are overshadowed by the enthusiasm for EHF, which has made the news media overwhelmingly support the study of EHF. If that publisher had printed Yu's friend's book with a chapter against EHF research, the book would have been severely criticized. Now that Yu has organized a group of scientists, newspapers, and magazines to attack EHF, his friend should be happy about the deletion.

In Yu's article, he complained that "those who are enthusiastic about ancient superstition have now introduced all the spiritual mid-wives [mediums] and spiritualists of foreign countries into China. Many rare names and terminologies of foreign spiritualists, previously unknown to the Chinese, have become familiar now in China." The names of the ESP institutions and spiritualists Yu referred to include those of Great Britain, the U.S., France, Japan, and the Soviet Union.

Yu also criticized Dr. Lee Shao Kung (Dr. Cyrus Lee), professor of psychology at Edinboro State College in Pennsylvania, who wrote an article, "Impact on America of Chinese Studies of EHF Children," published on page 3 of the September 30, 1981, issue of *EHF Report*. In the article, Lee stated that in the summer of 1980 the Chinese Education Department invited him to China for the arrangement of an exchange professor program between China and America. When he visited Wuhan University he made an agreement that Wuhan and Edinboro State College would make a joint effort in the next few years to study youngsters with EHF. Lee further obtained the support, and the eventual research cooperation, of many well-known American psychologists in the exchange program between Chinese and American scholars and experts. On the American side, the cooperating scholars and psychologists include Dr. Stanley Krippner; Dr. Arthur Hastings; Dr. Charles Tart; Thomas Hara, M.D.; Karl Menninger, M.D.; Daniel Anthony Snow, M.D.; Miss Barbara White; and Mr. Hugh Lynn Cayce. Obviously, Yu is not happy about involving foreigners in the publicity for EHF.

In his third article, Yu is even more blunt. The article, about 13,000 words long, was published in three parts. The essential points of Yu's criticism are:

1. He brands EHF as superstition, definitely not a fact.

2. Based on biology and physiology, he says that each of the five human functions—hearing, smelling, seeing, tasting, and touching—has its particular natural function. For example, eyes can see objects, but cannot see through objects. Ears cannot substitute for eyes; that would be contrary to science.

3. He agrees to having more discussions of EHF, but only on three conditions prescribed by him. The three conditions are:

    a. The discussions must be from the scientific point of view. (He means, of course, from the point of view of traditional orthodox science.)

    b. The subjects to be discussed must be based on psychology and physics. (There would be no room for discussion if the subjects were parapsychological or metaphysical.)

    c. The discussion must be done according to the principles of dialectical materialism. (If the discussion were from the viewpoint of idealism, then there would be nothing to discuss.)

Yu Guang Yuan, originally an economist, sees everything from the historical point of view of dialectical materialism. Anything contrary to the philosophy of the dialectical, materialistic point of view is, by definition, pseudo and ridiculous. When facts do not match with theory, this attitude says, the facts must be ignored and the theory upheld against all criticism.

At the Second Conference on EHF Science in Chungking, five scientists and technologists of China Science and Technology University jointly presented a report to the meeting. It said, in part,

> A human being has a physical body and an unseen body; existence has a physical world and also an unseen world. The world inhabited by unseen, or invisible, people is going to be discovered or developed. It is true that there are people beyond people, and a world beyond this world. Real or unreal—endless mysteries.

The report used the language of idealism, which Yu Guang Yuan considered intolerable, of course.

Ever since Yu published his first article on EHF, "Criticism of the Propaganda for 'Reading With Ears' in the Past Two Years," his followers have attacked the study of EHF. They published *Exceptional Human Function: Investigation Data* to counteract the *EHF Report.* Aligned with Yu's side are the EHF Investigation, Study and

Liaison Group, organized in October 1981 by the National Science and Technology Commission; the China Study Commission on Dialectical Naturalism; the Research Institute of Psychology of the Academia Sinica; *Knowledge Is Power;* Shanghai *Wen Wei Daily; China Youth; Social Science Front; News Front;* and others. In fact, a big debate has developed between the two sides for and against EHF, just as was the case for UFO research.

However, *People's Daily* has not been silent in the matter. On the day the debate started, *People's Daily* published only the news of the Academia Sinica calling for a discussion meeting on EHF, along with the article, "Summary of Criticism on the Propaganda for EHF Research in the Past Two Years." At the same time it also published an editorial note which I will paraphrase in proper editorial fashion to give the proper authoritative tone:

> We do not believe in "reading with ears." Our newspaper has published criticism of the propaganda for the so-called "reading with ears," which has been widely acclaimed by the readers. But some did not like the criticism. At the same time, some others, who were interested in EHF, complained against us. Why?
>
> It is because some science units and scientists insisted that reading with ears is science, a super science, a new and important discovery in the phenomena of human life and body. However, there were other science units and scientists who also insisted that EHF is a pseudo science, taking magic as science, and that some deliberately use the magic for cheating people. So, is it science or pseudo science? Our standpoint is that this kind of controversial subject should be resolved by authoritative science organizations, not by the *People's Daily.* Moreover, being a newspaper of political nature, we cannot afford to give sufficient space for printing so many articles on EHF. We expect scientific organizations to resolve the controversy.
>
> Luckily in October 1981, the Academia Sinica's Science and Technology Committee organized an EHF Investigation and Research Liaison Unit, which has so far published four issues of *Exceptional Human Function: Investigation Data.* Meanwhile, comrade Yu Guang Yuan, the Vice Chairman of the Academia Sinica's Science and Technology Committee, published a series of articles in *Knowledge Is Power* magazine criticizing EHF research. Some scientific magazines and newspapers also printed articles pointing out the falsehoods of EHF. Yesterday Academia Sinica called for a scientific meeting to criticize EHF.
>
> Today, while our newspaper reports the news about the meeting, we also publish a comprehensive report on the publicity in the past two years for EHF, together with our readers' analysis and judgment. In the last analysis, is EHF a science or pseudo science?

15
The Great
EHF Debate

Yu Guang Yuan's critique of Exceptional Human Functions in the October 1981 issue of *Knowledge Is Power* provoked an enthusiastic response which led to a heated debate. By a conservative count, sixty-eight newspapers and magazines, forty-two educational institutions, and a number of teaching and technology research staff members from fifty colleges and many TV and radio stations have been involved in the debate. Both sides aimed at the other directly, using names. Millions of people watched closely the development of the event.

Soon after Yu's article appeared, *The EHF Report* returned fire. On October 30, 1981, in an editorial called "The EHF Problems Raise New Arguments; We Will Continue the Discussion of EHF in Order to Explore a New Realm of the Scientific World," it stated

> In the last couple of years *Nature Magazine* has published over 20 articles about the scientific research of EHF. These articles indicate that the research work has advanced from the observation stage to the instrumental stage. By employing the techniques of modern science, it has been firmly established that EHF exists. Instruments and charts prove that those who possess exceptional ability are in many ways different from ordinary people. EHF is not magic, tricks or superstitions.

Printed on the same page as the editorial was an article by Shang Cheng-zuo, professor of Chinese at the Chungshan University in

Canton. The article, titled "Facts Are Undeniable, Facts Would Break up Empty-Talks" (a quotation from Lu Xun, China's literary mentor), criticized Yu and his followers for jumping to conclusions without detailed investigation. Shang said that scientists cannot deny anything that cannot be explained by science. He who holds such an attitude and claims himself scientific is actually unscientific, Shang declared. He noted that an EHF forum was held shortly before then in Chungking, and the attendants included doctors and psychologists. A similar meeting was held in Kunming with the presence of philosophers and scientists, he said, and these people did not deny that ears can read words. In his own college, he pointed out, an eleven-year-old daughter of a lecturer was able to recognize words not only by ears, but also with her fingers and feet. Moreover, she was able to distinguish color by ears, feet, and fingers too. "I myself have tested her many times," Shang said, "and each time she gave me a satisfactory answer." He then bluntly declared that people like Yu Guang Yuan would shut their mouths if they were shown the facts.

Finally, Shang quoted Lu Xun again as saying that very often experts speak mere rubbish. The experts are specialists only in their own field, but when asked for their opinions beyond their profession they often make mistakes, sometimes silly mistakes. "An expert specializes only in one field, not in all fields." Shang was obviously hinting that even a famed economist named Yu may know a lot about economics, but will not necessarily know everything.

The same issue of *EHF Report* also contains other interesting articles. A letter from the parent of a gifted child reflected his bitter feeling. He said that he reported the fact that his child could read words by skin because he is concerned with the growth of science in China. He has no intention of propagating feudalism or superstition, he said. Many science units have proved that skin reading is an undeniable fact. But still some people refuse to undertake research; they repudiate EHF as ridiculous and ignorant. This unreasonable denial is really discouraging and frightening, the parent wrote.

During the wave of heated debate, a most interesting letter was the one written by a former student of Yu. An engineer of Nanking Engineering Department, Yan Zi-hu, said in his open letter,

> It is irresponsible to use a few simple philosophical terms to deny the ever-emerging new facts of the vast scientific world. Teacher Yu's recent behavior is contradictory to what he had said at the Hereditary Conference in Qing Dao in 1956. On August 10, 1956, Teacher Yu told the conference:
>
> "We believe that we should behave in a scholarly manner in any discussions. We should respect the objectivity of facts. We must say things according to facts."

To illustrate further, Yan also referred to a Japanese story translated by Lu Xun. The story goes like this: Once two people saw something black on the ground. One said that it was a worm, the other said it was a bean. They argued about this. Finally the black thing began to move. So the one who said it was a worm declared that he was right. But the other person still did not give up and insisted it was a bean. In fact, they really did not have to wait for the worm to rise up. Why not just kneel down and take a good look?

The letter further said mockingly about Yu:

> Teacher Yu then emphasized, "Without sufficient proof one must be cool and be cautious not to denounce others as idealist, or to denounce others politically." As a student I am writing this letter to criticize my teacher, hoping that Teacher Yu will reflect upon what he said so impressively twenty years ago and not betray his teachings.

Many articles criticizing Yu were published. However, Yu responded to none of these criticisms. He continued to write his seven articles and let his followers and supporters answer his critics. Yu's followers did not give the critics an easy time. The *Exceptional Human Function: Investigation Data* published many pieces in a harsh tone to dismiss their opponents. They quoted Engels, Lenin, Lu Xun, and other important figures of dialectical materialism. The titles of these articles are pointed. They include, for example, "Ear-Reading Is Magic," "It Is Unbelievable that It Would Anger Them So Much by Telling the Truth," "Don't Let EHF People Heal Disease," and "The Real Face of Uri Geller."

Uri Geller, of course, is the well-known Israeli psychic who gained prominence for his metal-bending feats and for the heated attacks upon him by magicians and skeptics who claim he is a trickster without any paranormal power. It is interesting to note here the comments given by the *Exceptional Human Function: Investigation Data*, which said that since a feature story about Uri Geller appeared in the May 1980 issue of *Nature* magazine, many publications that supported EHF refer frequently to him. In the beginning Geller did amaze many Westerners. He amazed them by arranging ten aluminum cans together on a table with a metal ball hidden in one of the ten cans. Simply by touching these cans once he was able to locate the ball; every time he succeeded in doing that. Is this by chance, the magazine asked. It answered: No, that would be impossible. Did he touch the cans secretly? No, he performed before the public. Did he prearrange this with somebody else? It did not seem to be the case. Then what is the explanation? According to Uri Geller, the magazine commented, he contacted beings from outer space and got the inspiration from them. Of course, the comment continued, no one would believe this. At that time, it noted, *Nature* magazine of England had cast doubts on this. But some scientists protested that there should not be any doubts. They said that people would only believe in what they saw personally, and they had actually seen what happened. They said at first they could not believe it either, but they changed their minds after seeing Geller's performance. They said that the doubts raised by *Nature* were without basis. However, people later discovered that Geller was able to locate the ball simply by moving the table slightly. In his demonstration on August 1, 1973, Geller was not allowed to touch the table, and at once he failed to locate the ball.

The journal's editors said they were not sure if it is because spiritualists in China are uninformed that they still propagate this kind of "absurd" story in the eighties. At the same time, they related EHF with the "magic" of Uri Geller. But Geller, they said, was proved to be a fraud. The editors concluded that they just don't know how they should categorize the ear-reading phenomenon.

Whether Uri Geller is an extraordinary person or a fraud is unknown to me. However, research on psychic children shows that it is common for them to lose their extrasensory ability if they are in a low mood and, strangely, as they have grown older.

In this heated debate, a most remarkable response came from the Shanghai-based *Wen Wei Daily*. The newspaper published numerous articles opposing and denying EHF. However, in the midst of the organized opposition, *Nature Magazine* received a letter from an editor of *Wen Wei Daily*. I will paraphrase it using the first person point of view to retain the feeling of authenticity in the original letter:

> Comrade Editor:
>
> I am an editor of *Wen Wei Daily* and was very doubtful about the merits of the case for EHF. But after a personal encounter I must say that EHF absolutely exists.
>
> I support your position: recognize facts, respect science. I think we could make further progress by sticking to this position.
>
> My enclosed article focuses mainly on an observation experience. It aims at telling people what I have seen.

Together with the letter, the magazine published his article, "Recognize Facts, Respect Science." Again I will use the first person to speak as if I were the writer:

> My position in regard to EHF is that I would not believe what I was told and that I needed to see it personally. I had the opportunity to encounter that experience on the last national holiday of 1981.

On that afternoon, a special program was arranged with two psychic children performing their feats of EHF. The performance was held in the Workers' Stadium at the Hsu-Wei district of Shanghai. It was crowded with people. Before that, a qi gong show had won thunderous applause from the audience. At that time the two little girls who were ready for the next program were hanging around the place. One of the girls held a tin container like a soapbox in one hand and a rectangular plastic box in the other. Both girls were the same height, pigtailed, and dressed in simple suits. One was quiet, the other was active. I could not find any special traits in these children. They were just like ordinary students that could be found in any school.

Their performance was scheduled as the second program. When it first began, they sat on two chairs near the basketball net. They did not seem nervous, and impressed people as being experienced actors. An assistant then took a matchbox and a little piece of paper and came to the audience requesting someone to write words on it. I volunteered immediately. I wrote down the words, folded the paper, and put it into the matchbox. Another audience member wrote on another piece. The assistant did not pay any attention to us while we were writing. He then took the boxes back and put them into the container the two little girls had brought with them. I saw the little girls put the boxes under the armpit, then take the boxes out and put them near their ears. In less than a minute they went toward the blackboard and wrote down the words. The host asked me if these were the correct words. I nodded; so did the other person. The audience clapped their hands wildly.

The second time I wrote two Russian characters: ЯН . I did the same thing as what I had done and the same procedure was repeated. The quiet little girl then immediately put on the blackboard the two characters ЯН . The other girl said that she did not know what those words were but would write the shape of the character she visualized. Although she wrote Я as if it were R, I would say they were the same.

Similar tests on words and concrete things were made. And every time they amazed the audience. After that, an eighty-one-year-old pugilist Master Ma Yu Liang performed tai chi. Ma looked like sixty and stood firmly on the floor. When approached by his partner, he only pushed gently and the partner fell on the floor heavily.

I sought a chance to interview the two little girls. One was called Siao-hua, the other was called Siao-huang. Both were twelve. They were classmates in the fifth grade. I requested them to sign their names for me. I asked when they found they possessed a strange power, and they said at first they did not feel anything until last year when the teacher made a survey and found that they were among two of the several children who had the magic power. They were found the most sensitive and responsive and were put on training. I asked whether they could see things buried underground. They said that they had not tried that before. The girls appeared very honest and straightforward.

Since the girls did not use their eyesight, how could they read the characters in their mind? I asked. They said that in the beginning they would feel their hands numb and their ears buzzing, then their eyes would see different colors and finally the words appeared before them just like images shown on a television set. When we talked, people began to gather around us. The host then showed us to the office upstairs where we could rest for a while with Master Ma.

The office had two desks. We sat there facing each other. I asked Siao-huang why she had to put the container under her armpit. She said that by doing so she would feel the warmth and then a vague vision would appear. By touching her ears, the vision would become clearer and she could tell what characters or color they were.

"Could you see the vision if you did not put the box under your armpit and if you did not put the matchbox inside the container?" I asked. "Of course I could."

I got their agreement and did the test once more. I tore off a piece of paper. Siao-huang asked me if they had to withdraw for a while. I said it was not necessary. I then wrote words under the desk and folded the paper into a very small piece. Then I let them hold the paper. I watched Siao-huang closely. She was quite at ease. She put her hand on her face. Master Ma then said, "Let me help you a little bit." Then he pointed his finger sharply toward her. The girl smiled and immediately said that the word I wrote was "ye"(wild) and Siao-hua said that the word was "tung" (boy). I surrendered wholeheartedly.

I asked Siao-huang what she felt when Master Ma pointed his finger toward her. She said, "I have already read the word. But when Master Ma pointed at me, it made the vision clearer." She added that she saw a circle of light around the head of Master Ma. I asked Ma to do the same thing again. And I asked someone to take away Siao-huang for a while. Then I asked Siao-hua what she saw. She said she saw lighting above Master Ma's head and on his eyes too. I then told Siao-huang to come in and asked her the same question. She replied the same thing too.

By the time we left the office, Siao-huang said she felt a little dizzy—this is common to psychic children after a vision. Master Ma told them to stop. He held Siao-huang's hands tightly in one hand and with his other hand he pressed his thumb onto the acupuncture point on her hand for relieving headaches. This point is located at the top of the little bulge of flesh that occurs when the thumb is pressed alongside the forefinger. With his other hand he touched the forehead. After a few seconds he raised his hand a little bit. Then the girl looked at him and said, "I am all right." He did the same thing to Siao-hua and she also said, "I'm all right." I then said good-bye to them and was satisfied with what I had seen.

To detail the arguments of both sides would be too much to report here. Instead, I will list the names of the units that have involved themselves in the debate, so that readers can see the pro or con position that different groups have held. And I would like to suggest that the debate is not just an infighting among the groups, but is in fact a struggle in the entire science profession about the nature of human beings.

Below are the organizations and institutes that support the EHF research:

- China Society of EHF Research
- *Nature Magazine*
- The EHF Research Committee of Peking University
- The Peking Observatory
- The Research and Teaching Committee of Marxism-Leninism, Peking Economics Institute
- The Department of Physics, Peking Teachers' College
- The EHF Research Committee, Peking Ching Hua University
- EHF Research Committee, Nanking University
- Department of Philosophy, Nanking University
- The Nanking Research Society of Human Body Potential
- Shanghai Laser Technique Research Institute
- The Shanghai Chinese Medical Research Institute
- The Shanghai Educational Institute
- Acoustics Research Institute, The Chinese Academy of Sciences
- High Energy Physics Research Institute, The Chinese Academy of Sciences
- Yunnan EHF Research Institute
- Yunnan College of Chinese Traditional Medicine
- Yunnan University
- The Changchun College of Chinese Traditional Medicine
- Lanzhou University
- Hangzhou University
- Anhui Normal University
- Bethume University of Medicine
- Jilin Normal University
- Hubei Chinese Medical College
- Jinmusi Medical College
- Chungking Medical College
- Chungking EHF Research Institute
- The Popular Science Department, Chungking Science Institute
- The Chungking Laser Research Institute
- Commission in Charge of Science, Technology and Industry of National Defense, the #507 Institute
- The Guangdong Sanitorium
- Zhong Shan University of Canton
- Sichuan University
- Sichuan Medical College
- Science Research Committee, Zhe Jiang Textile Factory

- ☐ EHF Research Committee, Zhe Jiang University
- ☐ Hua Tung Normal College
- ☐ Central China Polytechnic
- ☐ The Minching Health Department, Minching County, Fujian Province
- ☐ Wuhan Physics Institute
- ☐ Nanking Number 54 Secondary School
- ☐ The Yunnan Qi Gong Research Institute
- ☐ First People's Hospital of Kunming
- ☐ Ningxia EHF Research Institute
- ☐ Biological Research Institute, The Chinese Academy of Sciences
- ☐ (Many other provincial medical units and science units are not listed)

Of course, all these groups engaged in the debate pointed their spearhead toward Yu Guang Yuan. The reason is not simply that Yu had written seven articles dismissing EHF, or that he refused to acknowledge the EHF Research Society as an official unit (which would block the society from obtaining government funding). The principal reason is that Yu acted so bureaucratically and dogmatically, even refusing to test the EHF children personally.

Yu's arguments, of course, have a semblance of legitimacy. He justifies himself by quoting the results of a failed test which was conducted on Jiang Yun on April 19, 1979, by the Chinese Academy of Sciences (see Chapter 10). He built up his case largely by adding up a few more experiments that have recorded failures by EHF children.

It is not reasonable to expect success every time EHF children are tested. There are different causes that may affect the strength of the children's psychic power, and even cause it to temporarily disappear. Tiredness, depression, frustration, wounds, and fears are some causes that can interfere with the effectiveness of the children's strange power. Those people who refuse to acknowledge the existence of such power usually treated the gifted children in an authoritarian manner when they were put to test. Or they would demand exceptional achievements from the children. Thus the children would find themselves under too much pressure and would become frightened. As a result, the test would fail. Then these people would claim that tests have been made which prove that EHF is nothing but cheating, and they keep on denouncing it. Such a biased attitude is too much for the public to accept. It is divisive and aggravates the situation rather than leading to clarification. The important thing is to know the truth, not to uphold dogma.

That is not to say that the EHF camp has a monopoly on truth.

Figure 15.1 Dr. Wu Xue Yu, right, of Otolaryngological Hospital of Shanghai First Medical College and Cheong Shon Liang (far left) of Peking University examining Tong Yu (middle) and two other EHF children.

It may be that there is some degree of cheating by some youngsters who are thought to have EHF. Even though EHF is proven in principle, there could be those who claim to have EHF but are, as Yu and others claim, mere tricksters. Skepticism and rigorous observation are always necessary, but when the evidence is in, the conclusion must be accepted, even though it is contrary to one's previous belief. In that regard, there is a very interesting article entitled "Respect the Truth, Explore the Truth," written by Dr. Wu Xue-yu, an otolaryngologist of the Shanghai First Hospital. He said that recently he heard about reading words by ears but did not believe anything about it. He thought it was ridiculous. An old friend of his wrote to him telling him that this was genuine. Xue-yu trusted the friend personally but would not believe a single line of the EHF story. However, since it was also part of his own research duties to investigate the otolaryngology phenomenon, Xue-yu had to take a look at it. When a meeting was held to discuss EHF, he went there with a very suspicious attitude and behaved rather stubbornly. On the day the meeting was held, he arrived very early and sat in the first row. He saw the test given to Wang Qiang and other children and began to change his mind. In the afternoon, he personally tested Wang Qiang, Jiang Yan, Tong Yu, and Xie Zhaohui. The test was conducted in his home, using a paper on which he himself wrote. All the children did an amazing job. He was finally convinced, and

137

thought of the Chinese maxim: "Practicing is the only way to test truth." He surrendered to the truth after he had tested it.

Another article is also worthy of noting here. It was written by Li Bao-shi, of the People's Liberation Army of the Second Region University. Again, I will recount it in the first person as if I were the writer:

> I attended an EHF forum recently and felt very grateful. Before the meeting I was very doubtful about the fact of EHF. Yesterday I personally watched the conducting of the test and believed there was no cheating. The children were very cooperative in making the test successful. The test proved that EHF does exist. It is an objective fact that ears and armpits can read words.
>
> Now I would say something more about EHF for your reference. Most of the human's sensory organs are not as sensitive as many people think. Our sensory perceptions, generally speaking, include vision, hearing, touching, smelling, and tasting. But none of these sensory abilities is that powerful. For example, when a cow begins to bellow, it can produce a sound that people may soon find they cannot hear clearly, although another cow may hear it clearly. If we observe more closely, we find that the cow is still making sound and that its neck is quivering. Although the sound the cow makes is inaudible to us, it does not mean that the cow has stopped lowing. The sound is beyond

Figure 15.2 Professor Li Bao Shi (front row, middle) from Shanghai Second Army Medical University, Professor Wu Xue Yu from Otolaryngological Hospital of Shanghai First Medical College (back row, left), and Professor Chen Han Kui from Shanghai Teacher's University (right in the back) with fourteen psychic children who attended the first EHF symposium. (Photo courtesy of Zhou Wen Bin)

what human ears can capture. What does this mean? It means that our hearing capacity is less sensitive than cows. Or take the example of bats. We all know that bats cannot see anything during the daytime. Even in the evening their.vision is very weak. But they can fly freely to seek food at night because bats are able to hear even a very weak sound. Because of their capacity to send and receive sound waves that humans cannot hear, bats can locate insects and other objects within a certain distance. We have never heard of bats killing themselves by flying into trees or walls. The reason is that they possess a hearing power more sensitive than human beings.

Our visual and touching senses are even worse. When night falls, we cannot see anything if we do not have the help of light. However, cats can still carry on their activities and catch mice in the evening. Another example: If we are bitten by a mosquito, we would only realize it after a while when we feel the itch. Many less intelligent animals survive because they possess special sensory organs.

All these indicate that what people often call "strange things" may not be strange. Human beings may possess other powers in the body that have not yet been discovered. The youngsters who are able to read in darkness or without eye vision are a concrete example. We should spend more time in exploring this area in order to make a break-through. Don't just listen to jokes. All researchers of the concerned parties have the responsibility to make further research on EHF. In addition, I would like to say that we should include this study of sensory organs of human body as an important subject in our future research efforts. Since there are children who are able to read words and characters by hand touching, this may mean that human hands may possess a visual sense capacity too. If that is true, will such sense be even more powerful than our eyesight? Or can it replace the function of eyesight? In sum, the point of my raising these questions is to say that I hope we will use the EHF issue as a basis for further research. I have thought about these questions in the last few days and I must admit that I am very satisfied with the results I saw yesterday. In order to discover more functions of our bodies, we should start from here, right now.

An old Chinese proverb says, "A fire in your neighbor's yard will attract the fish in your pool." The debate on EHF in the mainland also provoked interest in Hong Kong. Newspapers in Hong Kong also published many articles discussing the issue. Interestingly, most people in Hong Kong believe in the case for EHF. A certain Li Lian wrote an article in *Ming Pao Daily,* entitled "It May Not Be Absurd to Say that Ears Can Read Words." Yu Guang Yuan, in his second article, had already commented on Li's piece. He said that Li did not raise any original ideas, but repeated the age-old superstitions. Scholars and teachers in Hong Kong were interviewed on the subject. A reporter interviewed Dr. Fung Jian-yun of the department of physics of the University of Hong Kong. Their conversations went like this, I am told:

"I am not knowledgeable about this, but I will give my opinion based on what I know," Dr. Fung said. "I believe that this phenomenon is possible."

"Why?" the reporter asked.

"First we need to know how an image is produced," Dr. Fung said. "The process in which our eyes capture the image of external objects is constituted of two parts. First, light stimulates the nerves of the retinal cells. The cells then send messages which are carried by nerves to the brain, telling the brain what we have 'seen.' This is the first part.

"The second part is that these messages are reconstructed in the brain and the brain then tells us what the image is. If in our body we have other senses that perform the same functions as the retinal cells, the messages collected by these senses will also be transferred to the brain, which will tell us what we have seen. Thus we can 'see' things.

"This phenomenon happens to us very often. When we dream at night, we don't need our eyes to see. But still we can 'see' things. In fact, there is research showing that people can send out messages without necessarily using speech, writing, or any body motion. I believe that brain waves are messages produced by the brain while we are thinking. Under certain conditions people are able to capture and react to these messages. The sensitivity between twins is a good example.

"Thus it is not surprising that some people may possess a special sensitive power in their body that can produce signals via electromagnetic waves. Through the reaction of the object that receives the signals, the electromagnetic waves will bring back to the brain of the sender information such as the shapes and color of the object the waves encounter. The brain will then produce the image. This is not without probability. For those who can read words by ears, perhaps they possess some kind of special sensitive power of this kind in their body."

In conclusion, EHF research in China has laid down a foundation. Despite the interference of Yu Guang Yuan, I believe China may have already established a leading role in this research. Such research will probably challenge the orthodoxy of many sciences.

Although Yu has made a great effort to suppress the research into EHF, it does not mean that such research has been halted. On the contrary , it has received official sanction at the highest level of government in China. It happened this way.

When both sides were engaged in the debate, Dr. Qian Xue Sen, who supported EHF research, wrote a letter to the Central Propaganda Department. The exact content of Qian's letter is beyond my knowledge, but I am sure that his letter either requested the department to respect the freedom of science and to grant permission to carry on the research or to stop the debate. The Central Propaganda Department then directed Qian's letter to Chairman Hu Yao Bang. Finally, on May 13, 1982, Chairman Hu instructed the following. Since it is an official document intended for public dissemination, I will quote it:

> This is not a subject for our science research. Before any proof is established, the media should not propagandize, or make any comments [about the test or experiments]. I believe that these rules are appropriate and justified and that we should observe them. We may allow a minority group of people to continue their research and let them publish a small paper to report their research results regularly for the reference of the interested science workers, and let those who are intersted in EHF continue to read and continue their research efforts.

The Propaganda Department then issued a circular informing research units of all levels to obey the instruction. Since then, both sides have ended the debate and Yu has quieted himself. Only three of his seven planned articles have been published.

The Third
Mystery:
Qi Gong

16
Qi Gong:
Breath Control
and the Paranormal

While kung fu (more correctly, *wu shu*, meaning "Chinese martial arts") and tai chi chuan have become familiar terms to most Westerners, few have any idea of what qi gong is. This ancient deep-breathing technique (also spelled *chi kung*) is a key to developing paranormal abilities, and it has been known to the Chinese for centuries. Here is an example of what qi gong can do.

On March 20, 1979, the brightly lit Xian Stadium in Peking was packed with hundreds of people who came with great curiosity to watch a soul-stirring demonstration of qi gong by a master of the art, Hou Shuying. In the middle of the stadium field, a cast-steel bar was standing erect in the ground. The bar was one meter long with a cross section measuring about one inch. Hou Shuying would attempt to break it by hitting it with his foot.

Prior to this, the bar had been carefully examined by a committee of scientists, who attested that it was geniune and in no way prepared ahead of time in order to fool the audience with the illusion of solidity. The large gathering would not have taken place if, first, there were not widespread recognition of the master standing that Hou Shuying had in the practice of qi gong and, second, there were not public acceptance of the qi gong tradition itself. The thirty-eight-year-old master Hou's feats had been widely proclaimed, discussed, and acknowledged. Moreover, Chinese culture is thoroughly imbued with the concept of *qi*, the life energy or universal force that animates all living things, providing vitality to matter.

145

Further, Chinese philosophy holds that qi is the primal matrix of creation from which springs the yin and yang forces that give rise to substance and material forms. It is qi that is controlled and mastered in the practice of tai chi chuan and qi gong, and thus a master of qi is one who controls the very forces of life. Such a person can perform feats that are truly paranormal. However, the ultimate "miracle" of mastering qi is to become one with it so that your entire existence is simply yet wonderfully blended with the forces of the universe in a self-transcendent manner that marks the sage of cosmic equanimity and cosmic awareness.

When all was quiet in the stadium, Master Hou began to go through an exercise intended to concentrate qi energy in his foot. He was standing about ten feet from the bar. Suddenly he dashed straight toward it. For an instant, the audience gasped. It looked as if something tragic would happen because he had aimed his foot at the bar. But something quite different happened. Master Hou uttered a shout, "Hai," and it broke it in two. The audience applauded wildly in congratulations.

Qi gong of this kind is called hard qi gong; it is often demonstrated in China. There is another kind of qi gong, called nei yang gong (meaning the internal exercise of qi), which is not as often demonstrated and which is even more mysterious. Those who practice nei yang gong are able not only to improve their own health and to cure their own ills but to heal others as well. Two examples will demonstrate.

On a July day in 1980 at the Shanghai Institute of Traditional Chinese Medicine, an old man was sitting behind a patient who was paralyzed from the waist down. By projecting his vital energy (fa

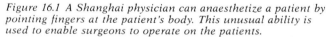

Figure 16.1 A Shanghai physician can anaesthetize a patient by pointing fingers at the patient's body. This unusual ability is used to enable surgeons to operate on the patients.

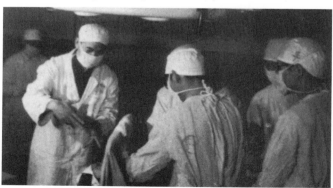

gong) through his fingers and eyes at the patient, the old man was able to place the patient completely under his control and cause the patient's limbs to quiver rhythmically and indefatigably for fully forty minutes.

At the Shanghai Medical College there is a qi gong master who can bring on local anesthesia in any part of a patient's body by simply pointing a finger at it. This unusual ability is used to enable surgeons to operate on patients.

It may all sound like science fiction, but the truth is that a qi gong master who has attained the apex of nei yang gong can kill a person from a distance of ten feet without so much as touching him. Use of lesser qi force will merely stun a person or knock him down.

Initial studies have discovered that the secret of qi gong (both the hard and the internal kind) lies in the bioelectricity emitted from the human body. In late 1978 the Bureau of Traditional Chinese

Figure 16.2
Heat measurement by thermogram shows the palm of Dr. Zhao Guang, a qi gong master in Peking, before he performs qi gong breath emission. The luminous spots on the palm show less heat. (Photo courtesy of He Qing Nian)

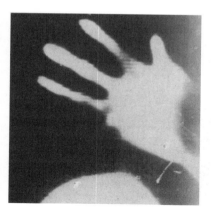

Figure 16.3
Eighteen minutes later, Zhao Guang's palm shows marked increase in heat (large luminous area); a wave effect is evident in the photo. (Photo courtesy of He Qing Nian)

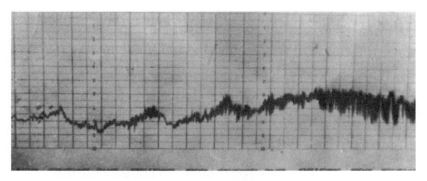

Figure 16.4 Zhao Guang holds his palm one meter in front of an infrared ray detection device and then emits breath to it. Compared to the signal obtained from an ordinary person (see Figure 16–5), Guang's showed a marked increase in signal. (Photo courtesy of Zhou Wen Bin)

Medicine under the Chinese Ministry of Health conducted a systematic investigation of qi gong masters throughtout the country. The bureau found that the bioelectricity emitted by qi gong masters can be tele-infrared electromagnetic waves, statics, biomagnetism, or some form of unknown energy. All these have been detected and recorded on instruments.

Subsequently, a research team in Jiatong University in Shanghai suggested the hypothesis of a "human body field." They hold that there is an electrical field in every human body which can release biological electricity. In September 1980 they began to develop an "actinograph" for the human body field. Since March 1981 research and experiments have been conducted in eight Shanghai hospitals. It has been proven that the human body can transmit and receive such

Figure 16.5 Signal obtained from an ordinary person tested for infrared emission. (Photo courtesy of Zhow Wen Bin)

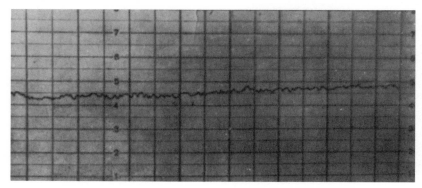

148

electricity through space. The results of the experiments are quite interesting. When a qi gong master moves his palm close to a heat image instrument, light spots appear on the screen of the instrument, but when an ordinary person moves his hand similarly, nothing happens unless he is in physical contact with a master.

There is an electrical field surrounding every human body, but a qi gong master, by virtue of his years or even decades of exercises, may have a field capable of producing bioelectricity several or even scores of times stronger than that of a layman and hence is much more effective. However, in projecting his power, a qi gong master will have to draw deeply upon his internal energy and, as a result, will experience fatigue afterward. Therefore in simulation of the bioelectricity generated through qi gong, the Peking Institute of Medical Instruments, the Qingdao Hospital of Traditional Chinese Medicine, and the Zhangjiakuo Medical College have cooperated in developing an electronic instrument for simulated qi gong treatment which can produce bioelectricity similar to qi gong, so as to take the place of qi gong masters in applying anesthesia and treatment to patients. The results have proved very successful. The instrument has a further advantage: It can be used to stimulate acupuncture points and thus can replace the acupuncture needles, eliminating the pain usually caused by them.

Figure 16.6 China developed an electronic instrument for simulated qi gong treatment. It can also be used to stimulate acupuncture points and to replace the acupuncture needles. (Photo courtesy of Zhou Wen Bin)

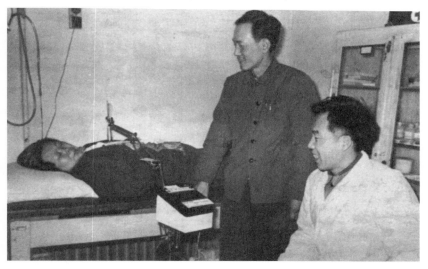

The success in developing this therapeutic instrument of qi gong is further evidence of the presence of an electrical field in the human body. What then, after all, is qi gong?

Qi gong is an ancient Chinese method of deep breathing to preserve health and prevent disease. Its origin dates back to the Warring States Era (403-221 B.C.). As noted in the classical Chinese medical work *Huang Di Nei Jing* (*The Yellow Emperor's Classic of Internal Medicine*), those who practice qi gong consistently can prolong life, and those who excel in its exercise can further bring hidden energy within their bodies into play. Since then various schools (mostly in the martial arts community) have developed use of the hidden energy to such a high level that a stroke of the hand can break a stone, a flip of a finger can break a branch, and even a literally fatal "killing glance" can be given to someone up to ten paces away without touching him.

Figure 16.7
Qi gong master performing hard qi gong. His hand can break a stone.

Mysterious though qi gong is, the method of mastering it is simple enough. In fact it is nothing more than the deep breathing as advised by doctors, except that it must be practiced with perseverance in order to have the desired result.

Normally, a person inhales and exhales once every three or four seconds, but the way of breathing in qi gong requires a longer interval than four seconds, and this interval is to be further prolonged from day to day. First inhale through the nostrils all the way down to the *dan tian* (which is the name for a vital center about two inches below the navel—the same center that the Japanese call the *hara* center) and keep it there for a second or two before exhaling through the opened mouth. For beginners the process of complete inhalation and exhalation takes about eight to ten seconds. For qi gong masters , however, it may be as long as five to fifteen minutes or even longer. Beginners may find it not so pleasant, but they will get used to it by and by. However much a beginner may feel uncomfortable in its practice, he will always have the feeling of being invigorated after twenty minutes of exercise in deep breathing.

Normally in breathing we use our chest, but a qi gong practitioner should use his abdomen instead. When inhaling, he must concentrate on his dan tian center, to which the inhaled air is to be directed. Chinese Taoists regard this center as the most important part of the human body; they call it the "fountainhead of internal energy." In other words, it is the central dynamo of the body. By practicing deep abdominal breathing, the qi gong practitioner compresses the diaphragm, rendering it more vigorous. Studies indicate that diaphragm muscles and the nerves governing their movement can produce relatively strong muscular electricity, the intensity of which varies with one's power of thought. So when you are conducting the inhaled air toward the dan tian center, you should imagine and firmly believe that "with the air in the dan tian center, my energy is enhanced." This cultivates the power of thought to enhance the physical efforts.

Chinese researchers in qi gong have pointed out that qi gong is "the physical exercise of the internal organs" under the command of the brain. Ordinarily, people doing physical exercises pay attention only to developing their muscles and bones, without giving much thought to strengthening their internal organs. Take for instance a Western boxer who may be capable of delivering a punch of one hundred pounds' force. He would undoubtedly be able to deliver a punch of more than one hundred pounds' force if he practiced internal exercises, plus the power of thought to direct it. That is why in recent years Chinese athletes have won many gold medals in international contests. I will tell you more about this in the last chapter of this section.

The internal exercise mentioned above does not depend on movements (such as jogging, high jumping, boxing, and so on), but on qi and thought. In other words, physical exercise is motion, while thought is stillness and relaxation. It seems paradoxical, but from the perspective of the qi gong tradition, stillness is the motive power of motion, and relaxation is the motive power of strength and hardness. Kung fu such as seen in movies and on TV is a kind of external power, emanating from the outside as in boxing. But a tai chi chuan master has his power emanating from inside—from a stillness and relaxation based on cosmic harmony. Hence kung fu is thought of as ying gong, meaning hard qi gong, while tai chi chuan is said to be nei yang gong, meaning the internal exercise of qi.

Qi gong is indeed a mystery. Scientists have found that apart from the changed way of breathing, qi gong depends further on two factors: time and direction. Nature has provided everything, and everything is arranged according to the law of nature. As we know, there are some kinds of flower that only blossom at a particular time and there are medicines that must be taken at certain hours. Bleeding from a cut in a finger has to do with the ebb and flow of the tide; bleeding is more profuse at the time of rising tide than at the time of ebbing tide. The strong or weak performance of an athlete varies with time. Do you know when is the most effective time to kill cockroaches? Chinese tradition does. Just as the various phases of the moon and the rising and setting of the sun follow the laws of the movement of celestial bodies, so also do the qi and blood of the human body. Traditional Chinese medicine has always regarded the early morning hours between 3 and 5 A.M. as the best hours for medical treatment. Likewise, qi gong tradition regards those hours as the time for qi gong exercises.

What about the factor of direction for qi gong exercises? Just as the position of a transistor radio or a TV set may affect its sensitivity to reception, producing static or low volume, so too have Chinese qi gong masters since ancient times always stressed the importance of direction. In practicing qi gong, magnetism is said to be the reason. It has been found through experience that a person is more apt to fall asleep when in a south-north direction and to suffer insomnia when facing east-west. Now, geomagnetism is one of the physical characteristics of the globe, and living beings are closely related to it, although science doesn't know just how. Research is going on to find if the human body, especially the brain, has magnetic receptors, just as it has light and sound receptors. Does sensitivity to the earth's magnetic field explain how some birds and animals migrate so unerringly? It is not known yet—only suspected. From the point of view of qi gong, however, the importance of geomagnetism on the human body is great, and the practitioner is taught to "flow with it" to his advantage. Orientation to the north-south lines of geomagnetic flow is said to reinforce the biomagnetism of the human body and hence to strengthen one's qi.

The experiments on magnetism therapy conducted in China in recent years have shown eloquently the effect of magnetism on the human body. Qi gong has been emphasized as a kind of natural therapy by magnetism. In light of the revelations of magnetism therapy, it is believed that the course of qi gong training may be shortened by making use of an artificial magnetic field. Thus, modern science is verifying why the ancient tradition says it is important to keep in a south-north direction while practicing qi gong—so as to harmonize with the action of nature's magnetic field.

17
Qi Gong's Relations to EHF and Acupuncture

Qi gong is sometimes misunderstood as being the same as kung fu. Actually, kung fu is a kind of martial art for self-defense, while qi gong is primarily intended for the preservation of good health and the prevention of diseases. It is a health technique, totally different from kung fu. The methods used in kung fu training are quite the opposite of those of qi gong. Whereas qi gong is an internal exercise directed to the internal functions of the human body, kung fu is an externally oriented exercise directed to the muscle, bones, and skin. In other words, the emphasis of qi gong is on developing an internal energy, and that of kung fu on external energy. To be sure, the two are related, inasmuch as kung fu depends on breath exercises to sustain its strength.

The methods of tai chi chuan follow more closely the principles of qi gong, for tai chi chuan stresses the overpowering of the "hard" by the "soft." In other words, qi gong is a kind of soft exercise, as is tai chi chuan. Hence, the practice of tai chi chuan can lead to good health as well.

Is qi gong also related to exceptional human functions? The answer is yes. Not only are they related, they actually supplement one another.

EHF is generally inborn and appears spontaneously; it comes as a surprise. However, the EHF a child is born with may gradually decline or even vanish when he or she reaches adolescence or early

Figure 17.1 A group of people in Peking practicing tai chi chuan early in the morning.

adulthood if no effort is made to keep it, just as athletic skill and strength decline. Qi gong exercises can help keep or prolong EHF. Furthermore, an ordinary person can also develop EHF if he or she has practiced qi gong over a long period of time. At present there are many qi gong masters in China who also possess EHF. Most surprisingly, by employing his power, a qi gong master can also induce EHF in a child not endowed with EHF. These facts, Chinese researchers say, indicate that qi gong and EHF are mutually supplementary. Both are rooted in the same deep potentials of the human body, and they develop in ways that can lead each to reinforce the other.

Here is a case to illustrate the point. Qi gong master Ou Hanrong's legs were paralyzed for many years. After having practiced qi gong for a year, function has been restored to his legs, and he has become a person with EHF. By using qi gong and his acquired EHF, he succeeded further in inducing and helping fifteen-year-old Yu Rui Hua (who had EHF but was originally only able to read with her ears) to acquire the power to see through objects. (See Chapters 12-13). Mou Feng Qin, another girl with her EHF already declining, was able, after induction and help by qi gong master Jiang Bo, not only to restore her EHF but further to develop the power of seeing through objects. As evidenced on experimental instruments, many similar phenomena such as tele-infrared electromagnetic waves and static electricity are detected both in diagnosing a child with EHF and in diagnosing a patient by qi gong.

Figure 17.2
A fifteen-year-old girl, Yu Rui Hua, who could originally only read with her ears, was able not only to restore her EHF after it was lost but also to develop the power of seeing through objects after induction and help by the qi gong master Jiang Bo.

To sum up:

1. EHF is inborn.
2. Qi gong is trained.
3. Qi gong exercises may lead to EHF and induce EHF in others.
4. Qi gong can reinforce EHF and keep it from declining or vanishing.

It may be asked if hypnotism can also induce EHF. The answer to this is also yes. Hypnotism depends on suggestions from another person, and by following them a kind of psychic power can be produced temporarily in someone. Likewise qi gong can release power (qi) externally into someone else. In releasing his qi, a qi gong master can project it into a human body to produce an effect, including psychic abilities.

Huang Rui-sen, a qi gong therapist with the Institute of Traditional Chinese Medicine in Zhejiang Province, is a well-known qi gong master who has been practicing qi gong since the age of fourteen and who has devoted himself to its study for forty years. Every day he projects his qi gong to treat patients (with particularly striking results for ailments of the nervous system). According to a 1980 book entitled *Qi Gong Treatments*, published in Tianjin City, one day as Huang was directing his vital energy at a paralyzed patient (who lay on a bed) under treatment, the patient was enabled to move his hand and legs. Amazingly, Huang could even rotate the patient on the bed *without touching him*! An average Chinese weighing between 130 and 160 pounds would be too heavy for most people to pick up, yet qi can cause him to move, and even turn head to foot, without touching him. What a miraculous power!

Clearly, qi gong is superior to hypnotism in inducing psychic power because qi goes directly into the human body (especially the nervous system) and makes its power felt directly without conscious effort by the patient.

Acupuncture can also activate EHF potential in a human body to induce, reinforce, and preserve the psychic power, as described in Chapter 12. By operating at certain acupuncture points, the channels in the body through which qi flows can be adjusted, thereby bringing into action the potentials in the body. To the extent that acpuncture can do this, it can also strengthen the effect of qi gong in its practitioners and shorten the time required for performing qi gong exercises. These are the facts that prove the inseperable relationship among qi gong, EHF, and acupuncture—a trinity such as exists among water, vapor, and ice or among electricity, magnetism, and gravitation, which interact and balance in the field of the universe.

What is the precise nature of the relationship among qi gong, EHF, and acupuncture?

Research has shown that qi gong is a remarkable system that can be used to restore health, preserve a robust condition of vitality, and develop the untapped psychic potentials with which one is born. The complementary relationship that qi gong has with acupuncture has been discovered through experimentation during the last twenty years, with the ascendance of acupuncture into the mainstream of modern medicine and scientific research. But the relationship of qi gong and EHF has only begun to be worked out during the past few years, due to widespread interest in EHF, and there undoubtedly is much more to discover.

But this much can be said. First, it is accepted by Chinese researchers that every person has inborn potentials, varying only in degree. However, only those who have strong potential are regarded as "persons with born EHF," while those whose EHF potential is weak have to train themselves or be induced by a qi gong master or by acupuncture in order to have effective EHF. And there are some people who apparently are not susceptible to induction at all. It is similar to the case where three persons tormented alike by headache seek treatment from the same acupuncturist. For person A, once is enough; for B, twice may be necessary; and for C, the treatment may be totally ineffective. This is because the organic functions and the nervous systems vary from person to person. Take, for instance, the treatment of hiccups by acupuncture. The effective rate is as high as 99 percent for just one treatment, but there are persons for whom the treatment has to be applied twice or three times before it can become effective. This is because such people have very different constitutions.

It is generally known that there are 949 acupuncture points (of which 361 are most often used) spread along 14 meridians or channels which in turn connect the various internal organs, the limbs, the muscles, the flesh, and the skin. Treatment by acupuncture or by qi gong follows the 14 meridians and aims at the free circulation of the qi and blood. The same 14 meridians are also followed in the exercises for inducing a certain psychic power in the human body.

A qi gong beginner starts with inhaling through the nostrils all the way down to the dan tian region before exhaling. A veteran qi gong practitioner can visualize the inhaled qi circulating thoughout his body, starting from the nostrils, then to the dan tian region, then gradually down to the perineum, then up the spine to *baihui* (the crown) and finally back to the dan tian region to complete the cycle before exhaling. This is what the Chinese Taoists call the "small cycle." There is, of course, the so-called "large cycle." Qi gong students need to complete the stage of small cycle before advancing into the stage of large cycle. In the large cycle stage, qi inhaled will run down from the perineum of the small cycle to the feet and then to toes and then move up again to the spine to baihui. From baihui the qi will travel to the eyes, ears, chest, and from the chest to the fingers. Finally it travels back to the abdomen and the dan tien region. Wherever the qi passes, it is felt at the acupuncture points it is passing through, just as during acupuncture, when the needle is applied at a point, the channel thus stimulated is made free of obstruction in a flash. Let me repeat here: Qi gong, acupuncture, and EHF interact in a way similar to electricity, magnetism, and gravitation, bringing equilibrium to the constitution. When equilibrium is attained, no disease will occur. To attain equilibrium, the human body requires adjustment so as to bring about the free circulation of the qi and blood. The adjustment depends on breath exercises, not on medicine.

Qi gong can indeed render possible the preservation of health and prevention of diseases. I have a friend fifty six years of age who is a stockbroker. Every day he climbs a steep hill to reach his office. At first he was always panting and felt tired after the climb, but after six months of exercising his qi, the panting was gone and he found his legs much stronger. The increased vigor and strength is due solely to qi gong—not to walking the hill itself, which he had been doing for years before he began qi gong.

Altogether, the research has shown that qi gong is a remarkable system that can be used to restore health, preserve a robust condition of vitality, and develop the untapped psychic potentials with which one is born. The complementary relationship that qi gong has with acupuncture has been discovered through experimentation during the last twenty years, with the ascendance of acupuncture into the mainstream of modern medicine and scientific research. But the relationship of qi gong and EHF has only begun to be worked out during the past few years, due to widespread interest in EHF, and there undoubtedly is much more to discover.

18
Qi Gong Mysteries

In *The Eagle Shooting Heroes* by Jin Yong, a very popular swords-man novel published in Hong Kong, there are five remarkable characters who were respected masters of traditional Chinese martial arts. The best of the five was Wang Chong Yang, who mastered an exceptional art called yi yang zhi (sun-ray finger). By pointing his finger toward an enemy, he could wound or kill him. The novel was later turned into a movie, and thus Wang's sun-ray finger became more widely known. Later, when *E.T.* was released in Hong Kong, people related the healing power of E.T.'s finger with that of Wang's sun-ray finger.

E.T.'s luminous red finger is an energy-producing finger. The strength of Wang Chong Yang's sun-ray finger is also produced by an energy or force generated inside himself—bioelectricity. We should remember that qi gong masters carry bioelectricity in their bodies. While qi gong masters usually use their eyes and fingers to project strong power, Wang Chong Yang's art, which every martial-art student should know, is a combination of qi gong and martial art. Thus when Wang pointed his finger toward any object, he could destroy the object at his wish.

Wang Chong Yang was an authentic figure in history. He was a famed Taoist of the Song Dynasty (960-1279). Taoism as a religion began in the Han Dynasty (206 B.C. to A.D. 220). The Han Taoists emphasized the practice of qi gong and research into acupuncture. According to historical records, Wang was the founder of Quan Zhen

Jiao, a Taoist sect. It was said that once, while someone was digging stone on the mountain, a piece of giant rock suddenly fell. Everyone was frozen in shock exept Wang. Wang shouted out loud and, amazingly, he was able to hold the rock from falling down. This happened centuries ago and, of course, there is no strong evidence to prove the authenticity of the story. However, we can refer to the example of Huang Rui Sen, a qi gong master mentioned in Chapter 17. Huang Rui Sen is able to turn a patient around by practicing qi gong at him (but without touching him) within a certain distance. Thus it is not surprising that Wang Chong Yang could hold the rock from falling if he possessed greater strength than Huang Rui Sen.

Understandably, people may doubt the story of Wang Chong Yang, since it happened long ago. But there are other stories that are recent and occurred in mainland China. The first instance is about Liu Chun Shan, who carries strong bioelectricity in his body. Liu is employed by a Tianjin watch factory. When news about his exceptionally strong bioelectric capacity became known, Zhou Wen Bin, reporter of the Peking *Guang Ming Daily*, and Xu Qian Wei, a member of the Tianjin Sciences Research Committee, came to visit him. After brief greetings, Zhou said, "When did you discover that you possess bioelectricity in your body?"

"In November 1973," Liu answered. "At that time I had just

Figure 18.1 Liu Chun Shan, a watch manufacturer in Tian Jing City, carries strong electricity in his body.

moved to a new house. The new stove there was not burning hot enough. I had to move the pot again and again from the stove to check if the stove had enough coal. However, each time I touched the pot, I felt shock on my shoulder. 'It is strange,' I thought, 'Is it that the pot carries electricity?' I was surprised and searched carefully to see whether the stove or the chimney were connected with any source of electricity. But I could not find anything. Then I used an electricity-detecting penlight to try the stove once again. When the pen touched the stove, its upper end detecting light flashed all of a sudden. Later, at work, when I touched my machine, I felt shocked again. Next year, officers from the Chinese Academy of Science's Research Department of Physics heard about this and came to see me. They did an experiment on me and found out that I do carry electricity in my body. At first, they found that I was wearing a nylon overcoat and thought that it might be the cloth of the coat that produced electricity. They told me to take the coat off, which I did. They started the test again, and again they found signs of electricity inside my body. At that time I was scared because my work in the watch factory required frequent contact with the machine and with gasoline. If the electricity inside my body were to ignite the gasoline, it would have unthinkable consequences. So I did an experiment myself with the gasoline and was greatly relieved that I did not start a fire. Since then I have felt relaxed and did not care too much about my body carrying electricity."

"Can you show us now?" Zhou Wen Bin asked.

Liu smiled and nodded. "You came at the right time. I am better able to show it in winter. In the summer, I don't think I can do anything." He then moved a plastic mat and stepped onto it. (According to Liu, he did this because he wore a pair of old shoes which would cause electric leakage into the ground. It was necessary to step on the mat to retain his full charge. If he wore a better quality shoe, he said, the mat would not be needed.) Then he used the detecting pen and touched softly on the machine. Surprisingly, the pen flashed a blue light. A minute later, he used the pen to touch the cement floor. Again, the visitors saw flashing light.

Then he put aside the detecting pen, took a small wire, and walked toward the machine. When the wire was about a meter from the machine, it produced signs of electricity—blue flashing sparks were seen. When he used the wire to touch the ground, a similar effect resulted. Liu said, "If we use the wire to touch people's skin, it will also produce flashes and make people feel shocked. In the past, my colleagues did not believe that I carry electricity in my body. After I gave them this test, they believed it. But the color of the flashes that resulted from touching the machine or the ground and from touching human skin are different. It was blue when touching the ground or the machine, and it was yellow when touching the human body."

Zhou then extended his hand and asked Liu to try on him. Liu took the wire and walked toward Zhou. About half a centimeter from Zhou, a yellow spark suddenly leaped out, followed by a clapping sound. Zhou felt a shock.

Involuntarily, Zhou withdrew his hand immediately. He was puzzled. Science knows that in the animal world, some fishes carry electricity. Cramp fishes can produce 350 volts of electricity; electric eels can produce 800 volts. But human beings do not possess such power. Biologists acknowledge that when the human heart is beating or when the brain is functioning, the human body produces a fraction of a volt of electricity. However, such a weak current can be detected only by special instruments. It is far too weak to make a detecting pen or wires such as Liu uses flash. So, what made Liu different from other people?

"Is your skin comparatively drier than other people's?" Zhou asked.

"No, my skin is not especially dry." While Liu was talking, he rolled up his sleeve and showed the visitors his shoulder. They did not find any special difference between his skin and their own.

"It is strange," murmured Zhou.

Liu then said laughingly, "It is not as strange as it is supposed to be. In our factory there is a comrade named Xu Gui Cheng. She carries electricity in her body too. She is a surveyor, and each time her eyes touch the sighting scope, there are crackles of electricity. At first she thought there might be electric leakage and she asked the electrician to examine the instrument. But the electrician said he did not find anything. Last April, after *Science Forum* published a story about me possessing electricity, Xu said to me teasingly, 'Hey, so you are something, Liu. You carry electricity in your body.'

'You might possess electricity in your body too, who knows,' I said.

"She took my words and tried the detecting pen on herself. The penlight flashed." Unfortunately, Xu did not come to work that day, so the visitors did not have the chance to talk to her.

"Is it possible that you can transfer the electricity in your body to me?" Zhou asked.

"Yes, it is possible," Liu answered. He passed the detecting pen to Zhou, and held Zhou's hand. Zhou then used the pen to touch the machine and the floor. Again he found that the detecting pen flashed.

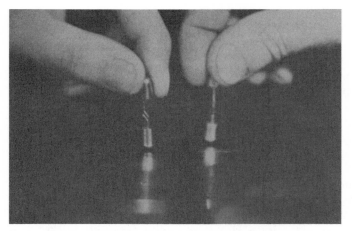

Figure 18.2 Liu Chun-shan and another are taking the same test on the electric detecting pen. While Liu can light it up, the other person cannot.

But once when Liu let go of Zhou's hand, the pen would not flash.

Liu, who still works in Tianjin, is living proof that the human body can carry a powerful charge of electricity. But his story does not mention anything about qi gong. I told it here to show a mystery that seems to be deeply connected with qi gong. Since researchers in China have proved again and again that qi gong masters can generate electricity, we can conclude that Wang Chong Yang, the master of sun-ray finger, might be an extraordinary person who learned superlatively both the technique of qi gong and a martial art.

Figure 18.3
Qi gong master Sun Min Xin from Henan Province. When he places his hand close to the cicadas, the cicadas on the tree crawl down the tree. It has been demonstrated a hundred times. The photo shows him performing the art.

164

How the human body generates electricity is a mystery—and also a fact. The body produces not only bioelectricity, but also tele-infrared electromagnetic waves, static electricity, biomagnetism, and some other kind of unknown energy. In Henan Province, there is a qi gong master named Sun Min Xin who is able to call cicadas to his hand. He has been observed to stand near a tree, and whenever he raised his hand near a cicada, the insect would crawl down the tree and be caught by him. What energetic means does he use to communicate with insects? What is the relationship between qi gong and body electricity? More research is needed.

Does Wang Chong Yang's special art of sun-ray finger exist today? Yes, the sun-ray finger of yesterday is today's *yi zhi chan* (one-finger art). In Shamen city of Fujian Province, there is a doctor of Chinese medicine named Liu Yong Yan. He has been practicing "one-finger art" for thirty years. When he treats patients, he uses his right forefinger to touch—actually, to jab—a specific acupuncture point on the body. However, there is an additional factor that he must consider in healing: the time of day. The use of one-finger art recognizes that acupuncture points respond differently at various hours of the diurnal cycle, and if the time of application is not right for the organ or area of the body associated with that particular acupuncture point, the treatment may not be effective.

There is a story told about Liu Yong Yan treating an officer from the Zuan Zhou military region who had been suffering from osteitis for many years. He came to Dr. Liu one day. After Liu jabbed the appropriate acupunture point several times, the officer found he was recovering from chronic pain. When he returned to his army camp, he showed the physician there the X-ray photo he had had taken after recovery. But the physician did not believe it. He thought the officer might have taken the wrong X ray—perhaps a copy from some other person. So the physician shot another X-ray photo of the officer, and when it was developed, amazingly, the osteitis was shown to be all gone.

The one-finger art can kill people as well as heal them. Those who know Chinese martial arts know what "point touching" means. It is a way of pointing at certain points of a human body—not necessarily acupuncture points. Whoever is the target might be wounded or killed if the person pointing is a martial art master. Why is point touching so powerful? Because the trained martial-art person can concentrate an enormous burst of energy in his finger, which will produce a special effect when pointed correctly toward an opponent. Similarly, when an acupuncturist treats a patient, he may give the patient local anesthesia by employing the point-touching technique instead of using chemical anesthesia. In some cases the patient can even undergo an operation this way. Martial-art masters, however, would use this technique only if attacked by an enemy and only, of course, if they are masters who can combine qi gong with their martial art. These people are very strict in adhering to their principles and would not hurt anybody without reason. Nor is it likely that an acupuncturist would make a mistake while applying acupuncture and thus hurt a patient. Treating a patient and attacking an enemy are two different things, and I have never heard of anyone being hurt by acupuncture or an acupuncturist who uses finger pointing.

Another story about one-finger art was published in the February 1981 issue of *Science and Life*. A reporter for the magazine, Chen Tse Ren, interviewed several qi gong masters and reported his experience. I will tell it as if I were the reporter.

> A Chinese medicine doctor, about thirty years old, would not disclose his teacher's name to us, but he was impressed in learning that we came from a long distance and was therefore willing to show us the art he learned. First he let us see how he "breathes." When he inhaled air into the abdomen, the abdomen swelled like a volleyball. Then the qi (air) seemed to reach to his chest and when we touched the chest it felt like a hard rock. When the air reached to the position of the throat, he told us to stab it with a sharp knife. "It doesn't matter, just go ahead," he said. (Apparently the doctor was not holding his breath, but was internally directing his qi through visualization.) But of course we were afraid to do so. We only used our fingers to probe his throat, which also felt as hard as a steel ball. The qi gong master next showed us his finger art. He took a red brick. After he gathered his qi, he held the brick with his left hand and used his right forefinger to make a hole in the brick. Turning his finger back and forth, after a while we saw his finger enter the brick while powder was falling from it! At this time, he asked us to pour cold water onto the brick. I did not realize what his intention was at that moment and I asked, "What's that for?" He said, "My finger is burning." It was because of friction that he felt burned. Later he continued to work a hole into the brick; after about a minute and half, the brick was pierced through. I examined his right forefinger and skin. The fingernail was not hurt and it did not look rough, either. I touched his finger and felt it was warm. And that's all.

There are many stories of people with exceptional ability in China's five thousand years of history, and many of the mystifying stories involved those who knew martial arts and qi gong. There is a common saying in China: "There always is a mountain higher than this one and there always is someone more able than this one." Many of the strange persons would not disclose their names to people. Thus when you meet someone, even though he may look like a common person, he may possess an amazing art.

The example of piercing a brick is the art of ying gong (hard qi gong), which is a branch of qi gong. That is dramatic, but unless a person is able to master the art of nei yang gong, he cannot really be called a master. Those who can master nei yang gong can reduce their body weight—that is they can levitate. To use a more common term that every Chinese knows, it is called *ching gong* (lightweight gong). The name of ching gong is strange to foreigners, but all Chinese know what it is. Although the swordsman novels always exaggerate this art, it does indeed exist.

In the Wen Zhou City Hospital in Zhe Jiang Province, there is a seventy-four-year-old doctor of Chinese medicine called Lin Hung Da. When he wants to, he can jump up from the ground and suspend himself in the air with only his hands touching a wall. He can even have his back touch a wall and by using the back muscles he can crawl higher and higher. This amazing art is called *bi hu gong*, which literally means "the tiger climbing up the wall."

Another Chinese medicine doctor, Ji Xin Ling, who works at the Wen Zhou City Si Tai Disease Prevention Center, heals patients only by using qi gong. He has practiced qi gong every day for many years (exactly how long is not known to me). When he gathers his qi he is able to raise himself from the ground and float in the air. This levitation ability is a fact. I personally saw this in Canton in 1981 with my friends. A qi gong master, Wu Zhen, moved up and down in the air from his sitting position.

I don't know what causes the body to lose weight or overcome gravity, but it is a concern to ufologists, as well as to qi gong researchers. I can only think of a related issue. Many UFO researchers believe that the flying saucers are carrying zero-mass matter. (Professor James A. Harder of the University of California is a proponent of the theory.) Is the ching gong phenomenon related to that of the flying saucers? I suspect so, and think this may lead us to a better insight about the "myth" of flying saucers. I think those who study anti-gravity should be aware of ching gong and examine it for clues to the UFO mystery.

Besides showing the visitors and reporters that he was able to hang his body on the wall, Dr. Lin also showed that he could lift a matchbox and move teacups through psychic means. According to reporter Chen Tse Ren, the table had a box of matches on it. Dr. Lin closed his eyes. Then he stretched out two fingers upon the matchbox. After a few seconds he removed his fingers and lifted his hand slowly. Then the matchbox also floated up. It seemed that the matchbox was stuck to Lin's fingers and would not fall. After that, the group touched Lin's fingers and felt they were only a little warmer.

Figure 18.4
Dr. Lin Hung-da, of Wen Zhou City, Zhejiang Province, has cured patients by means of qi gong. The picture shows him "magnetizing" a box of matches with his fingers. He puts his fingers flat on a box packed with matches, then by force of qi gong he makes the box float in the air for several minutes.

Lin treated the group to a cup of tea. When one person put down his cup (which was half full of tea) on the table Lin used his left hand to cover the cup. After a few seconds, he moved his left palm slowly around the cup and the cup also moved to the left direction. It just looked like the cup was an iron piece attracted to the magnetic palm of Lin.

Skeptics may object to this story about ching gong, claiming that Lin used trickery. But what about the following?

In February 1981 the Central Documentary Production Committee of *The Mysteries of Strange Power* went to the military front line of Fujian Province. There they visited the antiaircraft army division and shot a documentary film of an exceptional performance given by a People's Liberation soldier. The soldier could walk on top of an empty matchbox without crushing it.

Before an audience the soldier demonstrated how he could walk on empty matchboxes. When the performance began, the audience was standing around a Ping Pong table. The soldier wore an army cap, a white vest, a red cloth belt tied around his waist, and a pair of black shoes. He asked the audience for six matchboxes and arranged them on the table in two rows of three, right in the middle. Stepping onto the table, he stood quietly for a moment. Then he breathed deeply, held his breath and put his right foot on the first matchbox in the right row and his left foot on the first matchbox of the left row. Then he walked, step by step, on top of the matchboxes. They were not crushed. He made occasional turnings and walked fast, apparently as light as a feather. In order to prove his ability, he told the audience to remove four matchboxes and leave only two. Then he set his feet firmly on top of the two matchboxes. After a while, he lifted himself up and jumped from the matchboxes. The audience applauded thunderously.

Figure 18.5 Chinese and American women's volleyball teams lined up before the match.

Figure 18.6 China has issued a set of two stamps to commemorate the victory of the Chinese women's volleyball team at the Third World Championship of Volleyball.

How and where did the soldier learn such amazing art? When he was eight, he said, he studied under his grandfather to learn qi gong and martial arts. His grandfather was a master of ching gong, hard qi gong, finger touching, and various martial arts. He studied very hard under his grandfather and made progress. Unfortunately, his grandfather died when the soldier was thirteen, and the boy had only mastered the art of ching gong. Later he joined the army, and whenever he had time he would practice his art. He became known to people after giving a performance at an evening party jointly held in the Fujian Normal College and the army division. News of the performance and photos were published in the *Liberation Army Daily*.

Skeptics may doubt the soldier's claim, but they have to contend with the authoritative *Liberation Army Daily* plus the film of the soldier in *The Mysteries of Strange Power*.

It is impossible to include here every bit of information about the mystery of qi gong. My advice is that martial-art students, hypnotists, singers, doctors, antigravity researchers, and athletes should learn qi gong. A martial-art student without a qi gong foundation can never be a real master. The hypnotist who does not learn qi gong will be unable to hypnotise people who are strongly resistant. Singers who learn qi gong will find it helps a lot in singing.

And so will athletes. Chinese athletes have won so many awards in recent years because their training program includes acupuncture, massage, and qi gong.

When the Ninth Asia Olympics opened on November 19, 1982, in New Delhi, India, 5,000 athletes from 33 countries gathered there to compete for 196 gold medals. Chinese athletes won 61 first-place medals; and Japanese won 57. In the past Japan always was the first in the Asia Olympics. At the Eighth Asia Olympics of 1978, Japan took the lead; she won 70 medals while China won 51, ranking second. In the last few years, however, Chinese athletes learned qi gong and, they say, this helped defeat their Japanese opponents.

Japanese athletes are highly regarded around the world. The women's volleyball team of Japan is described by some people as the "Orient devil." However, the Japanese volleyball teams were beaten again and again by the Chinese in the last two years.

Just imagine: The Chinese are an average of three to seven inches shorter than the average white or black, and their strength is less too. However, the volleyball teams of both the U.S. and the Soviet Union were defeated by the Chinese in the last three years. What is the secret of China's ascendance in the arena of world athletics? Perhaps it is the mysterious phenomenon of qi gong.

The Fourth Mystery: Wildman

19
"Wildman": China's Bigfoot

The existence of Wildman remains a mystery to the world—a mystery that arouses curiosity and spurs enthusiasm for research. If Wildman does exist, it would be a matter of unusual significance. There have been stories about Wildmen in many countries, and China, with its traditional civilization and culture, is no exception.

Surprisingly, accounts of wild manlike creatures are found in large numbers in China's historical classics and local chronicles. In them the creatures are referred to by various names: *Renxiong* (man-bear), *Maoren* (hairy man), *Shangui* (mountain devil), *Xueren* (snowman), *feifei* (baboon), and, most commonly, *Yeren* (wildman).

The first mention of wildmen in the Himalayas was made in *A Dictionary of Anatomy for the Diagnosis of Various Diseases,* a late eighteenth century book published in the Tibetan language in Peking. The earliest scientific report on the topic appeared in 1932 and was subsequently followed with stories about wildmen in newspapers and periodicals.

In Fang County, Hubei Province, where more wildman sightings were reported in modern times than in the rest of China, an account was found in the local chronicle compiled two hundred years ago. The account, paraphrased, said:

> Large numbers of hairy men are found on Mt. Fang, which lies forty li [miles] south of the town, where the peaks are high, the valleys deep and the caves afford lodgings. They are more than ten feet tall and

173

covered all over with hair, and often come down the mountains and pillage the villagers, taking chickens and dogs for food. Any attempt at resistance is sure to evoke attack. People shot at them with firearms, but the lead falls without causing injury.

"Hairy man," of course, refers to hairy-coated Wildmen. More interesting is the discovery made during an archaeological excavation conducted in the area, when the fragment of a bronze lamp was found which bore the relief of the figures of "hairy man." The figures have heavy eyebrows and bear resemblance to apes. Curiously, as if to corroborate the evidence, in the Confucian temple at Qufu, Shandong, a mural on a stone done two thousand years ago in the Han dynasty (206 B.C.–A.D. 220) has been found which bears ape-like figures of hairy men. These point to the possible existence of some kind of manlike animals in many parts of China two thousand years ago.

Li Shizhen, the great pharmacologist of the Ming dynasty, in his great work *Compendium of Materia Medica* mentioned several varieties of wildmen, one of which was referred to as "feifei." He wrote:

Feifeis are also found in the mountains in western Sichuan and Chuzhou, where they are called "man-bears." People eat their paws and use their hide. Some are found in the mountains of Sha county in central Fujian, which are over ten feet tall and utter laughter when encountered by humans. People call them Shandaren ("the big men of the mountain"), Yeren ("wildmen") or Shangui ("mountain devil").

"Chuzhou" mentioned above is the present Lishui region, Zhejiang, where tales are told today of "man-bears" being observed and even hunted and killed.

Farther back in history, a "mountain devil" figures in the Nine Songs of Chu by the great poet Qu Yuan (339–278 B.C.), in which the animal was described as draped over with wild vines, disposed to laughing, drinking of the mountain springs and living in the forests. The model Qu Yuan took for his description was believed to be one of the Wildmen much rumored about in Zigui, the poet's hometown. Zigui is now the area round Shennongjia, Hubei, a place said to be haunted by Wildmen.

More popular are folk tales about Wildmen that have been handed down from generation to generation. One of the most widespread tales tells of a hairy Wildman in the forested mountains. The animal, it is said, lays firm grip on a person's arms and laughs so joyfully over the capture that it will swoon in its mirth without loosening the hold, and will eat up its victim when it returns to its senses. The traveler in the mountains, therefore, would be wise to arm himself with a pair of hollowed bamboo cylinders, which he should slip on his arms if he encounters a Wildman. When the latter grasps the bamboo cylinders and enters its swoon, the victim can thus escape or even kill the predator.

In recent years many stories have been told about encounters or sightings of Wildmen which were described as large in stature, with a coat of long hair, resembling both a human and an ape, and capable of standing upright. Of the numerous sighting stories, two involved witnesses who were scientific researchers.

One case which happened in the 1940s was told by Wang Zelin, a biologist. He said that he chanced to see a Wildman that had been killed in Gansu Province. He described it as being a female, about two meters tall, covered with thick grayish-brown fur, having big breasts, its facial features closely resembling those of the Peking Man. Here is his statement:

> It was in 1940 when I was working at the Yellow River Conservancy Commission. I was traveling from Baoji to Jiangluo township en route to Tianshui. I took a bus since there was not yet an express train on that segment of the Longhai Railway. When we reached Jiangluo and Niangniangba we heard gunfire not far ahead. Suspecting bandits, who were rampant in those days, the passengers asked the driver if it was necessary to stop and look. "Last thing to do in a case like this," replied the driver. "It would arouse suspicion and bring more trouble. Stow away your valuables, though, in case they search the bus." So we drove on. In a moment the firing stopped, and in another quarter of an hour we reached the scene and saw a crowd on the highway ahead. As we reached them, we asked what they were doing there.
>
> "We are hunters of the wildman," came the answer.
>
> "Where is the wildman?" we asked.
>
> "Here it is," was the answer. "We are going to haul it to the county government to see what to do with it."
>
> This aroused our curiosity, so we got off and took a look. Years have passed, but I still remember the details.
>
> Lying by the side of the highway was the wildman, still soft because it was just killed. I thought the body was still warm, though I didn't touch it. It was tall, about two meters, covered with grayish-brown hair which was thick and about one inch long. It lay on its face. A curious onlooker, one of my fellow passengers, turned it about, and we saw it was a female. It had breasts and the teats were red, suggesting a young had been newly born and was being breast fed. Some spectators, apparently of low taste, opened its legs to examine the pudenda. Its head looked not much larger than a human's, but the face was overgrown with hair which was shorter than that on the rest of the body. It had a narrow face, the nose was hairy, showing only the eyes. The cheekbones were high, making the eyes deepest. Its jaws were protruding. The hair on the scalp, about a foot long, draped over the

head like the plaster statue of the Peking man, but the hair was much longer and thicker than the latter's.

Limbs and body: The shoulders were rather broad, about eighty to ninety centimeters in breadth; there was conspicuous difference between hands and feet; the palms and soles were hairless; the hands very big with long fingers and fingernails; the feet were over a foot long and six to seven inches wide. I didn't examine the arch of the foot, nor remember the length of the arms.

According to local inhabitants, two wildmen had appeared and they had been in this neighborhood over a month, probably mates. They said that the wildmen were very powerful, used to stand upright, fast in movement. They climbed the mountains without difficulty, and it was impossible to overtake them. They had no language; they just uttered cries.

Another sighting was claimed by a geologist, Fan Jingquan, who said that he observed two Wildmen, a mother and baby, in the hilly regions near Baoji, Shanxi in the early fifties. The young one was 1.6 meters tall, and they looked like apes. Here is the story:

In the early post-liberation days I worked with a geological team under the Ministry of Heavy Industry and we operated in northwestern China. While making a year-long general survey, progressing westward south of the Longhai Railway (on the northern slope of the Qinling Mountain), we met two inhabitants of the region, both in their fifties, who had spent all their lives in the mountains. Their dwelling was a shack outside Baoji City, at some distance from the mountain forests. We employed them as our guides. Briefing us on the surroundings, they told us of the frequent appearance of wildmen whom, they said, they had observed more than a dozen times every year, mostly in the woods of wild chestnuts in autumn and winter. The wildmen, they told us, would not attack unprovoked, but the following should be observed in case of an encounter: 1. Avoid confronting it face to face, but keep track of it without its noticing; 2. Do not turn and run, but change your direction at normal pace; 3. In case of sudden close confrontation, give it some food to show friendship.

To our disappointment, we never chanced to meet any wildmen throughout our four weeks' activity within a radius of fifty li [miles] round their shack.

Upon conclusion of our work in this area we took a short rest before starting off to another place. Out of curiosity, I asked one of our guides to take me to the wild chestnut woods in the hope of meeting the wildmen, offering him five silver coins in reward. He gave his consent.

Toward evening of the next day I stole away from our camp with the guide and arrived at the woods some ten li from their shack. It was early spring. There was a carpet of fallen wild chestnuts of the previous year, which in places was almost five inches thick. While the twilight was dimming, there came a wildman with its young, the latter being at least 1.6 meters tall. The adult, which must have been a female, showed apparent vigilance caused perhaps by the novelty of my costume, and kept a cautious distance of about two-hundred meters. The young one, however was naive and bold enough to approach my guide and eat the wild chestnuts he picked. Its mother kept calling it back with a cry resembling that of a donkey or a horse. Our view was blocked sometimes by the thick growth of young trees. At sunset my guide became nervous about our safety, so we hurried back.

We made a second trip the following day without finding any more wildmen. Refusing to give up hope, we went again on the third day. Unexpectedly, the wildmen were already loitering in the woods when we arrived. They appeared less strained when they saw us. Following my guide's advice, I pretended to be picking chestnuts while moving closer to them.

At last the young one approached my guide, followed in a moment by its mother. I was afraid to stand up, but stole a good glance at it. It came so near that its private parts and even some blood scab on the hair of its leg came clearly into view. It looked quite the same as what had often been described. The brown hair on its knees was intact and smooth, a proof that it did not have the habit of moving on its knees.

In this way I passed about a minute of tension before the animals withdrew slowly. When they were over one hundred meters away I stood up and we hurried back.

On our way back my guide told me in a tone of pride that he had known the cub since it was born, and it was now seven years old. He described the habitat of the wildman as a large cave with a narrow opening, which they blocked with large stones against wild beasts. He told other interesting incidents that he had experienced. He impressed me with such simple honesty that I don't doubt the truthfulness of his stories.

There have been still other similar instances of sighting. One, for example, involved three witnesses who observed the same Wildman. Huang Xinhe, sixty-three, Party secretary of Malan Brigade, Hongta Commune, Fang County; Huang Xin Min, eighty-four; and Huang Xinkuei, seventy-four, all observed a wildman in 1922.

Recalled Huang Xinhe:

I was then not yet ten years old. One day I heard that a Wildman was being driven down by the village militia. I peeped out from a crack of the door and saw a Wildman walk up, followed by dozens of men under arms. Its body was tied by a heavy chain, with a long segment of the chain trailing behind. There were many onlookers, and two of them, Huang Xinmin and Huang Xinkuei, are in the brigade now.

The Wildman I saw was five to six feet tall, hairy all over. The hair was brown in the tip and red in the root. Its hands and feet were longer than a human's, and the fingers and toes were longer. The hands and feet were covered with long hair, and the hair on the torso was also long. The hair on the head stood up while that on the back of the head draped downward. It looked sturdy and strong and its eyes and nose were like those of xingxing (orangutan). I had seen a xingxing in the zoo in Wuhan which looked different from the Wildman. Xingxing had smaller hands and feet, its hair did not have red roots, and its face was not so broad. Xingxing walked on all fours most of the time, standing erect only occasionally, while the Wildman walked on its hind feet all the time.

Said Huang Xinmin:

I was then in my twenties. A Wildman was tied in chains and escorted through town by armed militiamen. The guards stopped at a restaurant on the way and then left with the Wildman. The Wildman's feet were more than a foot long, but they say this was the smaller kind. It was covered with hair of a reddish-black color. It walked on its hind feet sometimes, and sometimes on all fours. Its hands were like human's, but bigger. The hair on the back of the feet was lighter in color, and there was no hair on its palms and soles. It was said to have been captured in Shennongjia.

And here is Huang Xinkuei's description of the same event:

I was then seventeen or eighteen years old. The Wildman had a coat of red fur, which was mostly crimson and darker in some places. The armed militiamen escorted it along. Four guards carried a cage which was more than half a man's height. The Wildman walked on its hind feet, and it walked with a forward bend. When it refused to go they shut it up in the cage and four men carried it along. Its face resembled a monkey, the face big, the snout protruding. There was hair all over the head, and the hair was shorter on the face. It was taller than a man when standing erect, and sturdier and stronger. When the guards rested they tied the Wildman to a tree, binding only its torso and leaving the hands free. The Wildman was different from a bear; neither the head nor the hands were like a bear's.

In recent years more sightings of Wildmen were reported, the most remarkable of which were three incidents in 1976 in which the animal was seen by many spectators at the same time.

Case Number 1: On the morning of May 14, 1976, a strange animal was met by six officials of the Shannongjia forest region who were traveling on a jeep along the border between Fang County, Hubei Province, and the Shennongjia forest area. Upon encountering the animal the men disembarked from the jeep and encircled the animal. They did not venture to seize it, not knowing what harm it was capable of if it resisted, so at last they let it off. To their recollection, the animal was definitely not a bear. Here is how they described the incident:

The six went by jeep to Yunyang for a conference. When the

meeting was over, one of the party, Ren Qiyou, learned that his daughter was acutely ill, so they decided to speed to Songxiangping, a town in the forest region, the same night. They started off on a jeep at 6 P.M. on May 13. By 1 A.M. the next morning they reached Chunshuya, a village on the borders between Fang County and the forest region. They were on a point between mileposts 144 and 145 kilometers when they spotted an animal on the highway. Cai Xinji, the driver, who loved hunting, wanted to catch it, so he sped up the vehicle, switched on the headlights, and sounded the horn. Scared by the sight and din of the jeep, the animal rushed to a nearby cliff and tried to climb up it. Because the slope was too steep, it fell down midway, just as the vehicle reached it and almost ran over it. It turned about and stood on all fours, facing the headlights. In this posture it was taller in the hind part than in the front, the way a human would be, showing its big buttocks and genitals. While the driver remained in the jeep to keep tooting the horn, the other five got down and converged on the beast, two from one side and three from the other. They reached within one to two meters of it and did not go farther. Said Ren Qiyou: "I was closest and could have easily caught it by the leg." Said Shu Jiaguo, another of the party: "I have been hunting from early on and have seen all kinds of animals, but I have never set my eyes on a red-haired thing like this. I didn't touch it because I didn't know what it could do it me." A moment later Zhou Zhongyi, chief of the Agricultural Bureau, who was one of the party, picked up a stone and hit the animal on the hip. Instead of bolting suddenly, the thing turned aside, slid down the roadside ditch, mounted up the slope on the left and disappeared into the woods.

All six agreed that the animal had the following characteristics:

1. Its hair, soft and fine, was of a reddish-brown color, somewhat like that of a camel. When it stood on all fours the hair on its arms drooped down to the length of about four inches. There was a dark red stripe on the back. The face was light brown, and the feet had blackish hair. Never before had anyone seen such an animal.

2. Its limbs were thick and long, the thighs were as thick as a rice bowl, more slender below the knees. The forelimbs were short. Its feet had soft soles and enabled it to walk noiselessly. Its buttocks were big, its body plump, about eighteen inches across the waist. It was slow and clumsy.

3. Its eyes were like a human's, different from other animals', and had no light-reflecting qualities in the dark. Its face was rather long, broader in the upper part, like a horse's. It had protruding jaws, and the ears were larger than a man's. The forehead was covered by hair.

4. It had no tail, and it was about five feet tall. Cai, the driver, estimated its weight at not more than one hundred kilos.

Figure 19.1 Gong Yu Lan (center) with her son, reporting to the investigation team that she saw a wild man scratching himself on the tree.

Case Number 2: On the morning of June 19, 1976, a peasant woman, Gong Yu Lan, of Qunli Brigade, Qiaoshang Commune, Fang County, was cutting pig fodder on the mountain slope. She had her four-year-old boy with her. As she crossed a mountain ridge she suddenly spotted a reddish-brown animal five to six meters from her. It was rubbing against a tree to scratch itself, and it charged at Gong as soon as it saw her. The frightened woman picked up her son and ran down the mountain.

Interviewed by scientific researchers in September 1981, Gon Yulan recalled that the animal was abou 1.8 meters tall, its hair reddish-black. The hair on the scalp was long, and its hands and feet were both hairy. It walked like a man. "I was almost scared to death," she told the interviewer. "I ran with my boy in my arms. I didn't turn to look until I had run a li, and it was already out of sight. I reached the home of our brigade leader out of breath."

She replied to questions put to her.

Q: How did the thing rub itself?

A: It stood on its feet and rubbed against the tree the way a man does when he itches (she stood up and showed her questioner, moving her shoulder up and down. "Just like this," she said).

Q: How did it walk when it chased you?

A: On two feet, just like a man. Its paces were big. (At this Gong Yu Lan stood up and walked a few paces in big strides.)

180

Q: How tall was it? What color was its hair?

A: Very tall, about 1.8 meters. It was of reddish-black color. The hair on its head was long, and its hands and feet were hairy. It had a horrible face, especially the mouth.

The visitors showed her pictures of animals, asking her to point out which looked like the one she had seen. She shook her head when showed the picture of a bear. When she saw an orangutan, she exclaimed: "Just like this. But this has shorter hair than the one I saw."

Q: Was it male or female?

A: Oh, male, male! I saw that thing (meaning the genitals) very clearly. Its eyes were big and round and deep-set. Oh, they were fearful.

The brigade leader's wife gave an account of the day when Gong Yu Lan met the wildman. She said: "When Gong Yu Lan rushed to our door there were beads of sweat on her forehead, and she was panting for breath, muttering: "Wildman! Wildman!"

In September 1976 a small fact-finding team sent by the Chinese Academy of Sciences went to the scene where Gong Yu Lan met the Wildman. After nearly two months of investigation they procured much data for study. What was remarkable was that on the trunk of the tree on which the Wildman was said to have rubbed itself, the team found a quantity of hair at a height 1.3 meters from the ground. On September 26 another investigation team found the same kind of hair on the same tree at the height of 1.8 meters.

The initial examination showed the hair to be different from a bear's in shape and structure. It appeared not to belong to any ordinary animal, but to a primate.

Case Number 3: On the morning of October 18 of the same year, a schoolteacher, He Qicui of Anyang Commune, Fang County, took a dozen of her pupils to the neighborhood of Tianziping to pick wild fruit. By 3 P.M. a yellowish-red animal was seen northwest of the student group. It was walking on its hind feet, moving westward uphill. At the sight some older pupils ran down the mountain in horror. The teacher stayed with five of the younger pupils, watching the strange animal walk some dozens of meters till it went out of sight over a hill. As described by the observers, the animal stopped after a few paces, and made a clockwise circle before walking uphill. At the report some members of a survey team working in the neighborhood rushed to the scene. They proved after some investigation that what He Qicui and the pupils had seen was definitely a "hairy man."

It was these major sighting instances in 1976 that led Chinese scientists to decide on large-scale tracking and investigation in the area.

From the above brief account it can be seen that for more than two thousand years reports have been made about Wildmen in China, climaxed by recent instances of Wildmen being seen simultaneously by many persons. This can only mean that some kind of manlike animal, not yet scientifically identified, does exist in some parts of China. As to what the Wildmen are after all, the answer has to wait till sufficient scientific research is made and a specimen is captured.

20
Scientists Search for Wildmen

No matter how widespread folk legends about hairy Wildmen may have been, formal scientific investigation was undertaken only after the founding of the People's Republic of China in 1959. Investigation teams from relevant research departments in Peking, Shanghai, and other large cities have worked in a systematic manner to solve this mystery. Here in chronological sequence are the major results of their activities.

Investigation of the "Snowmen" of Tibet at the End of the 1950s

At the end of 1959, "snowman fever" struck China. Many countries sent investigation teams to trace "snowmen" in the southern foothills of the Himalayas. From then on, a substantial body of data on these creatures began to appear in China, including a photograph of a Snowman's footprint taken on the south slope of Pearl Peak by a British expedition, and the news that the scalp of a so-called Snowman had been discovered. This information aroused great interest in China, and a plan for climbing Pearl Peak was worked out by the State Physical Culture and Sports Commission. One of its objectives was to investigate the Snowman.

Composed mainly of researchers from the Chinese Academy of Sciences and biology teachers from Peking University, the investiga-

Figure 20.1
A set of "Snowman" stamps
issued by Bhutan (date of
issuance unknown).

tion team worked in the north slope area of Pearl Peak during May and July of 1959. It was said that while they were doing their fieldwork, a Tibetan guide claimed to have personally seen a Snowman and that once a Snowman's footprints were found beside a team member's tent. The most significant finding of this investigation was the discovery of a hair sixteen centimeters long alleged to be that of a Snowman. When examined under a microscope, the hair was found to differ in shape and nature from that of orangutans, brown bears, or rhesus monkeys. However, the investigators were still unable to prove whether or not it belonged to a Snowman or not. The results of this investigation were reported at a symposium held in 1959 in commemoration of the thirtieth anniversary of the discovery of the skull fragments of Peking man. Although many scientists, including the participants in this investigation, rejected the idea that Snowmen existed in this area, and assumed that it was probably a bear, the anthropologists Wu Dingliang and Zhou Guoxing, directors of the anthropology department of Fudan University in Shanghai, believed that the Snowmen of legend were probably huge primates.

184

As a matter of fact, these legends were widespread not only in Xizang (Tibet) and Xinjiang, but also throughout northwestern Yunnan Province.

Investigating Wildmen in the Xishuangbanna Forest of Yunnan Province in the Early 1960s

In 1961 the news emerged from the dense forests in the Xishuangbanna area of Yunnan that some railway construction workers had run across a Wildman and shot him on the spot. It was said that this Wildman was 1.2 to 1.3 meters tall, covered in black fur, could walk erect on two legs, had hands like a human being, and ears, breasts and genital organs also similar to those of humans. On hearing this, the Chinese Academy of Sciences immediately dispatched a team to investigate. However, they failed to obtain concrete evidence, and were unable to resolve the mystery of the existence of Wildmen. Some scientists maintained that it was probably the gibbon ape, known to live in these forests.

Nevertheless, during recent years, accounts have come repeatedly from southwestern Yunnan Province that further evidence of Wildmen had been discovered, and moreover, another one was reported to have been shot.

Investigations of Wildmen in Northwestern Hubei and Southern Shaanxi During the 1970s

Northwestern Hubei Province is an area where legends about Wildmen are even more widely spread and frequent. Since considerable investigation was carried out over the past few years, Shennongjia, the center of the region and the place purported to be the haunt of the Wildmen, has now become more and more important.

Situated at the eastern end of the Daba mountain range, Shennongjia is a 4,000-square-kilometer maze of steep, rugged mountains, most of which reach an altitude of 1,000 to 2,500 meters above sea level. The highest rises to 3,054 meters. This peak overlooks all of the thousands of mountains and valleys in northwestern Hubei and is known as the "peak of central China."

An area of dense forest since the Tertiary period, and possessing a wide diversity of climate as a result of local geography and its subtropical circulatory system, the region provides natural conditions for the growth and reproduction of a broad variety of flora and fauna. It contains one fifth of all the rare species under state protection in China. Recently the government decided to turn a 20-square-kilometer area around one of the main peaks into a nature preserve for the protection and study of local animal and plant life. It is, therefore, no surprise that the news of the activity of "hairy men" (Wildmen) in the area attracted particular interest.

Investigations of Wildmen in the Shennongjia region started as early as the 1970s. Initially they were carried out in a haphazard manner. Later, a large-scale investigation team was established under the leadership of the Chinese Academy of Sciences. More than one hundred people participated in the work, including geologists, anthropologists, and zoologists, as well as workers from the museum and zoo. Assisted by veteran hunters, soldiers, and local cadres, the team began its fieldwork in March 1976 and finished in November 1977. In those two years it investigated an area of 1,100 kilometers, traveling a total of 6,000 square kilometers. The team visited almost all of the places in Shennongjia and surrounding counties where traces of Wildmen had been reported.

After bringing all of its data back to Peking, the team held discussions with other research workers. The well-known anthropologist Zhou Guanzing made a summary of these analyses and discussions, which he later compiled into a work entitled *Are We Tracking an Animal That Doesn't Exist?*, published in 1980.

As far as the scale, number of participants, and time involved are concerned, this was an investigation the scope of which has rarely been seen in the history of the hunt for the Wildman. But unfortunately, although six team members had at one time or another come upon a Wildman, they had failed to catch it.

Following clues provided by local people, they had organized two large-scale searches during 1977, but without any success. On May 25 of that year, Cai Goyliang, a sixteen-year-old student, ran across a three-foot-high, strange brown animal at Dalong Gully on the slope of Lujia mountain. On receiving a report of the incident, the investigation team hurried to the place, but only discovered some footprints. The prints were about thirty centimeters in length. The toes were oval in shape and webbed.

On August 31 that year, while Xiao Xingyang, a young man, was working in a forest behind the Longdong Gully in Tienlu brigade, Panshui commune, he suddenly caught sight of a strange animal.

"I heard the leaves rustling by the edge of the gully," he said, recalling this encounter with the Wildman.

> I glanced in that direction and saw, about fifteen meters away, a round head emerging from the trees. Before long, a shoulder appeared with a hand stretching out to grab a branch. Having taken hold of the branch, the strange animal began to stand erect, so I saw all of it. It was 1.5 meters or so in height, covered with long fur, and it looked just like a

human being. Its fur was about an inch long, dark brown and pressed closely against the skin, whereas the hair on its head was about 1.2 inches long. After walking ahead a little, it suddenly turned around. I then saw its face very clearly: It looked like that of a very thin old man, with protruding teeth, sunken eyes, and upturned nose. I was very frightened and ran away instantly to my two companions.

Later on, the team members called on his two companions; one of them, Jian Hailing, told them:

When Little Xiao came running to us, he was all pale and out of breath, saying, "There's a strange animal. A strange animal." When I asked him what it looked like, he replied, "It has fur all over, walks upright, is tall and looks just like a human." Just then Mao Chengfu arrived and it was precisely at this juncture that we three heard the cry of "Wu—Wu—," the first a bit husky, the latter rather shrill. The cry sounded as though it was not far away from us; it was about fory meters or so. As Mao Changfu imitated the cry, it suddenly ceased. We all were scared so we didn't go over to take a look. After we went down the hill that afternoon, we reported it at once to our team leader.

After receiving a report of this incident, the investigation office at once urged some members to rush to the spot; and they also managed to inform the other member then working in another part of the region. Aided by a group of hunters, the investigators made a careful search and found three footprints on the ground, one of which happened to be fairly distinct, so Yuan Zhengxin, a team member, promptly made a mold of it.

On September 2, a detachment of the team rushed back to Longdong Gully from the Shennongjia forest and set out to search carefully through an area covering twenty-five square kilometers. Again they found many footprints, all of which were similar in shape to those discovered previously, following each other in single file. The space between them was about 65 cm. In addition to this, they also found some plants supposed to have been left by that animal. Also, not far away from the place where Xiao Xingyang had witnessed this strange animal, they found two piles of excrement around which were scattered similar footprints.

Despite the failure of the first search, the investigation team gathered seven more detachments and arranged to make a concerted effort again. From September 25 to October 26, they undertook another large-scale search. However, probably owing to the extremely rugged terrain and thick vegetation, they still found no such creatures.

Here is a brief look at the footprints collected: The prints are of an elongated foot, 24.5 cm in length; wider at the front, approxi-

Figures 20.2, 20.3
Scientists making a mold of
the Wildman footprints.

mately 11.4 cm; 6.5 cm wide in the middle; and approximately 6 cm at the back. The distance between the big toe and the tip of the second toe was 2.5 cm, with a bracket angle of 30 degrees between the big toe and the middle axis of the footprint.

After studying the plaster mold of the footprints and the investigation records, the anthropologist Zhou Gouxin held that, since the print was wider in front and narrower at the back and since there was no evidence of an arch, these were obviously not the footprints of a bear.

At the same time, he pointed out that the distance between the footprints was 65 cm and that they followed each other in single file, clearly indicating that the creature was walking erect on two legs. However, since the whole footprint bent toward the inside, the length of the toes was one quarter that of the whole foot, and the position of the big toe was lower than the other four toes and held to one side. These features proved that this type of foot has a certain amount of grasping ability, so it was relatively close to that of the ape. In addition, the comparative narrowness of the sole and the absence of an arch also indicated that its upright posture was still unsteady. Judging from the general nature of the foot, its erect posture was inferior to that of human beings, but superior to that of the apes known to us. It seemed that this footprint possessed characteristics of both the human being and the ape. However, it was basically closer to that of an ape.

Unfortunately, the extensive investigations and research failed to provide direct evidence proving the actual existence of Wildmen. Nevertheless, as a result of these activities, a great deal of firsthand material was obtained. Apart from the footprints, hair, and excrement, the team amassed a lot of information contributed by witnesses, thereby excluding groundless hearsay and confirming some valuable clues as a foundation for further investigation. They also collected considerable data on the region's geology, meteorology, vegetation, and fauna, including amphibians, reptiles, mammals, and bird life, all of which would assist further work on the potential existence of Wildmen in such an environment.

In short, through practical investigation, most of the team members concluded that although the centuries-old Wildman riddle remained unsettled, the veil of mystery and legend surrounding the matter was beginning to lift a little. It was possible that there existed a kind of manlike animal in the Shennongjia region.

From 1979 up to the present, investigation of these Wildmen was carried on in this region in a limited way. Although its scope has expanded farther to include the bordering counties of Sichuan

Province, no truly remarkable achievement has been made, possibly due to lack of sufficient personnel. Some of the team members, therefore, sighed, "It seems that our scientists are only good at developing spaceships or observing microbes. As for searching for the huge manlike ape which lives together with us on such a crowded globe, they are incapable and helpless."

1977 Eyewitness Accounts in Shaanxi Province

Feeling that some idea of the Wildmen could be obtained from eyewitnesses, the investigation detachment taped interviews with many people who claimed to have seen a Wildman. When the investigation detachment visited Zhou Zhi County, Shaanxi Province in 1977, a villager reported an encounter with a "hairy man" on the eastern side of Tai Bei Mountain. The Wildman, as the villager described it, was about two meters tall and could walk erect on two legs. The following is a typical account, as told by Pang Gengsheng, a thirty-three year old team leader in the Guifeng commune in Shaanxi's Zhouzhi County:

> One day in early June 1977, I went to Dadi Gulley to cut logs. Late that morning, I ran into a "hairy man" in the woods on the gulley slope. It came closer and closer. I got scared and kept retreating until my back was against a stone cliff and I couldn't go any further. The hairy man came to within seven or eight feet, and then to a distance of five feet. I raised my ax, ready to fight for my life. We stood like that, neither of us moving, for more than an hour. Then I groped for a stone and threw it at him. It hit him in the chest. He uttered some howls and rubbed the spot with his left hand. After that he moved off to the left and leaned against a tree, then walked away slowly toward the bottom of the gulley. He kept making a mumbling sort of noise.

Face to face with the Wildman at a distance of five feet, Pang Gengsheng had seen it clearly. He was

> ...about 2.1 meters tall, with shoulders wider than a man's, a sloping forehead, deep-set eyes, and a bulbous nose with slightly flared nostrils. He had sunken cheeks, ears like a man's but bigger, and round eyes also bigger than a man's. His jaw jutted out and he had protruding lips. His front teeth were as wide as a horse's. His eyes were black. His hair was dark brown and more than a foot long, and hung loosely over his shoulders. His whole face, except for his nose and ears, was covered with short hair. His arms hung down below his knees. He had big hands with fingers about six inches long and with thumbs only slightly separated from the fingers. He didn't have a tail, and his body hair was short. He had thick thighs, shorter than his calves. He walked

upright with his legs apart. His feet were each about a foot long and half that width—broader in front and narrow behind, with splayed toes. He was a male. That much I saw clearly.

The investigation of Wildmen in the area was carried out later on by a biological observation team from Shaanxi Province. They maintained that the Wildman of legend was probably a kind of huge primate.

The "Man-Bear" Discovered on Jiulong Mountain in Suichang County, Zhejiang Province, During the Early 1980s

As with other places in China, legends about a "man-bear" have long existed in the Jiulong Mountain area. The investigation work here was mainly organized by the Lishui district science committee; the team consisted of science workers and teachers from the relevant departments and colleges. Their most remarkable achievement was obtaining specimens of a man-bear's hands and feet.

Originally, these specimens were taken in 1957 immediately after a man-bear was discovered and shot on the spot. In the afternoon of May 23, 1957, a young female cowherd named Wang Congmei came upon a manlike animal while she was on her way home. It suddenly attacked, and the girl at once screamed for help. Hearing her cries, her mother rushed to her rescue and, with the assistance of some of the village women laboring nearby, beat the strange animal to death. They cut off its hands and feet and brought them instantly to the local government in the county town of Songyang to ask for a reward. Zhou Shouchong, a middle school teacher, took possession of the hands and feet, and immediately preserved them by soaking them in chemicals. Both the eyewitnesses and the villagers alleged that this strange animal was not a bear and not even a monkey, since its face was like that of a man. They all decided it was a Wildman, as described in local legend.

The recovery of this specimen by the investigation team twenty four years later instantly attracted great attention in scientific circles both at home and abroad. Nealy all the leading periodicals in China featured the news; it was also reported abroad that China had discovered an apeman's hands and feet.

It is fair to say that among the investigation team's achievements, this set of specimens was practically the first direct evidence proving the existence of Wildmen. But through careful comparison and analysis, the Chinese anthropologist Zhou Guoxing asserted that these hands and feet were not those of a Wildman, but of a huge stump-tailed macaque, since they closely resembled those discovered on Huangshan Mountain in Anhui Province. As such a huge animal had never been seen before, it might be thought of as a new genre in the stump-tailed macaque family.

In addition to those described above, there was also a small-scale investigation carried out around the Funiu Mountain district in Hunan Province. At the beginning of 1982, investigators found some footprints of the purported Wildman. But after analysis many anthropologists held that they were those of black bear.

In short, from all of the evidence cited above, it is clear that from the 1950s on, China has begun to search for Wildman in a systematic manner in the provinces of Sichuan, Yunnan, Hubei, Shaanxi, and Zhejiang. Up to now, however, with the exception of Zhejiang, the examples of footprints they obtained all proved to be something other than those of Wildmen. Investigation teams working in the other four provinces failed to obtain any concrete evidence that would justify the existence of Wildmen in China. What Chinese scientists obtained was merely hearsay, witnesses' accounts, and indirect evidence, such as footprints, hair, excrement, and so on.

However, many scientists still believe that since these areas have not only had a long history of folk legends about Wildmen, but also a considerable number of eyewitnesses, and since the Wildmen described were, on the whole, similar to one another in both appearance and habits, the existence of those manlike animals is not necessarily fictitious. What the Chinese scientists have been searching for in the dense forest is indeed a kind of unknown creature needed to be explained scientifically.

Science emphasizes ironclad evidence. To seek truth from facts is the method every scientific worker should employ. Considering all the data cited here, we must surely agree that the existence of Wildmen in China is not impossible. Interestingly, just as I was about to finish this chapter, a fresh report on the discovery of Wildman's tracks was published in the *Yangcheng Evening Paper*. When going once again into the dense Shennongjia's forest in September of 1981, the article said, three members of the investigation team witnessed a manlike ape, tall in stature and covered with reddish fur. This incident took place in the depths of a bamboo forest 8,200 feet high on the Shennongjia ridge. Since this manlike ape could run four times faster than a human, the researchers failed to get a photograph of it. Nevertheless, they found some footprints and excreta nearby.

Through the centuries, Chinese literary works and folk legends have told of large, hairy, manlike creatures. In days past, whenever children in mountain villages began to cry, their mothers would say

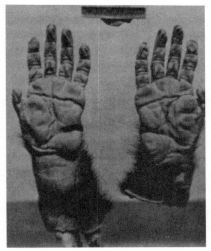
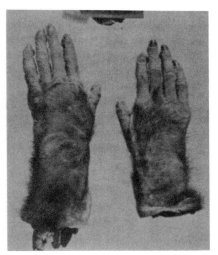

Figures 20.4, 20.5, 20.6 A "man-bear" was killed at Jiulongsan, Suichang County, Zhejiang Province, on May 23, 1957. A schoolteacher preserved and made specimens of the "man-bear" hands and feet by soaking them in chemicals. Zhou Guoxing examined the specimens and concluded that they are hands and feet of an ape.

to them: "Don't cry, my treasure. If you disturb the manlike ape, it will come and eat you up." Upon hearing this, the children would stop their crying at once. In numerous Chinese villages, this was an effective way of quieting children for a long time. Therefore, almost all of us had an image of a manlike ape from childhood—a huge, hairy Wildman who could eat a child in one mouthful. Such a widespread notion could hardly spring up without any grounds whatsoever. On the contrary, it resulted from the fact that many mountain villagers and their domestic animals were attacked by these Wildmen from time to time.

193

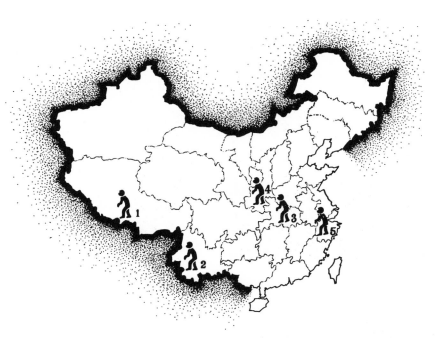

Figure 20.7 A map showing different phases of Wildmen investigation: Phase 1.
Investigation of Snowmen of Tibet at the end of 1950s; Phase 2. *Investigation of
Wildmen in the Xishuangbanna forest of Yunnan Province in early 1960s;* Phase
3. *Investigation of Wildmen in northwestern Hubei and southern Shanxi during
the 1970s;* Phase 4. *1977 eyewitness accounts in Shanxi Province; and* Phase 5.
*The "man-bear" discovered on Jiulong Mountain in Suichang County, Zhejiang
Province in early 1980.*

21
Zhou Guoxing
and Wildman Research

In 1977 China's Wildman research entered a new stage when a field investigation was carried out on a major scale in Shennongjia region. Rather than being of interest to a limited number of persons, the topic has become a matter of interest to the scientific world and the entire population of China, especially the government. In 1981 the Chinese Society of Natural Mysteries and the Chinese Society for Wildman Research were set up independently, and began to undertake study of the unknown manlike animal.

Among the scientists who shared the growing interest in this mystery of nature is the notable Zhou Guoxing, anthropologist, member of the Peking Natural History Museum and Research Institute of Natural History, leader of the Chinese Society of Natural Mysteries, and the chairman of the Chinese Society of Wildman Research. On the many investigation trips that have taken him around half of China, he has collected large amounts of Bigfoot data. Through his efforts, Zhou is endeavoring to place the study of Wildman in China on a solid scientific basis. He is the author of a series of books on the subject of the Wildman including, among others, *Wolf Boy, Snowman, Fossil of Fire, Mystery Yet to Be Solved* and *How Man Understands His Own Origin*. One of the most prominent Chinese scientists now engaged in the research, he is making important discoveries which command the attention of scientific circles.

While in Peking, I had the pleasure of meeting Zhou on many

Figure 21.1
Zhou Guoxing taking a rest in
the Shennongjia region.

Figure 21.2 The author, left, interviewed Zhou Guoxing, center, at
the Peking Natural History Museum in July 1981.

occasions. He gave me a special interview on the afternoon of July 5, 1981, during which he expounded elaborately on the subject. He gave me a far clearer picture than I previously had about the study of Wildman in China now and in the past.

196

An accomplished scholar, scientist, and author, Zhou is well known to Chinese readers of science books. He graduated in 1962 from Fudan University in Shanghai, where he studied anthropology under Professor Wu Dingliang (T.L. Woo). Upon graduation, he entered the Institute of Vertebrate Paleontology and Paleoanthropolgy of the Chinese Academy of Sciences and took up paleoanthropology. On the basis of his study of the tooth fossil of Yunnan *Homo erectus*, he determined the start of China's history at 1.7 million years ago. He made the discovery of two important Mesolithic Age ruins in south China, one at Lingjing in Xuchang City, Henan, and the other at Danawu, Yuanmou County, Yunnan. He led the latest excavation of the ruins of the famous Bailian Cave at Liuzhou, Guangxi Province.

Zhou's interest in and research on Bigfoot started in 1959, when he translated a series of foreign press reports on the Snowman in collaboration with Professor Wu Dingliang, and under the latter's direction started to explore the problem of the Snowman, approaching the subject from an unusual angle: the origin of man.

Generally speaking, anthropologists are reluctant to work on such unconventional subjects as the Wildman because it may subject the researcher to ridicule, censure, or even ostracism from scientific circles. However, in Zhou's opinion, the purpose of his study is the resolution of a scientific problem, and its success may not culminate in the capture of a Wildman. He points out that if such manlike animals actually exist in the world today, then the capture of one would not only be an important discovery in science, but would also help to resolve a number of theoretical problems about the origin of mankind. On the other hand, says Zhou, even if the work leads to the conclusion that the Wildman is utterly nonexistent, it should also be considered highly successful because this would resolve a mystery that has remained unsettled for a thousand years. An anthropologist, says Zhou, should not falter before jeering and disapproval, but should undertake to resolve the problem from an objective approach.

With such a scientific attitude, Zhou Guoxing is always ready to acknowledge facts. When a conclusion is confirmed, whether affirmative or negative, he sees that it is made public without delay, instead of attemping to conceal anything. In the meantime, he makes careful analysis of any material that comes to him. This accounted for the recognition given to his works on Wildman by academic circles at home and abroad. Zhou has been elected a member of the board of directors of the International Society of Cryptozoology, in which capacity he will contribute to the international endeavor to research Bigfoot.

Integrating the data from investigative trips over the years, Zhou Guoxing enumerates the characteristics of the rumored Chinese Wildman as follows:

1. Its height is between 1.2 and 2.5 meters, probably divisible into two categories: the taller and the shorter. The former is about 2 meters tall, the latter about 1 meter in stature.

2. It is capable of walking in an upright posture, but moves on all fours when running or climbing.

3. It looks like both human and ape, bearing mixed features, especially in the face.

4. Its scalp is covered with hair of different lengths, the shorter being 3 to 4 cm in length, while the longer reaches the shoulders. Body covered with thick hair, colored brown, red, or black. White found occasionally. Some have lighter color in the chest area.

5. It is similar to humans in hands, ears, and male's genitals.

6. The female has clearly prominent twin breasts.

7. Its footprints are of two kinds. The larger is 30 to 40 cm in length, with four toes closely parallel while the big toe points slightly outward, the whole foot closely resembling human; the smaller is about 20 cm in length, with the big toe apparently diverging from other toes, more inclined to resemble that of ape or monkey.

8. It has no syllabic language; utters monotonous cries.

Its ecological characteristics as described by Zhou are:

1. It is mostly active individually, more seldom in couples or one female with its cub.

2. It is capable of winter activity; apparently it has no habit of hibernation.

3. It feeds mainly on plants, such as berries, nuts, tender stalks, tree sprouts, and root tubers. There are instances reported of it eating insects. It raids ripened corn crops in autumn, when it is more active and therefore often encountered.

4. No evidence has been found of it using tools for procuring food or defending itself.

5. It is capable of activity during the night. Its eyes do not have the light-reflecting quality in the dark as do those of other animals.

6. It lives mainly in uninhabited virgin forests, and is very agile in avoiding humans. If unprovoked it does not attack when encountered.

However, Zhou says, this does not mean that all the strange animals observed by the numerous witnesses are of the same type. He believes the Wildman that people claimed they have seen or heard about may have been the image of objects in different circumstances. Probable cases are the following.

Some, he says, may have come in sight when the witness was nervous or frightened, or the witness observed from a distance where visibility was low. Others may have been some animal unknown to the witness; still others were misrepresented or exaggerated when the story was told and retold till it became downright falsehood.

There have been cases in which some monkeys (golden monkey, macaque, Sichuan stump-tailed macaque), serows, or bears (black bear, brown bear) have been mistaken or alleged to be Wildmen. A most notable instance of a monkey being mistaken for a Wildman happened in 1957 when an animal said to be a man-bear was killed at Jiulongshan, Suichang County, Zhejiang Province, and its hand and foot were cut off and shown in public. Zhou Guoxing examined the amputated parts and proved they belonged to a monkey instead of to a Wildman. He further pointed out that this could serve to prove that some Wildmen or xingxing (orangutans), said to have been spotted in many parts of China, could actually have been a certain kind of large stump-tailed macaque. He believed that these macaques may have caused illusions which figured in stories about 1.2-meter-tall Wildmen in Xishuang Banna and western Yunnan, and likewise about xingxing in Shennongjia and Huangshan, Anhui.

That bears have been mistaken for Wildmen was proved in investigations conducted in the Shennongjia area. When Zhou led a research team around the summit of the Shennongjia mountains in 1977, inquiries were made into allegations among local peasants about the existence of a kind of man-bear (also called Wildman) which was able to walk erect and break off corn cobs without damaging the stalk. The conclusion was that they had been black bears.

Zhou placed special emphasis on checking stories about the hunting and killing of Wildmen in the Shennongjia area. Every instance that could be confirmed was found to be the killing of a black bear. More significant was the case when a Wildman's foot said to have been preserved for generations was sent from a district in Henan Province for examination. This was likewise confirmed by Zhou to be a bear's foot. These led him to conclude that the Wildmen involved in some of the reported discoveries had actually been black bears.

Notwithstanding the unraveling of various cases of misjudgment or even false stories, Zhou still believes in the possibility of the existence of certain manlike animals in some of China's virgin forests whose identity remains unknown to scientists. His belief is based on years of research and analysis, and in particular on his investigation in Shennongjia area which lasted almost a year. What led to his hypothesis has also been the fact that tales about the sighting of Wildmen have been reported over a long period, and they have been restricted to certain definite areas. This, argues, Zhou, could be indicative of a certain objective existence. Further, some of the reported instances, such as the three sightings in Shennongjia in 1976, warrant scientific explanation and cannot be dismissed arbitrarily as nonexistent.

If, one may ask, some kind of large, man-shaped animals do exist, whatever could they be? I approached Zhou with this question. His answer was that he is not positive about it, since any scientific conclusion must be based on physical evidence, and in the absence of it, one could only make presumptions. Field investigation convinced him that, as has been pointed out by other scientists, the unidentified animal could not have belonged to the human race such as, say, a remote descendant of primitive man. The reason is the Wildman's inability to make and use tools and its lack of language and social structure. Besides, Zhou stressed, throughout the investigation no apparent trace was found of the Wildmen living in groups. These, he pointed out, are qualities that all primitive human beings possessed.

Zhou reasoned that if any such large manlike animals do exist, they are most likely to have been the descendants of gigantopithecus, a giant ape which lived in the period between 1 million and 200,000 to 300,000 years ago, and whose fossils were discovered in southern China and India.

He pointed out that in the quaternary period of geological history, south China was extensively populated by members of the stegodon animal family, including such typical mammals as the giant panda, orangutan, golden monkey, gigantopithecus, rhinoceros, tapir, and horse. With the change of geological history, many of them became extinct in China, but some species still exist in certain areas. Most notable is the giant panda, which still lives in northwestern Sichuan and the border regions between Gansu and Qinghai, while tapirs are still found in Malaysia and orangutans in Indonesia.

It is to be noted, said Zhou, that most of the places where Wildmen were reported belonged to areas of virgin forests which remain largely in closed or semi-closed state. The existence of certain tertiary trees points to the environmental antiquity of these forests. Apparently the devastation by quaternary glaciers there had been slight, making it possible for certain prehistoric animal species to survive. Couldn't any of these species still exist in some south China virgin forests? The answer is yes, he says.

There may have been chances, Zhou believes, for the gigantopithecus to survive by changing its living habits and evolving into Wildman. A branch of its descendants may have crossed the Bering land bridge to reach the Americas, where they became Sasquatch, while another branch remains extant on the southern slope of the Himalaya and has evolved into the Yeti. The Wildmen in various parts of the world may differ in their physical characteristics. This may mean they belong to various types of descendants of the gigantopithecus, or else the differences reflected the influence of the place of habitat or the stage of evolution.

"Of course, this is only presumption," Zhou said.

"But about the significance of the study of Wildman..." I asked.

"Tracking down the Wildman," said Zhou, "is not a purposeless effort. But we can't tell what the animal is before a specimen is actually captured; its value in science can only be conjectured. If we can eventually prove it to be the remote offspring of the ancient ape, it would be of immense scientific value to the research into the origin of man.

"The evolution from ape to man is a historic process so remote that it can only be inferred and reconstructed with the aid of their fossils and the tools they used which we have dug up from underground. Since the fossils are fragmentary and incomplete, scientists have not been able to give a thoroughly clear account of how ape changed to man and in what way prehistoric man developed. Many aspects of it remain controversial.

"Take, for example, upright walking, one of the main characteristics of man. How did the habit come into being? In what way is it related to the emancipation of the hand? Did the process start with the use of the forelimbs for work, which led to the need to stand erect, or, on the contrary, did man form the habit of standing on his hind feet over a long period of evolution, which made it possible for him to handle tools with his hands? This has been a point of dispute for lack of concrete evidence. Further, as regards the gigantopithecus, some contend that it was an ape of large size which might not have been able to stand erect. Opponents to this notion believe that it was the prehistoric man, or man himself in primitive stage; that on its way of development toward modern man it deviated on the path of growing bigger and bigger and failed to survive; and that it was able to use natural tools and walk in an upright posture.

"Which is correct? Though a point of disagreement concerning the gigantopithecus, the problem involves one of the crucial aspects of the development of man, namely, the ability to stand and walk in an upright posture and the formation of that ability. The strange animal active in the Shennongjia area was said to be able to stand and walk upright. In the meantime, no evidence has been found of its having used any natural tools. Such being the case, how did it come to possess the ability of standing erect? If any such manlike animal is captured at Shennongjia, and if it is ultimately proved to be a gigantopithecus, it would mean the resolution of the long disputed problem of the classification of the gigantopithecus in systematic zoology. It would also provide information concerning the development of the upright posture."

Zhou further pointed out: "Another manlike strange animal directly connected with the descendant of the primitive man is the Yeti or Snowman, which is sometimes thought to be the still-living offspring of the Neanderthal people. In the last two years there have been reports about the existence of an 'X' (unknown) animal in Kenya, East Africa, which in the opinion of French sociologist Dr. Roumeguere might be the descendant of the *Homo habilis* or *Homo erectus*. The latter, however, is still unconfirmed conjecture.

"The X animal is extremely interesting because East Africa has been the site where wide varieties of fossils of the genus *Homo* were found in large quantities over recent years, which provided abundant data for the study of the origin of man. If the descendants of these fossils have survived, and if they are found alive in the forests and a specimen can be captured, it would have inestimable value in science. It would be an inexhaustible source of information about the life of man in his early stage, his language and way of thinking, his mode of propagation, etcetera—information not in terms of rigid fossils, but of flesh and blood. What a thrill that would be for scientists! This, however, may be a wild dream which can never come true.

"If, on the other hand, the animal in question is ultimately proved to be none other than an existing ape, I would also call it a discovery of tremendous importance. The reason is that the places of habitat of modern apes are restricted to Africa and certain parts of South Asia; if some are also found living in the medium latitude area of Shennongjia, it would mean a breakthrough which outmodes existing theories concerning the distribution of apes and which raises new questions for study.

"If we could prove by investigation that the unknown animals are neither Wildmen nor apes, but brown bears or big monkeys, we would also have done a great job because the discovery would bring to light the thousand-year-old mystery of the Wildman and provide clues for the resolution of similar rumors circulating in other parts of the world.

"As I see it, such is the significance of the research into the mystery of Wildman," said Zhou in conclusion. He warned against the practice of playing up the Wildman stories. He said: "Natural mysteries such as the Wildman are interesting, and for this reason they are apt to be misrepresented, exaggerated, and acquire an element of miracle and wonder. Some of the stories spread about became downright falsehood. Worse still, some people even went so far as to fabricate stories for purposes of deception and swindle. All this tends to discredit any discussion of the Wildman, which in itself raises a scientific issue to be dealt with in earnest. We must admit that of the colossal amounts of sighting reports and relayed stories, scarcely any has been of scientific value. In these circumstances it is not surprising that many scientists adopt a skeptical attitude toward the matter, and some who hold biased views or confine themselves to existing theories even dismiss the reports as sheer nonsense.

"In China, the investigation of the Wildman has enlisted numbers of scientific and technical personnel. But it must be noted that not all were enough versed in such fields as animal colony, ecology, primate, paleovertebrate, paleoanthropology, and constitutional anthropology. As a result, data collecting and interviewing witnesses were often carried out without a scientific and down-to-earth attitude, while seriously faulty stories have appeared in the press. It becomes necessary, therefore, that all data and information be handled cautiously so as to avoid possible hazards they might cause to the research work.

"However," said Zhou, "I believe that these obstacles will gradually disappear with the progress of the work and with our continued appeal for greater accuracy."

Zhou was deighted to learn that this book was to be published and wished it success. At the end of the interview he told me that since the study of Wildman is a scientific undertaking of worldwide significance, he would be glad to establish academic ties with professional and amateur scientists abroad so as to join their efforts in the resolution of this enigma of nature. Interested readers may write to him in care of the author.

Mr. Paul Dong
P.O. Box 2011
Oakland, CA 94604

Conclusion

A Chinese proverb says, "In ten years human affairs reverse themselves nine times." It has been more than fifteen years since the first appearance of these chapters, and new information on developments concerning China's major mysteries is now available. This concluding chapter provides an update on the continued study of and controversy over paranormal activity in China.

UFOs

All those who study UFOs are keenly aware of the great explosion that occurred around the Siberian town of Tunguska in June, 1908, felling trees in all directions over 1,200 square miles of forest. Eyewitnesses to the event said a fiery object had come from space, and after a tremendous crash, the entire forest had disappeared, with only smoking embers remaining. This later led to a spirited debate, with some calling it a UFO incident and others convinced it was a meteorite from space. Still others said it was a small comet that had crashed into the earth. Though many have strongly advocated their positions, there remains no final proof, and Tunguska continues to be the subject of speculation (its inclusion in the popular American television series "The X-Files" is proof of this) and many UFO books claim it as a UFO incident.

In actuality, the events in Tunguska present little difficulty in the final analysis: it is perfectly reasonable to say it was caused by a meteorite. The incident of the "strange vehicle in the sky" that appeared in the early November morning on the northern fringes of Guiyang city, in China's Guizhou province, however, is more perplexing and difficult to explain. The Guiyang incident also attracted a great deal of attention in the Chinese press. The *Zhejiang Daily* reported, "Strange Vehicle in Sky Raids Guiyang." The following is a description of the event from start to finish.

At approximately 3:30 am on the morning of November 30, 1994, a large area of land in the Duxi forest region north of Guiyang city was "attacked" by a sudden UFO event. The phenomenon caused the destruction of 160 square meters of forest, cutting through three-meter tall trees. Strangely, between the fallen trees were trees that were left completely untouched.

Lan Derong, the foreman of a stonecutting yard in Duxi, said he suddenly heard a great booming sound that gradually drew closer. When it came close to his home, the sound was frightening. Then, when Lan and his family tried to open the door to their house to investigate, the door was stuck. They felt "like a mysterious force was going to swallow everything." There were about thirty eyewitnesses to the event. One elderly man said that when the "strange vehicle in the sky" came, he saw two fireballs rolling, one red and one green, after which the trees were broken.

Not surprisingly, the story of a mysterious force destroying a forest overnight spread instantly, and it was reported in over ten newspapers, including *Guiyang Daily, New People's Evening News, Chinese Science News, Beijing Youth News, UFO Investigation,* and the journal of the Chinese UFO Research Association.

After the news had spread around the country, investigators and curiosity seekers quickly descended on Guiyang. The local authorities saw it as a "wealth creation opportunity" and immediately spent twenty-thousand yuan in order to "preserve" the area. They then charged an admission fee of three yuan (about US$.38) to any wishing to see the site. From the first of the new year, 1995, 70 to 80 busloads of curiosity seekers arrived daily, and the number of visitors soon rose into the thousands. The whole event was so exciting that some nearby hotels even arranged to bring their guests to the scene.

On January 8, 1995, journalists from Guiyang television came to film a story about the event. When they arrived at the site of "the first landing," the magnetic control for the film image frame changed, and the image fell to one-fifth its original size. Moreover, when a reporter tried to take a picture, he discovered his camera would not work properly.

Less than a week later, on January 12, Guizhou's Science Commission and Provincial Science Association organized a team of 12 scientists to investigate the site, including specialists in aviation, astronomy, forestry, meteorology, environmental protection, and physics. Six days later, the Chinese Academy of Sciences, the National Science Commission, the Academy of Construction Material Science, the Chinese Environmental Protection Agency, and Beijing Qiankun High Technology Development Company sent their own experts to visit the site and conduct their own investigations.

The Guiyang incident resulted not only in the destruction of a large swath of forest. It also mysteriously stripped away pieces of wood, glass, and copper and brick tiling from the roof of an engine house in the locomotive yard of the Guiyang Railroad, five kilometers north of Duxi forest. It was said that when the fireballs left the locomotive yard, they also tore down the walls on the northeast side. After the fireballs passed, the starry night sky returned to stillness.

The investigators took note of another perplexing phenomenon. The pieces of wood and brick tile that were pulled off fell to the ground nearby, but all pieces of glass and copper had disappeared, or had been carried away by an unknown force. The search team scoured the area as far as the hills five kilometers away, but to no avail. Asbestos tiles from the roof of a work shed in the nearby Guiyang Baiyun Forestry Chemical Plant had fallen to the ground, and its iron sheeting had disappeared without a trace. A shed in a nearby rock quarry also lost the iron sheeting from its roof, except for one piece that was caught in the branches of a pine tree and thrown against a tree trunk eight meters high.

The Duxi incident in Guizhou province, 1994.
Some trees are felled while others are left standing.

The investigators were amazed by one point. A railroad engine house with a carriage containing 50 tons of copper was pushed over 20 meters, and of four copper pipe poles ten centimeters in diameter, two were bent out of shape, and two were "cut apart" cleanly. What kind of power could do this? However it may have happened, this tremendous force was remarkably merciful to people. Not one person was injured in the course of the Guiyang incident.

The scientists investigating on site expressed many opinions about what had happened in Guiyang. One proposed it was the effect of a tornado, but another meteorologist countered that there hadn't been any tornadoes in Guizhou province in 70 years of recorded weather, and the terrain and climate of Guizhou are not conducive to tornadoes. Could this event in early winter be an exception to the rule? Another suggested that the timber workers in Duxi had extracted too much rosin oil from the trees, making them become brittle and easily felled, because the point at which the trees were broken was just where rosin oil would be extracted. However, others objected that this only explained why the trees were susceptible to being broken, but not what force actually broke them. Another scientist hypothesized that a large energy source would have to release its energy in the manner of an earthquake. If the strong magnetic force under the earth in this spot were released suddenly, it could have created an atmospheric glow in the sky and felled the trees. Another believed the phenomenon could have been caused by some sort of flying machine. The machine could have been carrying strongly magnetized material, and as it approached, it could exert a powerful force of attraction over iron deposits in the ground. When it flew away, this could have pulled the trees apart. While there were known to be iron deposits in the area of the Guizhou auto factory, nobody could confirm that any flying machine had passed over the region that night.

Amid this entire debate, a UFO hypothesis was inevitable. Some said it was a visit by a flying saucer to Guiyang, because a flying saucer would produce a great deal of energy, and it would not be surprising for it to break up trees under its flight path. The saucer could also give off some sort of cosmic rays and this was the speculation concerning the broken copper pipes. But had anyone seen a flying saucer? Could the two Guiyang fireballs be flying saucers?

Another Chinese proverb says, "Fortune can come from misfortune." Whether the incident was caused by a UFO or some phenomenon of nature, it did bring benefits: Firstly, Guiyang has become a tourist attraction, helping the city economically. Secondly, since Guizhou province is an underdeveloped region of barren land where people live in difficult conditions, this event clearly gives it a chance to improve its name recognition in China and the world while becoming a target for UFO research.

Two months after the Guiyang event, at 9am on February 9, 1995, as Zhongyuan Air flight B737-2946 from Guangzhou (Canton) to Guiyang was in the air, the display of the collision avoidance system showed a UFO that was changing shape and color. The pilot took evasive action and dramatically altered the flight path, after which the plane touched down safely. Ma Yinglin, secretary of the Communications and Guidance Department of the Guizhou People's Aviation Commission, said that considering all the circumstances, the UFO encountered by the plane was probably the same as the UFO that raided Guiyang's forest the previous November.

Wuhan's "Extraterrestrial Snow"

On the evening of November 16, 1998, a stunning event took place. Around eight o'clock that evening, a UFO appeared over the southeast side of Wuhan city in central China for half an hour. The most unbelievable thing was the "extraterrestrial snow" the object sprinkled over the ground around the Qingshan boat yard along the Yangtze River. Crowds of people witnessed this strange scene in the districts of Qingshan, Hongshan and Jiangxia.

According to descriptions by various witnesses, when they discovered one big and two small luminous objects in the sky giving off a green glow, they thought it must have been flashes of lightning from behind the clouds, but when they looked closely, they saw three ellipsoid objects chasing after each other and *crashing into each other* from time to time. When the objects crashed together, something like ashes would fly off. Sometimes the objects would come together, when they would appear larger than a washbowl. When they split apart, they were a bit smaller.

The object(s) had a ring of light with an elongated black center and was flying rather slowly. The entire event lasted about 30 minutes, but Wang Xiguang, a witness from Hongshan district, said the UFOs moved faster than an airplane and chased each other, sometimes circling, sometimes crashing into each other and giving off a green glow, and sometimes hovering motionless in the sky.

In Dawu county, not far from Wuhan, two villagers named Dan Naigui and Wu Dashen described their experiences. At the same time as the group of witnesses from Wuhan's Qingshan boat yard were witnessing the event, the villagers discovered that white flakes were floating down from the sky, falling on the ground and glittering. Some of it fell on people's backs (it was a hot day and many people had their shirts off to cool down), and they felt a strange itching feeling, the substance being difficult to wash off. After the material continued falling for ten minutes, the ground was covered with a thin layer of it. According to local residents there, the same thing had happened twice before. A staff member from Wuhan's environmental protection service who went to the site to collect data and investigate said he had never seen such a material before and it was an anomaly.

This UFO incident was reported in Shanghai's *Wen Hui Bao,* Gansu's *Journal of UFO Research* and Taiwan's *China Times* and the *Ufology Journal.*

UFO Phenomenon Filmed in China

The latest news from China includes one particularly noteworthy item: a report of November 19, 1999 from the Yunnan province city of Kunming stated that China had released to the public the first video of a UFO. This event too place at the "Chinese Space Science Education Exposition" held in Kunming, and attracted great interest from the audience as well as internationally.

The video was filmed in the northwest of Kunming on October 3, 1998 by Han Jianwei, a worker for the city's railroad service. After this, he treated it as a priceless treasure and secured it in his home. On the day of the incident, Han had gone on an excursion with several friends. Around 11:50am, he happened to see a silvery white luminous object that appeared to be several kilometers away in the sky. Its brightness was gradually decreasing and it soon disappeared in the clouds. About three minutes later, it reappeared and Han immediately turned on his video camera and started filming the flight of the UFO. The whole process of its transformation and final disappearance lasted about two minutes.

The UFO could change color. At first it was silver, then became lighter, then turned orange. Strangely, about half a minute later, with a flash of light it changed shape from a cylinder to the disk shape usually associated with flying saucers.

After viewing Han's video, some Chinese scientists affirmed its research value. A member of Beijing's "Chinese UFO Research Association" said that although there have been a number of videos of UFOs in all parts of the world, few filmed sightings are as long as two minutes. Over the last two decades, China has gathered thousands of eyewitness accounts of UFOs. Some say the purpose of publicizing this video was to tell everyone that UFOs have an objective existence in the material world and we humans should pay attention and strengthen our investigations and research.

UFO Appears over Shanghai

Just as I write this, the *Sing Tao Daily,* a well-known Chinese language newspaper published in San Francisco, devoted a one-half page article to report a UFO that appeared over Shanghai on December 2, 1999 under the headline, "UFO Appears in Shanghai for Half Hour." At 3:50pm on that day, an orange UFO appeared in the western district of Shanghai and was witnessed by over a hundred residents. The most convincing evidence was that two Shanghai television stations had broadcast a video about the incident, but it was not clear from the report whether this was a scene of its flight or an interview with witnesses.

Some witnesses said the UFO was a "round disk of golden flashing light," while others said it was cone-shaped with two glowing strips of light. But all agreed that it moved slowly in the air for over an hour, and it hovered in one spot for ten minutes. The first to discover the object was Jiang Xiaoyuan, a former researcher at Shanghai Observatory. As he was walking along the street, he happened to notice it in the sky. Meanwhile, a city resident called the story in to the Shanghai newspaper *Wen Wei Daily,* and a science reporter immediately rushed to the top of the building to watch it. Sure enough, he saw a luminous object in the western sky. At that moment it was standing still.

Seven days later, on December 9, as I was watching an evening television news broadcast from Mainland China's Central Television, it was reported that the same UFO appeared again over Shanghai. This time the broadcast showed the entire flight. We were fortunate to get a full view of the UFO. It was formed of two strips of light, but unlike before, the strips were crossing each other.

In an interview published in Nanjing Service Guide Report, Wang Enchao, a researcher for the Chinese Academy of Sciences at the Mount Zijin Observatory, and a specialist in asteroid research, concluded that the object had to be a special flying machine. He ruled out cloud reflections and smoke trails from jet exhaust because the object was seen to maintain its form for over an hour. He also ruled out any unknown airplane because it would generally take only 20 minutes to fly over Shanghai, and he said a helicopter or blimp would have caused much more noise than was reported. He said a special flying machine could have released dust particles that reflected sunlight to cause the orange glow people observed, but he said there was not enough evidence to conclude that it was of extraterrestrial origin. Wang also remarked that while it was fortunate the event was recorded on video, there were not any close-up observations by telescopes, surveying instruments, or radar to allow the estimation of the object's size, altitude, or speed. Wang suggested that observation of such unexpected objects was a new challenge for astronomers and others who monitor the skies.

EHF

After many years of EHF research, China has begun devoting more time and money to scientific experimentation. Of course, this includes many different research areas, but two of the most exciting fields in recent years have been in EHF induction and "see-through" vision.

Beginning in March 1992, a team of seven Hangzhou University researchers led by Tian Weishun and Zhu Huizhong conducted experiments in the induction of reading with the ear involving 1,222 elementary and high school students over a period of six months. In one experiment, they trained schoolchildren aged seven to eighteen in one afternoon and then tested them. The results showed that younger students tended to have increased EHF ability, and as age increased that ability also decreased. In addition, it was shown that females tested higher for EHF ability than did males.

The scientists recalled that in the days when China's EHF research was just getting started, Chen Shouliang and He Muyan conducted separate experiments on EHF induction with two groups comprising over 40 teens and children. Chen and He found that EHF was most common among children of a certain age: between seven and thirteen years old.

The March, 1992 tests were conducted in four elementary and high schools in four districts of Hangzhou (a city popular with tourists) with 623 male students and 599 female students, whose ages ranged from seven to eighteen. Before the test, the scientists explained to the subjects the concepts of EHF and reading with the ear, told them the experimental procedure and the indications they hoped to discover. In addition, they requested that the students concentrate and clear their minds of any distractions. Both Tian and Zhu said it took most people a long time in their first trial, so they would need confidence and patience. Further, for ease of monitoring, the students were not allowed to place anything on their desks, even books or paper. The tests were also witnessed by the head teachers from the students' respective elementary, middle, and high schools.

The results of the Hangzhou tests were that the majority of those with the ability to read with the ears were aged seven to thirteen. In this age group, 12.35 percent were found to have the ability, while none of those from age 14 to 17 had the ability. The best results were with the nine-year-old subjects, who demonstrated a 20 percent success rate. Of the 17- and 18-year-olds, only one female had the ability.

After this, they prepared a test one afternoon with the freshmen and sophomores in the high school associated with Hangzhou's Zhejiang University. The results showed that in one group four people could read with their ears, and in the other group five had the ability. But their report did not show how many students there were in each group.

According to Tang Jianmin's *My Research on EHF*, Xu Baoyi of China's Bangbu Medical Institute conducted experiments with 1,388 teenagers and discovered that 180 possessed special vision powers. Among them, the greatest number were 12 years old, and the fewest were over 16.

On one occasion, Mr. Shao Laisheng and Ms. Zhu Yi-yi, editor of China's *Nature Magazine*, published a report of experimental results of EHF induction of youths aged 18 to 20. They discovered that less educated young working people were easier to train. The rate of success with university students was lower and their powers were less stable. The older they were and the busier they were with their classes, the lower their success rates. At the same time, ordinary workers had higher success rates, because they had simple jobs that required less mental effort.

Zhu Yi-yi is one of the leading figures in China's EHF research. She revealed that scientific researchers tried EHF induction with some children in six districts of Shanghai. Their success rates were very high. Sometimes they were successful in bringing out the ability in about 30 percent of the children after one training session, and at other times, the final success rate was 90 percent after more extensive training. Zhu Yi-yi said that this universal discovery provided further confirmation of the reality of EHF and gave a solid basis for further research on this as yet untapped human potential.

China has more females than males with EHF. The same holds true for reading with the ear, but only by a little. Researchers believe the reason is that girls generally tend to be more quiet and focused, while boys are active and hard to calm down.

From 1982 to 1986, the "Human Body Informatics Research Group" in the electrical engineering department of Shanghai's Fudan University conducted experiments in EHF induction with small numbers of people. They trained 40 men and women in Shanghai's Putuo district, and discovered that it was just as easy to induce EHF in teenagers as it was in children, and they could all attain varying degrees of EHF after a little more than ten days of training. Another time, an EHF training class was held on the campus of Fudan University. The subjects comprised 11 young workers (six males and five females) aged 18-20. The workers practiced three hours every day and achieved satisfactory results after 18 days of training. They stated that the main idea in EHF induction was contained in the following words: "Steady, constant repetition, advancing from easy to hard."

In a new set of planned EHF induction experiments conducted from 1986 to 1993, researchers trained a total of 46 young people, of whom 18 were male and 28 female. Almost all of them attained some level of skill in ESP and psychokinesis. It generally took from four to ten training sessions for the abilities to appear. This indicates that EHF is possessed by the great majority of people and has gradually faded through disuse in our advanced society, but can be recovered, and even strengthened by suitable training and exercise. It should be mentioned, however, that after completing the experiments, the subjects experienced dizziness or throbbing of the head as well as general physical fatigue. For this reason, they participated in only four tests a week, each test no longer than one hour in duration.

As the Fudan University researchers disclosed, these experimental subjects were not participating out of a devotion to the cause of EHF research. Rather, they were doing it to earn extra money in their spare time. As soon as the experiments ended, the subjects gave up on continuing the training themselves.

However, there are two sides to all things. As the Fudan University researchers stated: as more people who actively develop EHF, the risk of those using the ability for unethical or illegal purposes might increase, thereby threatening social order. Given China's population of 1.2 billion, the idea of a "psychic war" may not be as ludicrous as it sounds.

See-through Vision

See-through vision (a derivation of the more popular term "X-Ray" vision), is a very appealing prospect. Not only can one look into a patient's body to view a diseased part, one can also look inside objects or under the ground. A number of people in China have used this ability to find underground sources of water and oil.

Du Yongcheng, a man known as "the fire and metal eye" (a common Chinese phrase for this phenomenon), lives in Beijing. Du can see through the concrete of the street to a depth of approximately one meter. One case when he used this power took place in relation to the gasoline supply pipes to the foreign embassy quarters in Beijing.

Unlike ordinary citizens who buy gas at gas stations, the embassies fuel their cars from their own special pipes. One day, the pressure in the pump was low, which indicated a possible rupture in the pipe. The engineers of the Beijing municipal construction department and design bureau, however, could not find any leak. It was then that someone suggested letting Du Yongcheng, then 20 years old, examine it. As a car from a service station with a camera drove along the street, Du Yongcheng duly followed, looking at the roadway as he went. The car had to drive very slowly. After going several meters at a snail's pace, the road repair engineer's patience wore thin and he started to complain. Suddenly, Du Yongcheng found the leak in the pipe, and after digging down they were able to repair it.

Du Yongcheng's father, Du Wensheng, is an engineer for Peking Observatory. After he discovered his son's gift of see-through vision, he specially invited his good friend, Nanjing University Astronomy Chairman Zhu Cansheng, to put Du Yongcheng to the test. As we know, the atmosphere of the earth is layered, but the ability to discern the layers falls well beyond the range of normal vision. On this occasion, however, Du was asked to look into the air to see how many layers were contained within the earth's atmosphere. In only a few moments, he correctly replied that there were five layers.

In another test, Du was asked to view the distribution of gold deposits in Gaoyao county, Guangdong province. The test was held in the second-floor conference room of the armed militia. A total of 13 people were present for this test, including the manager of a mining company and an engineer for the Guangzhou Nonferrous Metal Research Institute. At the start of the experiment, they spread open a map and showed Du some sample mines. After an on-site visit, Du found five mineral deposits in six mining camps. He was then driven to the land between the number 9 range and number 19 range and was asked to trace the course of the gold veins. In only 15 minutes, he pointed out the direction of three lodes that coincided closely with that previously given by a surveying team.

Medical diagnosis by see-through vision uses those with natural-born ability to see into the human body. It is a contribution to humanity that these people use their powers to help the sick. It is also an intelligent choice not to waste the social resource of these abilities. This kind of diagnosis is simple, economical, and beneficial.

Xinjiang People's Liberation Army Hospital conducted 117 tests of children with see-through vision. In 22 cases of examining the head for eight different diseases, they were completely correct in 17 cases, mostly correct in four cases and incorrect in one case. In 53 cases of looking into liver patients, they were completely correct 43 times, mostly correct five times, and incorrect four times. In one case they couldn't see clearly. In 19 trials of viewing fetal position, they were correct or mostly correct 16 times and wrong three times. In looking into 23 other kinds of cases of 13 different diseases, their diagnostic effectiveness was lower, although these particular cases included a wide variety of complicated conditions.

Later, in the conclusion of their report, "Preliminary Investigation of Modern Medical Verification of EHF," Assistant Director Yang Junpeng of the Xinjiang People's Liberation Army Hospital stated, "We believe the use (of see-through vision) is feasible and has clinical value," reflecting the objective reality of diagnosis by EHF see-through vision.

Many people see the importance of medical diagnosis by see-through vision, mainly because it saves time, work, and money. Nowadays, people are afraid to go for X-ray photography, because if the radiation level is too high, it is said to harm the body or even cause cancer. If they instead use a person with EHF, it works right away, simply, and without any hazardous side effects. We now present one more example of see-through vision.

Di Rong is the daughter of Professor Di Huaichun of Xi'an Communication University. Her eyes are called "more penetrating than an X-ray." On October 12, 1986, Shaanxi's Weiyang College of Chinese Medicine sent a car to pick her up for a demonstration of see-through vision. Di Rong went to the hospital with her mother. Dr. Liu, the director of the department of external medicine, asked Di Rong to look at the left leg of an old worker and tell what was wrong with the man's leg, which was covered with a towel. After concentrating on it for about five minutes, she then said she saw that the bone was broken into three pieces and pointed to the places. Her diagnosis was correct down to the slightest detail.

EHF researchers say that in one four-month period, Di Rong used her see-through vision for 300 people with over 40 different diseases, and her accuracy was over 90 percent!

Perhaps because of inaccurate descriptions of the power ascribed to see-through vision, many people (perhaps women in particular) may fear that people could see through their bodies. In reality, this ability does not allow one to "see through at a glance." When a man or woman with see-through vision exercises this power, it generally requires one to six minutes to see the target. Unless they deliberately try, they won't be able to "look through" anyone, and few people would be unscrupulous enough to want to do that.

Professor Tang Jianmin, a longtime EHF researcher, said, "Through personal experience over many years of researching EHF, I have become strongly convinced that strengthening the eye's see-through ability comes by the same process as raising the eye's frequency in the electromagnetic spectrum, and this process is connected with strengthening the vision. This is a long-term process which requires a quiet environment and a calm and patient emotional state, and especially a reduction in the amount of strain placed on the eyes in activities such as reading, watching television, driving a car, and reduction or elimination of some stressful forms of work. These conditions are required to strengthen the eye's see-through vision capabilities. Only in these conditions can the see-through vision power be preserved. Otherwise, not only will a person not be able to develop see-through vision, even one who originally had strong see-through vision will gradually lose the power and it will disappear after not very much time."

Professor Tang also said, "Among the population of people with EHF, there are more females than males, more teens and children than adults, more rural people than city people, more American children than Chinese children, more Chinese adults than American adults." Why these differences? He gave simple explanations. For example, in the case of the male-female difference, he said it was because "Females enjoy much greater stability and ability to select comfortable living environments than males in China. Females take part in fewer stressful activities than males, and their work places much less stress on their eyes than males."

The reason children are more numerous than adults was due to "the eyes of teens and children still being in the developmental stage, and making it easier to train their powers. They also do much less work requiring tense concentration of vision than adults. For this reason, there are many more children with EHF than adults."

And why do more rural people than city people have this power? "The Chinese countryside has a slow and easygoing pace of life. The amount of work requiring concentration of vision is much less than in the city. Analyzing the results of the experiments, we found that the rate of success of university students who used induction to try to create EHF was low, while youth in the countryside had higher rates. These completely different outcomes can be explained by the enormous difference in the amounts of time these two groups spend in concentrated use of the eyes."

Dr. Tang's reason why American children had more EHF ability than Chinese children was quite interesting:

"Tests by two professors in Beijing University, Wang Zhong and Shi Youxin, and by Han Qingyuan in Minnesota State University proved that American children also were generally receptive to induction of EHF and in fact were easier to 'induce' than Chinese children, in particular on the first time. What causes this difference? They believe that Chinese children spend much more time studying at home than American children, and of the time they spend studying in school, the American children study less than Chinese children....the different results reflect the different amounts of time they spend with their eyes focused on one thing."

Conversely, the reason why American adults had weaker

vision than Chinese was "most people over the age of 16 drive their own cars and like to participate in high-stimulation activities, so that the U.S. adults spend much more time in concentrated vision than in China."

Tang also quipped, "I believe you cannot find anyone with EHF among China's adult professional drivers. If anyone is interested in this, you can go test it for yourself." Of course, I take his word for it.

Beginning in 1979, Chinese scientists have found over 5,000 children with exceptional psychic powers. This huge figure includes children with natural-born abilities as well as those who developed it through Qi gong or induction. Those with only a little power perform to the delight of audiences nationwide, while those with considerably more power serve their country and are kept under national protection. Those with advanced EHF can often perform many different kinds of services, such as predicting earthquakes, looking through the ground to find underground waterways for well-digging, prospecting for gold and mineral resources, examining the body for medical purposes, performing healing, and, perhaps not surprisingly, participating in military drills awaiting the onset of a "psychic war."

Qi Gong

Although the mysterious powers of qi gong are fascinating, its main role is in heath and healing, particularly for chronic diseases. Therefore, I want to emphasize the ability of qi gong to cure cancer to allow readers to gain a broader perspective on it.

Qi gong is an ancient Chinese health exercise. It was used as a means of cultivating the mind and spirit by Taoists, Buddhists, and Confucian scholars, and used as a medical treatment by ancient doctors. All these groups kept the knowledge of qi gong to themselves, and so only a limited number of people knew about it. In the decades since 1979, Chinese scientists have discovered that qi gong can be used to treat not only all types of chronic illnesses, but even cancer. At first no one believed this, but later, more facts proved that cancer patients who practiced qi gong exercises could achieve higher rates of remission, recovery, and improvement in their physical and mental condition. Word of the power of qi gong spread, and the Chinese came to view qi gong as a wonder cure for cancer.

Many medical specialists from around the world have come to China to observe qi gong firsthand.

If a person has cancer or another disease that cannot be treated using conventional means, then he or she should do something else in an effort to cure the disease. This is a very straightforward idea. And yet, there are people who have an unreasoning faith in medicine, who believe that if medicine is helpless, there can be no other way. A Chinese proverb says, "Heaven always provides another way out." The natural world and the human body are products of Heaven, and both are gifted with the mysterious ability to mend themselves. The human immune system is one aspect of this mysterious ability. By regulating and strengthening the immune system, it is possible to resist many illnesses.

Perhaps the best way to regulate the immune system is through appropriate exercise. Qi gong is an exercise, but in contrast to vigorous exercises like sports, running, or even martial arts, qi gong is relaxed, more like dancing, morning calisthenics, and the popular tai chi exercises. This latter kind of exercise would seem more suitable for a person weakened by disease. It is in this sense that qi gong is useful for curing sickness.

Everyone knows that exercise is good for one's health, but a patient who is a defeatist or pessimistic state of mind—exacerbated by already having accepted his or her fate as a result of disease or illness—may not even try it. For any sick person it is important to have a positive attitude, an unwavering will, and a calm emotional state while choosing an appropriate program of exercise—or choosing qi gong, an exercise that has already proven its effectiveness in China. By persisting in the exercise, one will definitely see a great improvement in one's physical and psychological health. Of this there is no question.

The idea of striving for a new lease on life by exercising is actually not a new invention; it is already known and documented in medical literature. It's just that we have neglected to keep it in mind.

If one is the sort of person who has an unquestioning faith in medicine with a suspicious attitude toward qi gong, I offer the following: continue to see the doctor, and use whatever medicine, chemotherapy or other treatment the doctor advises. At the same time, however, practice qi gong exercises. This intelligent approach, realizing that the two ways of healing are not mutually exclusive, is the most suitable method to recovery.

I have no wish for the reader to have a suspicious attitude toward qi gong. In China, nearly everyone knows about qi gong cancer therapy, and medical specialists from U.S. institutions such as the prestigious Harvard Medical School are also aware of it. I take a sincere attitude in presenting this information to the general reader outside China, and this chapter is based on my own experiences and observations. I am not a medical specialist, and my knowledge of the mechanisms used by qi gong to cure cancer is not extensive. It is just my belief that a good life-saving method should be made known to the public in a timely way, and one doesn't need to be a medical specialist to be qualified to make such a report. I was hesitant to write these lines concerning qi gong and the treatment of cancer until I was inspired by the cover story from the March 1988 issue of *Life* magazine. That article reported the case of actress Gilda Radner, who was undergoing cancer treatment with a major emphasis on developing a positive emotional and mental state, which is also a primary benefit of qi gong.

Qi gong is an ancient medical practice with its roots in the forgotten past in China, but its recent revival is due largely to Guo Lin, the pioneer of qi gong cancer treatment. Guo Lin, an elderly woman artist, was diagnosed with advanced uterine cancer. After two unsuccessful operations, she was at death's door. She turned to qi gong and created her own unique set of exercises, the "New Qi Gong Therapy." After months of diligent practice, her cancer went into remission. As a result of Guo Lin's efforts, qi gong has become phenomenally popular in China.

There is also a growing surge of interest in qi gong in the West. Teams of doctors and medical professionals from the United States have visited China to study qi gong. They have taken a particular interest in qi gong's potential as a treatment for AIDS, since the primary principle of qi gong therapy is to strengthen the immune system, and it is precisely the debilitation of the immune system which makes AIDS so terrible.

In considering a new or unfamiliar phenomenon such as qi gong, it is important to keep an open mind and evaluate factual evidence calmly rather than jumping to conclusions. Many scientists and doctors refuse even to consider the possibility that a simple exercise could cure the human body of cancer. A well-known Chinese author, Ke Yan, was originally skeptical of qi gong's power. She was struck with cancer in early 1981, and after several months of medication and chemotherapy, her condition worsened. At this point, she reluctantly joined one of Guo Lin's qi gong therapy classes. In less than half a year, her cancer was cured, and she changed from a skeptic into a strong supporter of qi gong. After that, she published a famous article entitled "Cancer Does Not Equal Death" in the July 1982 issue of *Beijing Literature*. Her article called on the medical community to look at the facts regarding qi gong cancer therapy rather than rejecting it out of hand. In this article, Ke Yan revealed that she had taken doctors to visit Guo Lin's cancer therapy classes, and the doctors were all impressed with the usefulness of qi gong for cancer patients.

The key elements underlying qi gong's effects on cancer are exercises to strengthen the internal organs, deep breathing to ensure healthy oxygen supply, chanting to harmonize the workings of the internal organs, and meditation to promote a positive mental state and mobilize the body's latent power. All of these practices contribute to strengthening the body's immune system in order to fight cancer.

The exercise of the internal organs is a very important feature unique to qi gong. This distinguishes it from activity sports, such as swimming or aerobics, which are all external exercises with no capabilities of curing cancer. Only a combination of internal and external exercises can generate enough power to cure cancer.

Deep breathing helps the body take in more oxygen, which is understood to be particularly effective against cancer. Cancer cells grow under conditions of insufficient oxygen and die when oxygen is abundant. Chanting is similar to deep breathing in this respect, but in addition it causes the internal organs to vibrate with a kind of resonance and thus revives their weakened functions.

Meditation encourages relaxation, a feeling of euphoria, and freedom from trivial annoyances. Under these conditions, energy will be mobilized by the power of the human will, which plays a very important part here. It is well known that confidence and willpower can work wonders on a patient. Guo Lin had a profound grasp of this principle, and therefore offered elements in her therapy program specifically designed at building self-confidence and willpower.

All these mechanisms contribute to qi gong's ability to strengthen the immune system and build good health. Over a hundred ailments can be overcome by practicing qi gong. The human body, just like Mother Nature, regulates itself. The practice of qi gong is designed to enhance this inherent self-healing property and harness it in order to rid the body of disease.

I have introduced China's use of qi gong to cure cancer to suggest to those cancer patients who have not achieved any improvement using Western medicine that there is nothing to lose by trying qi gong therapy. On the contrary, it may bring surprising benefits. Moreover, the technique for practicing qi gong is extremely simple. Patience and confidence are all that is needed.

Wildman

In China, after news spread concerning the existence of the wildman, interest in the topic has continued unabated, including a hope to capture one and bring it to public view to fulfill people's interest and conduct further research. The Chinese yearning to see a living wildman is the same as that of the American public to see a flying saucer land on the White House lawn.

As for the wildman, like the elusive Bigfoot of America's Pacific Northwest, nobody has captured one. Although photographs do exist, they are from too far away and not satisfying. Some even say those photos that do look like something are fakes.

Does the wildman really exist? As a great deal of documentation shows, it clearly does, but it is not the 400-pound hairy giant of our imagination, walking on two legs, with menacing eyes, the female having well-developed breasts and living in a cave, and so on.

Within the boundaries of China, there are five places where the wildman is said to make its rare appearances. These are Xishuangbanna in Tibet and Yunnan; the northwest of Hubei Province; the south of Shanxi Province, and the Mt. Suichang region of Zhejiang Province. Shennongjia in northwest Hubei is most famous for its wildman stories. It is a vast region with a great, largely untouched forest sparsely inhabited by people, and indeed suitable for long-term residence by wildmen. Chinese scientists have gone into this region many times to investigate, but unfortunately they never came up with anything conclusive.

In the past decade, people have turned their attention to Bhutan, Nepal, and Pakistan on China's borders, and Tibet and the Himalayan region in search of the wildman. In Tibet, a "Himalayan Mystery Research Association" was formed and dispatched teams to investigate the wildman on expeditions lasting as long as two months, but they found nothing. On another occasion, the government of Sikkim organized many groups to go into the mountains, but their search also was fruitless. The record of these search teams goes back at least to 1959, when a U.S.-organized team investigated the snowman in Nepal, but again to no avail.

Chinese wildman researchers Wang Rong and Wang Liche, in their book *The Last Hidden Land,* say they once put the question to villagers in Bangxing village, Motuo county, in Tibet. Since they all said the wildman was real, why not catch one and prove it? They replied with their traditional beliefs: "Our forefathers have passed down to us the belief that if we see a wildman we will get sick, so we must avoid them." They further said, "If we hear the wildman crying, we will die." That is why no one would try to catch a wildman.

Yi Wenzheng, a member of the Himalayan Mystery Research Association, revealed that many signs of wildman activity exist in the 10,000 square kilometers of mountain forest in Motuo. This mountain region alone may have as many as 11 wildmen. Two of these, however, disappeared in the 1980s. In 1991, according to testimony by over 20 hunters, besides the original nine wildmen, they also discovered signs of wildman activity in two other places. But nobody dealt with the question of whether the two wildmen who disappeared from Motuo had moved to a new area. The two new wildmen were said to live in the Bari ravine, a distance of about three days by foot from Motuo. All described the wildmen as having a body covered with long brown hair; big feet; walking upright; able to throw rocks; making rapid hand and foot motions when laughing; a large mouth; glowing red eyes; white teeth which it generally bared if people approached; and often crying out when far away from people. The female had small but long breasts. Chairman Bai of the Motuo county government (who is also a hunter), said he could not understand why people still debated the existence of the wildman, saying "There are many wildmen around my home village, but the debate goes on and on!"

One hunter followed a wildman that was about 1.7 meters tall, and concluded that the creature prefers to live alone. One time he watched for three days, and the wildman left its cave only once. While it was gone, the hunter entered the cave, the floor of which was covered crudely with twigs and soft grass. There were some animal bones in the cave, and outside the cave was some waste.

Motuo is covered with primeval forest over a large area. Its valleys are studded with rock caverns and tree hollows, and it has many wild fruits, providing ideal conditions to support many wildmen. The Himalaya region also has a large area, very few people, and is said to be inhabited by kind people who have never disturbed the wildman. This is precisely the kind of place where the wildman could thrive.

There are many fascinating things about the wildman. According to a report by the Himalayan Mystery Research Association, in an investigation of two and a half months, they heard the recollection of a villager. One time when going into the forest for firewood, he smelled a scent of burning, and a little later heard something like a human voice calling. When he turned to look, he saw two red-haired "monsters" standing at the entrance to a cave. His whole body was trembling with fright, and he ran away rapidly. After returning home, he was sick for several months. Another story said that when several local hunters went into the forest to catch monkeys, a wildman suddenly came out of the undergrowth at the side of a lake. The wildman broke off a tree branch and ran quickly toward them. The hunters fled in terror, hearing wild laughter behind them as they ran.

In the Himalayan region of Tibet and Nepal, there are many tales of the Yeti, or snowman. An Italian explorer has even said there are over a thousand snowmen there. It is not only the Chinese who come here to investigate the snowman, but also Japanese, British, Polish, Italians, and Americans. The wildman and the snowman, like Bigfoot, remains a target of international research.

In the coming years the Chinese Academy of Sciences will form a new and much larger wildman investigative team with the aim of making a deeper and more comprehensive investigation. In the foreseeable future, we should have a convincing answer at last to the question of the wildman's existence.

Index

Paul Dong